DEPARTMENT FOR EDUCATION AND SKILLS
NATIONAL ASSEMBLY FOR WALES
SCOTTISH EXECUTIVE
NORTHERN IRELAND DEPARTMENT OF EDUCATION
HIGHER EDUCATION STATISTICS AGENCY
NORTHERN IRELAND DEPARTMENT FOR EMPLOYMENT AND LEARNING

Education and Training Statistics for the United Kingdom

2004 Edition

London: TSO

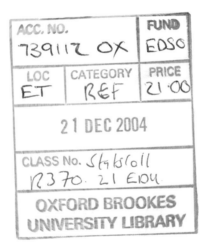

Contents

Introduction

This is the eighth edition of *Education and Training Statistics for the United Kingdom*, providing an integrated overview of statistics on education and training in the UK. It largely follows the format of last year's volume, however, the previous Chapters 4 (Qualifications) and 5 (Destinations) have been combined into a single Chapter 4 'Qualifications and Destinations'. Consequently, the 'Population' Chapter is now Chapter 5, and International Comparisons is now Chapter 6. There have also been a few changes to the tables in the 2004 volume:

- In Table 2.9, Key Stage 1 information for England is based on results for trial LEAs, where just teacher assessments were submitted to DfES, and non-trial LEAs, who continued to submit both test/task and teacher assessments.

- Table 3.2, reports 'participation' data for a single year only, i.e. 2001/02, as earlier years in the standard time series await the publication of revised pre-2001 population estimates;

- Table 3.11 from the 2003 edition, reporting FE students in the first year of their course of study, has been dropped;

- Tables 3.12–3.15 reporting data on Work-based learning for young people provision in England replace the previous tables 3.13–3.15;

- Table 4.5 no longer reports GNVQ/GSVQ figures;

- In part (i) of Table 4.7, targets no longer subsumed within the Public Service Agreement (PSA) targets for England have been dropped. In part (ii), Lifelong learning targets for young people and for adults have been added for Wales;

- Old tables 5.1 and 5.3 reporting destinations of school leavers and full-time first degree graduates, respectively, are now numbered 4.11 and 4.12. Old table 5.2, reporting destinations of Work-based learning for young people leavers, has been dropped;

International Comparisons chapter

The International Comparisons chapter (Chapter 6) largely reports data available from the Organisation for Economic Co-operation and Development (OECD) publication *Education at a Glance 2004*. Table 6.5 now reports results from the Progress in Reading Literacy Study (PIRLS) 2001.

Regional Analyses

Where regional analyses are given they are on the basis of Government Office Regions (GORs) – the primary classification for the presentation of regional statistics since April 1997.

Contributions

The efforts of the statistics teams in DfES, National Assembly for Wales, Scottish Executive, Northern Ireland Department of Education and Northern Ireland Department for Employment and Learning, who have contributed data for the volume, are again greatly appreciated. In DfES the people responsible for bringing all the data together and producing the 2004 volume were the UK and Local Statistics team within the Data Services Group (DSG) and, in particular, Martin Johnson, Graham Devonshire and Dave Walton.

Chapter 1
Expenditure

CHAPTER 1: EXPENDITURE

Key Facts

- Expenditure on education services by central and local government in the UK in 2002-03 was £53.8 billion, including £3.2 billion directly on under fives, £30.5 billion on schools, £6.6 billion on further education and £6.6 billion on higher education. £35.2 billion was spent by local education authorities and £18.6 billion by central government. (**Table 1.1**)

- Expenditure on education services by central and local government in the UK increased by 26 per cent in real terms between 1995-96 (£42.6 billion) and 2002-03 (£53.8 billion). (**Table 1.2**)

- Expenditure on education services by central and local government in the UK in 2002-03 represented 5.1 per cent of Gross Domestic Product - an increase of 0.2 percentage points from 2001-02. (**Table 1.2**)

- In 2002-03, UK identifiable expenditure on education services in the UK represented £908 per head of population, compared with £754 per head in 2000-01. Identifiable expenditure ranged from £883 per head in England to £1,169 per head in Northern Ireland. (**Table 1.3**)

CHAPTER 1: EXPENDITURE - LIST OF TABLES

1.1 EXPENDITURE
Education expenditure on services by function[1], 2002-03[2]

United Kingdom				Financial year 1 April to 31 March				£ million
	Local education authorities	Central govern- ment	Total		Local education authorities	Central govern- ment	Total
Under fives				**Student support (inc mandatory awards & access funds)**			
Total current [3]	2,976.7	189.4	**3,166.1**	Total current [3]	75.9	1,583.7	**1,659.6**
Total capital [4]	5.6	31.5	**37.1**	Total capital [4]	-	1.4	**1.4**
Total under fives	**2,982.4**	**220.9**	**3,203.2**	**Total student support**	**75.9**	**1,585.1**	**1,661.0**
Schools				**Other education services**			
Total current [3]	26,818.4	1,561.4	**28,379.8**	Total current [3]	2,305.5	2,542.3	**4,847.8**
Total capital [4]	1,981.9	166.2	**2,148.1**	Total capital [4]	195.4	188.5	**383.9**
Total schools	**28,800.3**	**1,727.6**	**30,527.9**	**Total other education services**	**2,500.9**	**2,730.8**	**5,231.7**
Further Education				**GRAND TOTALS**			
Total current [3]	711.2	5,373.6	**6,084.8**	**Total current [3]**	**32,887.9**	**17,489.7**	**50,377.6**
Total capital [4]	115.4	359.8	**475.2**	**Total capital [4]**	**2,298.3**	**1,139.7**	**3,438.0**
Total further education	**826.6**	**5,733.4**	**6,560.0**	**TOTAL Education Expenditure**	**35,186.2**	**18,629.5**	**53,815.6**
Higher Education							
Total current [3]	-	6,239.4	**6,239.4**				
Total capital [4]	-	392.4	**392.4**				
Total higher education	**-**	**6,631.7**	**6,631.7**				

Source: HM Treasury - Public Expenditure Statistical Analysis

1 Total Expenditure on Services (TES) is a definition of aggregate public spending and covers most expenditure by the public sector that is included in Total Managed Expenditure (TME), where TME is a measure of public sector expenditure drawn from components in national accounts produced by the Office for National Statistics (ONS). TES broadly represents the sum of current and capital expenditure of central and local government, and public corporations, but excludes general government capital consumption and other accounting adjustments.

2 Provisional.

3 Including general administrative expenses and purchases of goods and services which are not of a capital nature.

4 Comprising expenditure on new construction, the purchase of land, buildings and other physical assets, less the proceeds from sales of similar assets and the value of net changes in the level of stocks. Also includes grants to the private sector, nationalised industries and other public corporations.

1.2 EXPENDITURE

Summary of expenditure on education services[1] - time series

	United Kingdom	Financial Year 1 April to 31 March		£ million
	1995-96	2000-01[2]	2001-02[2]	2002-03
Local education authorities				
Current	23,962	28,119	30,903	32,888
Capital	1,202	1,810	2,151	2,298
Total	**25,165**	**29,929**	**33,055**	**35,186**
Central Government				
Current	9,703	13,866	15,751	17,490
Capital	706	555	928	1,140
Total	**10,408**	**14,421**	**16,679**	**18,629**
All public authorities				
Current	33,665	41,985	46,654	50,378
Capital	1,908	2,365	3,079	3,438
Total	**35,573**	**44,350**	**49,733**	**53,816**
Gross Domestic Product (GDP, cash)[3]	729,389	963,508	1,005,150	1,055,190
Education expenditure as a percentage of GDP	**4.9**	**4.6**	**4.9**	**5.1**
GDP deflator[3]	83.414	94.251	96.721	100.000
GDP in real terms[4]	874,420	1,022,279	1,039,226	1,055,190
Total education expenditure in real terms[4]	**42,646**	**47,055**	**51,419**	**53,816**

Sources: HM Treasury - Public Expenditure Statistical Analysis; Office for National Statistics

1 Total Expenditure on Services (TES) is a definition of aggregate public spending and covers most expenditure by the public sector that is included in Total Managed Expenditure (TME), where TME is a measure of public sector expenditure drawn from components in national accounts produced by the Office for National Statistics (ONS). TES broadly represents the sum of current and capital expenditure of central and local government, and public corporations, but excludes general government capital consumption and other accounting adjustments.

2 Includes revised data.

3 Source: Office for National Statistics - March 2004 National Accounts release.

4 At 2002-03 prices.

1.3 EXPENDITURE

UK identifiable[1] expenditure on education services[2] by country - time series

	Financial Year 1 April to 31 March			cash £ million
	1995-96	2000-01[3]	2001-02[3]	2002-03
By country				
England	28,314	35,799	40,298	43,766
Scotland	4,075	4,597	5,079	5,233
Wales	1,799	2,223	2,557	2,825
Northern Ireland	1,377	1,716	1,789	1,983
United Kingdom	**35,565**	**44,335**	**49,723**	**53,807**
				£ per head[4]
By country				
England	579	728	816	883
Scotland	793	908	1,003	1,035
Wales	617	765	879	968
Northern Ireland	832	1,020	1,059	1,169
United Kingdom	**607**	**754**	**842**	**908**

Sources: HM Treasury - Public Expenditure Statistical Analysis

1 A small amount of expenditure cannot be disaggregated to individual country level. Therefore, the figures in this table are slightly different from those shown in Table 1.2.

2 Total Expenditure on Services (TES) is a definition of aggregate public spending and covers most expenditure by the public sector that is included in Total Managed Expenditure (TME), where TME is a measure of public sector expenditure drawn from components in national accounts produced by the Office for National Statistics (ONS). TES broadly represents the sum of current and capital expenditure of central and local government, and public corporations, but excludes general government capital consumption and other accounting adjustments.

3 Includes revised data.

4 Comparisons of expenditure per head between countries should be made with caution e.g. different countries have different proportions of young people within their population.

Chapter 2
Schools

CHAPTER 2: SCHOOLS

Key Facts

- There were 10.1 million full-time and part-time pupils in 34,600 schools in 2003/04, compared with 9.3 million pupils in 34,600 thousand schools in 1990/91. **(Tables 2.1, 2.2, 2.3)**

- There were 290,700 full-time and part-time pupils with statements of Special Educational Needs (SEN), or Record of Needs in Scotland, in 2003/04, representing 2.9 per cent of all pupils, with 64 per cent of SEN pupils with statements being educated in mainstream schools. **(Table 2.4)**

- There were 510,200 full-time qualified teachers in the United Kingdom in 2002/03, of which almost 70 per cent were female. Eighty-six per cent of full-time teachers were employed in maintained nursery, primary and secondary schools. **(Table 2.5)**

- There were, on average 41 pupils per maintained mainstream nursery school in 2003/04, 227 pupils per primary school and 943 pupils per secondary school. **(Table 2.6)**

- The average class size in primary schools in the United Kingdom in 2003/04 was 25.9 pupils. The average class size in secondary schools in England and Wales was 21.8 pupils. **(Table 2.7)**

- The average size of one-teacher classes in primary and secondary schools in England in 2003/04 was 26.2 pupils and 21.8 pupils respectively. **(Table 2.7)**

- The average pupil/teacher ratio in nursery schools in 2003/04 was 23.6. In primary schools the ratio was 21.9 and in secondary schools it was 16.4. The average pupil/teacher ratio for all schools was 17.5, compared to 17.3 in 1990/91. **(Table 2.8)**

- 72 per cent of boys and 83 per cent of girls in England achieved Level 4 or above in the 2004 Key Stage 2 English test. 74 per cent of boys and 84 per cent of girls in Wales achieved Level 4 or above. **(Table 2.9)**

- 74 per cent of both boys and girls in England achieved Level 4 or above in the 2004 Key Stage 2 Maths test. 77 per cent of boys and 80 per cent of girls in Wales achieved Level 4 or above. **(Table 2.9)**

- In 2003/04, 14.5 per cent of pupils in maintained nursery & primary schools were taking free school meals, compared with 14.0 per cent in 1990/91. In maintained secondary schools, in 2003/04, 14.8 per cent of pupils were known to be eligible for free school meals, but only 10.7 per cent of pupils were taking free school meals. The proportion of pupils in maintained special schools taking free school meals was 31.3 per cent. **(Table 2.10)**

CHAPTER 2: SCHOOLS - LIST OF TABLES

2.1 SCHOOLS
Number of schools, by type of school – time series

United Kingdom — Numbers

	Academic years					
	1990/91	1995/96	2000/01	2001/02	2002/03[1]	2003/04
UNITED KINGDOM						
Public sector mainstream						
Nursery[2]	1,364	1,486	3,228	3,227	3,394	3,438
Primary	24,135	23,441	22,902	22,800	22,638	22,509
Secondary[3]	4,790	4,463	4,337	4,306	4,284	4,255
of which						
middle deemed secondary	491	400	316	300	294	279
modern	171	113	145	130	130	130
Grammar	222	231	231	232	234	234
Technical	3	1	3	3	2	4
Comprehensive	3,696	3,509	3,443	3,450	3,436	3,420
of which 6th form colleges	116	.	.	.	.	.
Other	207	209	199	191	188	188
of which Specialist schools[4]	.	107	536	685	992	1,446
Non-maintained mainstream	2,508	2,436	2,414	2,409	2,380	2,524
Special - maintained }		1,456	1,401	1,387	1,367	1,360
}	1,830					
- non maintained }		109	97	96	104	103
Pupil referral units	.	315	338	340	390	457
ALL SCHOOLS	34,627	33,706	34,717	34,565	34,557	34,646
ENGLAND						
Public sector mainstream						
Nursery	566	547	506	494	475	468
Primary	19,047	18,480	18,069	17,985	17,861	17,762
Secondary[3]	3,897	3,594	3,481	3,457	3,436	3,409
of which						
middle deemed secondary	491	400	316	300	294	279
modern	171	113	145	130	130	130
Grammar	152	160	159	161	163	164
Technical	3	1	3	3	2	4
Comprehensive	3,042	2,876	2,825	2,836	2,823	2,807
of which 6th form colleges	114	.	.	.	.	.
Other	38	44	33	27	24	25
of which Specialist schools[4]	.	107	536	685	992	1,446
Non-maintained mainstream	2,289	2,266	2,205	2,206	2,180	2,330
Special - maintained }		1,191	1,113	1,098	1,088	1,078
}	1,380					
- non maintained }		72	62	63	72	70
Pupil referral units	.	291	308	312	360	426
ALL SCHOOLS	27,179	26,441	25,744	25,615	25,472	25,543
WALES						
Public sector mainstream						
Nursery	54	52	41	40	37	34
Primary	1,717	1,681	1,631	1,624	1,602	1,588
Secondary[3,5]	230	228	229	227	227	227
of which 6th form colleges	2	.	.	.	.	.
Non-maintained mainstream	71	62	54	56	59	60
Special (maintained)	61	54	45	44	43	43
Pupil referral units	.	24	30	28	30	31
ALL SCHOOLS	2,133	2,101	2,030	2,019	1,998	1,983
SCOTLAND						
Public sector mainstream						
Nursery[2]	659	796	2,586	2,597	2,782	2,836
Primary	2,372	2,332	2,278	2,271	2,258	2,248
Secondary[5]	424	405	389	387	386	386
Non-maintained mainstream	131	87	129	122	119	117
Special - maintained	343	164	195	197	189	192
- non maintained	.	37	35	33	32	33
ALL SCHOOLS	3,929	3,821	5,612	5,607	5,766	5,812
NORTHERN IRELAND						
Grant aided mainstream						
Nursery[6]	85	91	95	96	100	100
Primary[7]	999	948	924	920	917	911
Secondary	239	236	238	235	235	233
of which						
Grammar	70	71	72	71	71	70
Other (Secondary intermediate)	169	165	166	164	164	163
Non-maintained mainstream	17	21	26	25	22	17
Special (maintained)	46	47	48	48	47	47
ALL SCHOOLS	1,386	1,343	1,331	1,324	1,321	1,308

Sources: Department for Education and Skills; National Assembly for Wales; Scottish Executive; Northern Ireland Department of Education

1 Includes revised data.
2 Nursery schools figures for Scotland prior to 1998/99 only include data for Local Authority pre-schools. Data thereafter include partnership pre-schools.
3 From 1993/94, excludes sixth form colleges in England and Wales which were reclassified as further education colleges on 1 April 1993.
4 Operational from September of the first year shown.
5 All secondary schools are classed as Comprehensive.
6 Excludes voluntary and private pre-school education centres (383 in total in 2003/04).
7 From 1995/96, includes Preparatory Departments in Grammar Schools (19 in total in 2003/04).

2.2

SCHOOLS
Full-time and part-time pupils by age, gender [1] and school type, 2003/04 [2]

United Kingdom   Thousands

| | Maintained schools [3] | | | | | | | | Non-maintained | | | All schools |
	Nursery Schools [4,5]	Nursery Classes	Other Classes [6]	Total Primary Schools	Secondary Schools	Special schools	Pupil Referral Units [7]	All maintained schools	Special schools	Other Schools [8]	All non-maintained schools	
Age at 31 August 2003 [9]												
All												
2–4 [10]	150.4	314.6	605.0	919.6	0.1	5.8	-	1,075.9	0.1	71.0	71.1	1,147.0
5	-	-	662.9	662.9	-	3.9	-	666.9	-	32.9	32.9	699.8
6	-	-	695.3	695.3	-	4.6	-	700.0	0.1	33.8	33.9	733.9
7	-	-	684.7	684.7	0.1	5.0	0.1	689.9	0.1	34.6	34.7	724.7
8	-	-	693.1	693.1	0.1	5.6	0.1	698.9	0.2	36.6	36.8	735.7
9	-	-	681.7	681.7	25.1	6.6	0.2	713.5	0.2	39.6	39.8	753.3
10	-	-	680.4	680.4	30.7	7.3	0.3	718.7	0.3	40.2	40.4	759.2
11	-	-	76.7	76.7	643.6	9.7	0.3	730.2	0.5	53.9	54.4	784.6
12	-	-	16.9	16.9	709.3	10.6	0.9	737.6	0.6	54.7	55.3	792.9
13	-	-	0.1	0.1	717.9	11.1	1.7	730.8	0.7	55.1	55.8	786.6
14	-	-	-	-	705.0	11.3	3.3	719.6	0.8	54.7	55.5	775.1
15	-	-	-	-	701.0	11.5	6.2	718.7	0.9	54.7	55.5	774.3
16	-	-	-	-	265.7	4.6	0.2	270.5	0.6	42.9	43.5	314.0
17	-	-	-	-	193.9	3.3	-	197.2	0.4	40.3	40.7	237.9
18	-	-	-	-	19.5	2.3	-	21.9	0.3	6.3	6.5	28.4
19 and over	-	-	-	-	1.1	-	-	1.1	0.2	2.4	2.6	3.7
Total [11]	150.5	314.7	4,796.7	5,111.4	4,013.1	103.2	13.4	9,391.6	5.9	653.6	659.5	10,051.1
of which												
England	39.0	281.9	3,970.7	4,252.5	3,325.0	86.9	13.0	7,716.4	4.8	613.6	618.5	8,334.9
Wales	2.1	24.0	254.7	278.7	214.3	3.8	0.4	499.3	-	9.8	9.8	509.2
Scotland [5]	103.1	-	406.0	406.0	318.4	7.7	.	835.3	1.1	29.3	30.3	865.6
Northern Ireland [4]	6.2	8.8	165.3	174.2	155.4	4.8	-	340.6	-	0.8	0.8	341.5
Males [1]												
2–4 [10]	24.5	160.5	309.5	470.0	-	3.8	-	498.4	-	34.7	34.7	533.2
5	-	-	338.9	338.9	-	2.7	-	341.7	-	15.8	15.9	357.5
6	-	-	355.2	355.2	-	3.2	-	358.5	-	16.3	16.3	374.8
7	-	-	350.6	350.6	0.1	3.5	0.1	354.3	0.1	16.9	17.0	371.3
8	-	-	354.0	354.0	0.1	3.9	0.1	358.1	0.1	17.9	18.0	376.1
9	-	-	347.5	347.5	12.9	4.7	0.2	365.2	0.1	19.5	19.6	384.8
10	-	-	346.5	346.5	15.6	5.2	0.3	367.6	0.2	19.7	19.9	387.5
11	-	-	39.1	39.1	328.0	6.8	0.2	374.2	0.4	26.4	26.8	401.0
12	-	-	9.0	9.0	359.8	7.4	0.8	376.9	0.5	26.5	27.0	403.9
13	-	-	0.1	0.1	364.9	7.7	1.3	374.1	0.5	26.6	27.1	401.2
14	-	-	-	-	356.8	7.8	2.6	367.1	0.6	26.4	27.0	394.2
15	-	-	-	-	353.3	7.9	4.4	365.6	0.6	26.5	27.1	392.8
16	-	-	-	-	126.3	2.8	0.1	129.2	0.4	20.7	21.1	150.3
17	-	-	-	-	90.0	1.9	-	91.9	0.2	19.6	19.8	111.7
18	-	-	-	-	10.2	1.4	-	11.5	0.2	3.3	3.5	15.0
19 and over	-	-	-	-	0.5	-	-	0.5	0.1	1.3	1.4	2.0
Total	24.6	160.5	2,450.5	2,611.0	2,018.4	70.8	10.2	4,734.9	4.1	318.1	322.3	5,057.2
Females [1]												
2–4 [10]	22.8	154.1	295.5	449.6	-	2.0	-	474.4	-	35.4	35.4	509.8
5	-	-	324.0	324.0	-	1.2	-	325.2	-	15.7	15.7	341.0
6	-	-	340.1	340.1	-	1.4	-	341.5	-	16.2	16.2	357.7
7	-	-	334.1	334.1	-	1.5	-	335.7	-	16.3	16.4	352.0
8	-	-	339.1	339.1	-	1.7	-	340.9	-	17.3	17.4	358.2
9	-	-	334.1	334.1	12.2	1.9	-	348.3	0.1	18.5	18.6	366.9
10	-	-	333.9	333.9	15.2	2.1	-	351.2	0.1	18.6	18.7	369.8
11	-	-	37.5	37.5	315.6	2.8	-	356.0	0.1	25.2	25.3	381.3
12	-	-	7.9	7.9	349.4	3.2	0.1	360.6	0.2	25.4	25.5	386.2
13	-	-	-	-	353.0	3.4	0.4	356.7	0.2	25.6	25.8	382.6
14	-	-	-	-	348.2	3.5	0.7	352.4	0.2	25.3	25.5	378.0
15	-	-	-	-	347.7	3.6	1.8	353.1	0.2	25.2	25.4	378.5
16	-	-	-	-	139.4	1.8	0.1	141.3	0.2	19.4	19.5	160.8
17	-	-	-	-	103.9	1.4	-	105.3	0.1	18.4	18.6	123.9
18	-	-	-	-	9.4	1.0	-	10.4	0.1	2.6	2.7	13.1
19 and over	-	-	-	-	0.5	-	-	0.6	0.1	1.0	1.1	1.7
Total	22.8	154.1	2,346.2	2,500.4	1,994.7	32.4	3.3	4,553.5	1.7	306.2	307.9	4,861.4

Sources: Department for Education and Skills; National Assembly for Wales; Scottish Executive; Northern Ireland Department of Education

1 In Scotland gender split is not collected by age but has been estimated according to figures collected in September 2003. In Northern Ireland a gender split is not collected by age but is available by year group and so this is used as a proxy. For example pupils in Year 1 are counted as age 4, pupils in Year 2 are counted as age 5 etc.
2 Provisional. Data for Wales refer to 2002/03.
3 Grant-aided schools in Northern Ireland.
4 Excludes 5,913 children at voluntary and private pre-school centres in Northern Ireland in places funded under the Pre-School Expansion Programme which began in 1998/99.
5 Nursery schools figures for Scotland include pre-school education centres. The "All" figures include nursery school pupils which cannot be split by gender.
6 Includes reception pupils in primary classes and, in Northern Ireland, pupils in preparatory departments of grammar schools.
7 England and Wales only. Figures exclude dually registered pupils.
8 Age 2-4 includes pupils less than 2 years of age in England.
9 1 July for Northern Ireland and 31 December for non-maintained primary and secondary school pupils in Scotland.
10 Includes the so-called rising five's (i.e. those pupils who became 5 during the autumn term).
11 Includes pupils with unrecorded gender and ages unknown for Wales and Scotland.

SCHOOLS
Full-time and part-time pupils by gender and school type - time series

United Kingdom   Thousands

| | Maintained Schools [1] | | | | | | | | Non-maintained | | | All schools |
| | Nursery schools [2,3] | Primary Schools | | | Secondary schools [5] | Special schools | Pupil Referral Units [6] | All maintained schools | Special schools | Other schools | All non-maintained schools | |
		Nursery classes	Other classes [4]	Total Primary Schools								
1990/91												
All	104.9		4,954.5	4,954.5	3,473.3	107.7	.	8,640.4	6.4	613.4	619.7	9,260.2
Males	54.0		2,529.4	2,529.4	1,753.6	70.6	.	4,407.7	4.2	323.8	328.0	4,735.6
Females	50.9		2,425.1	2,425.1	1,719.7	37.1	.	4,232.8	2.2	289.6	291.8	4,524.5
1995/96												
All	84.2	367.1	4,971.2	5,338.4	3,676.8	107.7	..	9,207.0	6.7	602.7	609.4	9,816.5
Males	43.4	188.2	2,536.9	2,725.1	1,853.0	71.6	..	4,693.2	4.6	314.4	319.0	5,012.2
Females	40.8	178.9	2,434.4	2,613.3	1,823.7	36.1	..	4,513.9	2.2	288.3	290.4	4,804.3
2000/01 [7]												
All	152.2	30.3	4,413.7	5,297.7	3,916.9	107.7	9.7	9,484.2	5.7	626.1	631.8	10,116.0
Males	79.2	15.5	2,254.5	2,706.6	1,973.7	72.8	7.4	4,839.7	4.0	321.9	325.8	5,165.5
Females	73.1	14.9	2,159.3	2,591.0	1,943.2	34.9	2.4	4,644.6	1.8	304.2	305.9	4,950.5
2001/02												
All [8]	149.5	330.0	4,915.5	5,245.5	3,949.3	106.4	10.4	9,461.1	5.7	635.0	640.7	10,101.8
Males	26.3	168.3	2,510.7	2,678.9	1,990.0	72.4	7.8	4,775.4	4.0	324.6	328.6	5,104.0
Females	24.4	161.8	2,404.8	2,566.6	1,959.3	34.0	2.6	4,586.9	1.7	310.4	312.1	4,899.0
2002/03												
All [8]	153.9	323.1	4,855.1	5,178.2	3,995.0	105.6	12.4	9,445.2	5.9	643.5	649.5	10,094.6
Males	25.4	164.6	2,480.1	2,644.7	2,011.3	72.1	9.3	4,762.9	4.2	327.6	331.7	5,094.6
Females	23.5	158.5	2,374.3	2,532.8	1,983.7	33.4	3.1	4,576.4	1.8	315.9	317.7	4,894.1
2003/04 [9,10]												
All [8]	150.5	314.7	4,796.7	5,111.4	4,013.1	103.2	13.4	9,391.6	5.9	653.6	659.5	10,051.1
Males	24.6	160.5	2,450.5	2,611.0	2,018.4	70.8	10.2	4,734.9	4.1	318.1	322.3	5,057.2
Females	22.8	154.1	2,346.2	2,500.4	1,994.7	32.4	3.3	4,553.5	1.7	306.2	307.9	4,861.4

Source: Department for Education and Skills; National Assembly for Wales; Scottish Executive; Northern Ireland Department of Education

1 Grant aided schools in Northern Ireland.

2 For 1990/91 and from 1999/00, nursery schools includes some nursery classes in primary schools for Scotland. From 1999/00 nursery schools figures for Scotland include pre-school education centres.

3 Includes children at voluntary and private pre-school centres (5,913 in 2003/04) in Northern Ireland in places funded under the Pre-School Expansion Programme which began in 1998/99.

4 Includes reception pupils in primary schools and, in Northern Ireland, pupils in preparatory departments of grammar schools.

5 From 1993/94 excludes sixth form colleges in England and Wales which were reclassified as Further Education colleges from 1 April 1993.

6 England and Wales only. Figures exclude dually registered pupils.

7 A spilt between nursery classes and other classes in primary schools is not available for 2 - 4 year olds in England. Figures are included in the Total Primary Schools column only.

8 Includes nursery schools figures for Scotland which cannot be split by gender.

9 Provisional. Data for Wales refer to 2002/03.

10 Includes non-maintained 'Other schools' figures for Scotland which cannot be split by gender.

SCHOOLS
Full-time and part-time pupils with Special Educational Needs (SEN) [1] by type of school, 2003/04 [2]

United Kingdom

Thousands and percentages

	UK	England[3]	Wales	Scotland	N Ireland
ALL SCHOOLS					
Total Pupils	10,057.0	8,334.9	509.2	865.6	347.4
SEN pupils with statements	290.7	247.6	16.0	16.1	11.0
Incidence(%) [4]	*2.9*	*3.0*	*3.1*	*1.9*	*3.2*
MAINTAINED SCHOOLS [5]					
Nursery [6]					
Total Pupils	156.4	39.0	2.1	103.1	12.2
SEN pupils with statements	1.8	0.5	-	1.3	0.1
Incidence(%) [4]	*1.1*	*1.2*	*0.6*	*1.2*	*0.5*
Placement(%) [7]	*0.6*	*0.2*	*0.1*	*7.8*	*0.6*
Primary [8]					
Total Pupils	5,111.4	4,252.5	278.7	406.0	174.2
SEN pupils without statements	712.6	685.7	..	..	26.9
SEN pupils with statements	83.0	69.6	5.8	4.0	3.6
Pupils with statements - Incidence (%) [4]	*1.6*	*1.6*	*2.1*	*1.0*	*2.1*
Pupils with statements - Placement (%) [7]	*28.5*	*28.1*	*36.1*	*24.8*	*32.6*
Secondary					
Total Pupils	4,013.1	3,325.0	214.3	318.4	155.4
SEN pupils without statements	461.3	450.1	..	..	11.2
SEN pupils with statements	92.3	78.5	6.1	4.8	3.0
Pupils with statements - Incidence (%) [4]	*2.3*	*2.4*	*2.8*	*1.5*	*1.9*
Pupils with statements - Placement (%) [7]	*31.8*	*31.7*	*38.0*	*29.7*	*26.9*
Special [9,10]					
Total Pupils	103.2	86.9	3.8	7.7	4.8
SEN pupils with statements	98.1	84.3	3.7	5.7	4.4
Incidence (%) [4]	*95.0*	*96.9*	*98.5*	*73.9*	*90.8*
Placement (%) [7]	*33.7*	*34.0*	*23.3*	*35.3*	*39.9*
Pupil Referral Units [9,11]					
Total Pupils	13.4	13.0	0.4	.	.
SEN pupils with statements	2.4	2.3	0.1	.	.
Incidence (%) [4]	*17.9*	*17.6*	*25.5*	.	.
Placement (%) [7]	*0.8*	*0.9*	*0.7*	.	.
OTHER SCHOOLS					
Independent					
Total Pupils	653.6	613.6	9.8	29.3	0.8
SEN pupils with statements	8.1	7.8	0.3	-	..
Incidence (%) [4]	*1.2*	*1.3*	*3.0*	*0.1*	..
Placement (%) [7]	*2.8*	*3.1*	*1.9*	*0.2*	..
Non-maintained Special [9]					
Total Pupils	5.9	4.8	.	1.1	.
SEN pupils with statements	5.1	4.7	.	0.4	.
Incidence (%) [4]	*86.0*	*97.2*	.	*34.7*	.
Placement (%) [7]	*1.7*	*1.9*	.	*2.3*	.

Sources: Department for Education and Skills; National Assembly for Wales; Scottish Executive; Northern Ireland Department of Education

1 For Scotland, pupils with a Record of Needs including some who also had an Individualised Educational Programme.
2 Provisional. Data for Wales refer to 2002/03.
3 Includes new codes for recording SEN status following the introduction of a new SEN Code of Practice from January 2002. Data are not therefore directly comparable prior to 2001/02.
4 Incidence of pupils - the number of pupils with statements within each school type expressed as a proportion of the total number of pupils on roll in each school type.
5 Grant-Aided schools in Northern Ireland.
6 Includes pupils in Voluntary and Private Pre-School Centres in Northern Ireland funded under the Pre-School Expansion Programme which began in 1998/99.
7 Placement of pupils - the number of pupils with statements within each school type expressed as a proportion of the number of pupils with statements in all schools.
8 Includes nursery classes (except for Scotland, where they are included with Nursery schools) and reception classes in primary schools.
9 England and Wales figures exclude dually registered pupils.
10 Including general and hospital special schools.
11 England and Wales only.

2.5 SCHOOLS
Qualified teachers by type of school and gender — time series

(i) Full-time teachers
Thousands

	Public sector mainstream schools		Non-maintained mainstream schools	All Special schools	Total All Schools [2]
	Nursery and Primary	Secondary[1]			
All teachers					
Great Britain					
1990/91	200.3	223.2	44.9	18.2	**486.6**
1995/96	203.3	212.2	48.6	16.6	**480.6**
United Kingdom					
2000/01 [3,4,5]	211.2	225.7	52.3	16.5	**505.7**
2001/02 [3]	211.2	227.1	52.8	16.3	**507.3**
2002/03 [6]	209.0	230.5	53.6	17.1	**510.2**
of which:					
England & Wales [7]	179.5	197.3	51.0	14.3	**442.1**
Scotland	21.5	23.1	2.5	2.1	**49.1**
Northern Ireland	8.1	10.1	0.1	0.7	**19.0**
Males					
Great Britain					
1990/91	35.8	116.0	20.6	5.8	**178.2**
1995/96	33.8	103.4	21.1	5.3	**163.5**
United Kingdom					
2000/01 [3,4,5]	32.1	102.9	21.3	5.0	**161.3**
2001/02 [3]	31.8	102.6	21.5	4.9	**160.8**
2002/03 [6]	31.4	102.6	21.6	5.1	**160.7**
of which:					
England & Wales [7]	28.4	88.1	20.6	4.5	**141.6**
Scotland	1.6	10.4	1.0	0.5	**13.5**
Northern Ireland	1.4	4.0	-	0.1	**5.6**
Females					
Great Britain					
1990/91	164.5	107.1	24.3	12.4	**308.4**
1995/96	169.5	108.8	27.4	11.3	**317.0**
United Kingdom					
2000/01 [3,4,5]	179.1	122.8	30.9	11.6	**344.4**
2001/02 [3]	179.4	124.5	31.2	11.4	**346.5**
2002/03 [6]	177.7	127.9	32.0	12.0	**349.6**
of which:					
England & Wales [7]	151.1	109.2	30.4	9.8	**300.5**
Scotland	19.9	12.6	1.5	1.6	**35.7**
Northern Ireland	6.7	6.0	0.1	0.6	**13.4**

(ii) Full-time equivalent (FTE) of part-time teachers
Thousands

	Public sector mainstream schools		Non-maintained mainstream schools	All Special schools	Total All Schools [2]
	Nursery and Primary	Secondary[1]			
All teachers					
Great Britain					
1990/91	..	..	..	..	**30.0**
1995/96	18.7	17.6	8.9	1.5	**46.7**
United Kingdom					
2000/01 [4,5]	21.9	16.7	10.2	1.6	**50.4**
2001/02 [3]	23.4	17.4	10.4	1.8	**53.0**
2002/03 [6]	24.0	17.8	11.1	1.7	**54.6**

Sources: Department for Education and Skills; National Assembly for Wales; Scottish Executive; Northern Ireland Department of Education

1 From 1993/94 excludes sixth form colleges in England and Wales which were reclassified as further education colleges on 1 April 1993.
2 Excludes Pupil Referral Units (PRUs).
3 Includes revised data.
4 Includes 1999/00 pre-school data for Scotland.
5 Includes 2001/02 data for Northern Ireland.
6 Provisional. Includes 2001/02 pre-school and 2003/04 school data for Scotland.
7 A gender breakdown of public sector teachers in England and Wales is only available from the Database of Teachers Records (DTR) where some in-service teachers may be shown as not in service because their service details are not recorded. A more complete coverage of teachers in England and Wales is available from the Form 618G survey, and published in "Statistics of Education: School workforce in England (including teachers' pay for England and Wales)".

United Kingdom	(i) Number of schools											Numbers
	25 and under	26 to 50	51 to 100	101 to 200	201 to 300	301 to 400	401 to 600	601 to 800	801 to 1,000	1,001 to 1,500	1,501 and over	Total
United Kingdom												
Public sector mainstream												
Nursery [3,4]	1,566	1,066	959	231	2	-	-	-	-	-	-	**3,824**
Primary [5]	342	1,082	2,673	5,967	6,711	3,236	2,277	214	20	1	-	**22,523**
Secondary [6]	6	9	13	48	84	141	492	750	921	1,491	300	**4,255**
Pupil referral units	304	73	44	29	5	-	-	-	-	-	-	**455**
Non-maintained mainstream [7]	313	219	346	556	340	228	234	122	88	75	2	**2,523**
Special	177	319	604	338	23	2	-	-	-	-	-	**1,463**
All schools	**2,708**	**2,768**	**4,639**	**7,169**	**7,165**	**3,607**	**3,003**	**1,086**	**1,029**	**1,567**	**302**	**35,043**
England												
Public sector mainstream												
Nursery	3	50	298	117	-	-	-	-	-	-	-	**468**
Primary	73	553	1,874	4,639	5,692	2,738	2,000	177	16	-	-	**17,762**
Secondary	1	1	4	23	58	102	357	581	739	1,275	268	**3,409**
Pupil referral units	281	70	41	29	5	-	-	-	-	-	-	**426**
Non-maintained mainstream [7]	266	200	317	524	325	210	219	112	83	72	2	**2,330**
Special	72	245	518	294	17	2	-	-	-	-	-	**1,148**
All schools	**696**	**1,119**	**3,052**	**5,626**	**6,097**	**3,052**	**2,576**	**870**	**838**	**1,347**	**270**	**25,543**
Wales												
Public sector mainstream												
Nursery	3	13	19	2	-	-	-	-	-	-	-	**37**
Primary	54	165	265	514	403	133	64	4	-	-	-	**1,602**
Secondary	-	-	-	-	-	7	33	51	48	71	17	**227**
Pupil referral units	23	3	3	-	-	-	-	-	-	-	-	**29**
Non-maintained mainstream	19	6	8	9	4	5	4	4	-	-	-	**59**
Special	-	8	22	11	2	-	-	-	-	-	-	**43**
All schools	**99**	**195**	**317**	**536**	**409**	**145**	**101**	**59**	**48**	**71**	**17**	**1,997**
Scotland												
Public sector mainstream												
Nursery [3]	1,198	970	561	105	2	-	-	-	-	-	-	**2,836**
Primary	191	267	318	560	482	279	142	9	-	-	-	**2,248**
Secondary	5	8	9	10	7	12	48	68	94	115	10	**386**
Non-maintained mainstream	20	10	17	22	10	13	11	6	5	3	-	**117**
Special	102	59	47	16	1	-	-	-	-	-	-	**225**
All schools	**1,516**	**1,314**	**952**	**713**	**502**	**304**	**201**	**83**	**99**	**118**	**10**	**5,812**
Northern Ireland												
Grant aided mainstream												
Nursery [4]	362	33	81	7	-	-	-	-	-	-	-	**483**
Primary [5]	24	97	216	254	134	86	71	24	4	1	-	**911**
Secondary [6]	-	-	-	15	19	20	54	50	40	30	5	**233**
Non-maintained mainstream	8	3	4	1	1	-	-	-	-	-	-	**17**
Special	3	7	17	17	3	-	-	-	-	-	-	**47**
All schools	**397**	**140**	**318**	**294**	**157**	**106**	**125**	**74**	**44**	**31**	**5**	**1,691**

Sources: Department for Education and Skills; National Assembly for Wales; Scottish Executive; Northern Ireland Department of Education

1 School size on a pupil headcount basis.
2 Provisional. Data for Wales refer to 2002/03.
3 Nursery schools figures for Scotland include pre-school education centres.
4 Northern Ireland figures include 383 Voluntary and Private Pre-School Centres including 5,913 pupils, funded under the Pre-School Expansion Programme which began in 1998/99.
5 Includes 19 preparatory departments attached to Grammar Schools in Northern Ireland.
6 Includes Voluntary Grammar Schools in Northern Ireland.
7 Includes City Technology Colleges and Academies.
8 Includes pupils in nursery classes in primary schools in Scotland.
9 Includes pupils in nursery classes and reception classes, except for Scotland - see footnote 8.

CONTINUED
SCHOOLS
Schools and pupils by size of school [1] and school type, 2003/04 [2]

United Kingdom				(ii) Number of pupils								Thousands
	25 and under	26 to 50	51 to 100	101 to 200	201 to 300	301 to 400	401 to 600	601 to 800	801 to 1,000	1,001 to 1,500	1,501 and over	Total
United Kingdom												
Public sector mainstream												
Nursery [3,4,8]	22.4	38.8	66.6	28.2	0.4	-	-	-	-	-	-	156.4
Primary [5,9]	5.8	41.9	203.4	921.5	1,619.6	1,117.9	1,041.1	141.7	17.3	1.0	-	5,111.4
Secondary [6]	0.1	0.4	1.0	7.9	21.6	49.7	248.9	532.3	829.9	1,809.4	511.8	4,013.1
Pupil referral units	2.7	2.7	2.9	3.9	1.2	-	-	-	-	-	-	13.4
Non-maintained mainstream [7]	3.9	8.0	25.7	82.9	84.4	78.3	113.5	84.3	78.6	89.2	5.0	653.6
Special	2.2	12.3	44.4	44.3	5.2	0.7	-	-	-	-	-	109.1
All schools	**37.2**	**104.1**	**344.0**	**1,088.6**	**1,732.4**	**1,246.6**	**1,403.5**	**758.4**	**925.7**	**1,899.6**	**516.8**	**10,057.0**
England												
Public sector mainstream												
Nursery	0.1	2.0	22.4	14.5	-	-	-	-	-	-	-	39.0
Primary [9]	1.3	21.9	144.0	722.6	1,370.9	945.5	915.1	117.4	13.8	-	-	4,252.5
Secondary	-	-	0.3	3.8	14.9	36.0	181.7	412.3	666.8	1,552.0	457.1	3,325.0
Pupil referral units	2.6	2.6	2.8	3.9	1.2	-	-	-	-	-	-	13.0
Non-maintained mainstream [7]	3.3	7.3	23.6	78.2	80.6	72.5	105.4	78.0	74.1	85.6	5.0	613.6
Special	1.1	9.7	38.2	38.1	3.9	0.7	-	-	-	-	-	91.8
All schools	**8.4**	**43.6**	**231.3**	**861.2**	**1,471.4**	**1,054.6**	**1,202.2**	**607.7**	**754.6**	**1,637.6**	**462.1**	**8,334.9**
Wales												
Public sector mainstream												
Nursery	0.1	0.5	1.3	0.2	-	-	-	-	-	-	-	2.1
Primary [9]	1.0	6.3	19.9	77.3	96.9	45.5	29.0	2.7	-	-	-	278.7
Secondary	-	-	-	-	-	2.3	16.4	36.7	43.5	86.6	28.9	214.3
Pupil referral units	0.1	0.1	0.2	-	-	-	-	-	-	-	-	0.4
Non-maintained mainstream	0.3	0.2	0.5	1.3	1.0	1.7	2.0	2.8	-	-	-	9.8
Special	-	0.3	1.5	1.5	0.4	-	-	-	-	-	-	3.8
All schools	**1.5**	**7.4**	**23.5**	**80.3**	**98.4**	**49.6**	**47.4**	**42.2**	**43.5**	**86.6**	**28.9**	**509.2**
Scotland												
Public sector mainstream												
Nursery [3,8]	17.0	35.3	37.8	12.6	0.4	-	-	-	-	-	-	103.1
Primary	3.1	9.9	23.3	84.6	118.8	96.7	63.5	6.1	-	-	-	406.0
Secondary	0.1	0.3	0.7	1.5	1.7	4.3	24.4	48.2	84.0	136.1	17.2	318.4
Non-maintained mainstream	0.3	0.3	1.3	3.2	2.5	4.1	6.0	3.5	4.5	3.6	-	29.3
Special	1.1	2.0	3.2	2.2	0.2	-	-	-	-	-	-	8.7
All schools	**21.5**	**47.9**	**66.4**	**104.1**	**123.7**	**105.1**	**93.9**	**57.7**	**88.4**	**139.7**	**17.2**	**865.6**
Northern Ireland												
Grant aided mainstream												
Nursery [4]	5.3	1.0	5.0	0.9	-	-	-	-	-	-	-	12.2
Primary [5,9]	0.4	3.8	16.2	37.1	33.0	30.2	33.4	15.6	3.5	1.0	-	174.2
Secondary [6]	-	-	-	2.6	5.0	7.1	26.4	35.2	35.7	34.7	8.6	155.4
Non-maintained mainstream	0.1	0.1	0.2	0.2	0.2	-	-	-	-	-	-	0.8
Special	0.1	0.3	1.4	2.4	0.7	-	-	-	-	-	-	4.8
All schools	**5.9**	**5.2**	**22.8**	**43.1**	**39.0**	**37.3**	**59.9**	**50.8**	**39.2**	**35.7**	**8.6**	**347.4**

Sources: Department for Education and Skills; National Assembly for Wales; Scottish Executive; Northern Ireland Department of Education

See previous page for footnotes.

SCHOOLS
Average class size [1], by Government Office Region [2] - time series

United Kingdom

	One teacher classes		All classes [3]	
	Primary	Secondary [4]	Primary	Secondary [4]
1990/91				
Great Britain	..	..	26.4	21.0
North West	26.0	20.6	26.5	21.6
North West	27.1	20.4	27.5	21.1
Yorkshire and the Humber	25.9	20.5	26.4	21.2
East Midlands	26.1	20.1	26.5	20.9
West Midlands	26.3	20.6	26.8	21.1
Eastern	26.0	20.9	26.4	21.7
London	25.8	20.7	26.2	21.4
South East	26.7	20.7	27.1	21.4
South West	26.4	20.9	26.7	21.4
England	26.3	20.6	26.8	21.3
Wales	..	19.5	24.8	21.0
Scotland	..	..	24.7	18.5
Northern Ireland	..	..	..	..
1995/96				
Great Britain	..	..	27.1	21.6
North East	27.1	22.0	27.2	22.5
North West	27.7	21.8	28.0	22.0
Yorkshire and the Humber	27.6	21.9	27.9	22.1
East Midlands	27.6	21.6	27.8	21.9
West Midlands	27.3	21.8	27.6	22.0
Eastern	26.6	21.3	26.8	21.6
London	27.0	21.7	27.3	22.0
South East	27.3	21.4	27.4	21.6
South West	27.3	21.8	27.4	22.0
England	27.3	21.7	27.5	21.9
Wales	..	..	25.9	20.2
Scotland	..	..	24.8	19.5
Northern Ireland	..	..	..	..
2000/01				
United Kingdom	..	..	26.4	22.1 [5]
North East	25.8	22.1	25.9	22.2
North West	26.7	22.0	26.8	22.1
Yorkshire and the Humber	26.6	22.1	26.8	22.3
East Midlands	26.7	22.1	26.8	22.2
West Midlands	26.5	21.9	26.6	22.1
Eastern	26.4	21.8	26.5	22.0
London	27.0	22.1	27.2	22.2
South East	27.0	22.0	27.1	22.0
South West	26.7	22.2	26.8	22.3
England	26.7	22.0	26.8	22.1
Wales	..	..	24.8	21.3
Scotland	24.3	..	24.4	..
Northern Ireland [6]	..	..	23.9	..

Source: Department for Education and Skills; National Assembly for Wales; Scottish Executive; Northern Ireland Department of Education

1   Maintained schools only.
2   Government Office Regions in England and each UK country.
3   Includes classes where more than one teacher may be present.
4   Figures throughout the table exclude sixth form colleges in England and Wales, which were reclassified as further education colleges from 1 April 1993.
5   England and Wales.
6   Excludes preparatory departments attached to Grammar schools, but includes reception pupils integrated into P1.
7   Provisional.

CONTINUED
SCHOOLS
Average class size [1], by Government Office Region [2] - time series

United Kingdom

Numbers

	One teacher classes		All classes [3]	
	Primary	Secondary [4]	Primary	Secondary [4]
2001/02				
United Kingdom	..	..	26.0	21.9 [5]
North East	25.3	21.8	25.4	22.0
North West	26.1	21.8	26.3	21.9
Yorkshire and the Humber	26.4	22.0	26.6	22.1
East Midlands	26.3	22.1	26.4	22.1
West Midlands	26.1	21.9	26.3	22.0
Eastern	26.1	21.6	26.2	21.7
London	26.9	22.1	27.1	22.2
South East	26.4	21.8	26.5	21.8
South West	26.2	22.1	26.3	22.2
England	26.3	21.9	26.4	22.0
Wales	..	..	24.4	21.2
Scotland	24.2	..	24.3	..
Northern Ireland [6]	..	..	23.6	..
2002/03				
United Kingdom	..	..	26.0	21.9 [5]
North East	25.2	21.8	25.4	21.8
North West	26.1	21.8	26.2	21.8
Yorkshire and the Humber	26.3	22.0	26.5	22.1
East Midlands	26.3	21.9	26.4	22.0
West Midlands	26.2	21.9	26.4	21.9
Eastern	26.1	21.6	26.2	21.6
London	26.9	21.9	27.0	22.1
South East	26.4	21.8	26.5	21.8
South West	26.2	22.3	26.2	22.3
England	26.3	21.9	26.4	21.9
Wales	..	..	24.4	20.5
Scotland	24.0	..	24.0	..
Northern Ireland [6]	..	..	23.3	..
2003/04 [7]				
United Kingdom	..	..	25.9	21.8 [5]
North East	25.1	21.7	25.2	21.8
North West	26.0	21.8	26.1	21.8
Yorkshire and the Humber	26.3	21.9	26.5	21.9
East Midlands	26.3	21.9	26.4	21.9
West Midlands	26.2	21.7	26.4	21.8
Eastern	26.2	21.7	26.3	21.7
London	26.6	21.8	26.8	21.9
South East	26.4	21.7	26.5	21.7
South West	26.3	22.1	26.3	22.2
England	26.2	21.8	26.4	21.9
Wales	..	..	24.5	20.6
Scotland	23.7	..	23.7	..
Northern Ireland [6]	..	..	23.1	..

Source: Department for Education and Skills; National Assembly for Wales; Scottish Executive; Northern Ireland Department of Education

See previous page for footnotes.

SCHOOLS
2.8
Pupil/teacher [1] ratios [2] by type of school and Government Office Region [3] - time series

United Kingdom

Numbers

	Public sector mainstream			Non-maintained mainstream schools	Pupil Referral Units	Special schools		All schools
	Nursery Schools	Primary Schools [4]	Secondary Schools [5]			Maintained	Non-maintained	
1990/91								
United Kingdom	21.6	22.0	15.2	10.7	.	5.9	..	17.3
North East	19.3	22.3	15.6	12.5	.	6.1	4.7	18.0
North West	19.3	22.8	15.4	12.6	.	5.7	5.0	18.1
Yorkshire and the Humber	18.1	21.9	15.5	11.6	.	5.8	4.7	17.6
East Midlands	19.1	22.4	15.2	10.5	.	5.7	5.4	17.5
West Midlands	24.0	22.4	15.5	10.6	.	6.3	3.9	17.7
Eastern	18.7	22.4	16.2	10.7	.	5.8	5.0	17.6
London	16.9	20.6	15.3	11.6	.	5.1	4.8	16.6
South East	18.1	22.8	16.2	9.9	.	7.0	4.8	17.0
South West	19.2	22.4	16.0	9.8	.	6.5	4.9	17.2
England	19.1	22.2	15.7	10.8	.	6.0	4.8	17.4
Wales	20.6	22.3	15.4	9.8	.	6.3	.	18.2
Scotland	25.7	19.5	12.2	10.5	.	4.5	..	15.2
Northern Ireland	24.7	22.9	14.7	11.0	.	6.9	.	18.1
1995/96 [5]								
United Kingdom	21.3	22.7	16.1	10.3	..	6.3	.	18.0 [6]
North East	21.3	23.7	17.1	11.9	5.7	7.1	5.0	19.3
North West	20.0	23.7	16.6	11.7	4.1	5.8	4.5	18.9
Yorkshire and the Humber	18.7	23.8	17.0	11.3	4.6	6.5	3.8	19.2
East Midlands	19.2	24.1	16.8	10.1	2.9	6.2	5.2	18.9
West Midlands	23.3	23.5	16.7	10.4	3.1	7.1	3.6	18.7
Eastern	19.3	22.7	16.5	10.1	4.3	6.6	4.1	17.9
London	16.4	21.6	15.8	10.8	5.2	5.5	5.5	17.0
South East	17.0	23.0	16.7	9.4	3.9	7.1	4.7	17.2
South West	20.4	23.6	17.1	9.4	4.1	6.9	4.9	18.2
England	19.2	23.2	16.6	10.2	4.3	6.7	4.6	18.2
Wales	19.5	22.5	16.0	10.1	..	6.7	.	18.7 [6]
Scotland	24.3	19.5	12.9	11.0	.	4.8	3.7	15.5
Northern Ireland	24.1	20.7	14.8	10.9	.	6.7	.	17.2
2000/01 [5]								
United Kingdom	23.1	22.3	16.5	9.7	..	6.3	.	17.9 [6]
North East	19.9	22.6	17.0	11.4	4.4	7.1	5.0	18.6
North West	18.1	22.9	16.6	10.7	6.8	6.4	4.9	18.4
Yorkshire and the Humber	16.9	23.1	17.3	10.9	5.5	6.3	4.3	19.1
East Midlands	16.7	23.5	17.3	9.9	4.1	6.2	5.3	18.9
West Midlands	21.2	23.1	17.0	9.9	3.4	7.0	3.5	18.5
Eastern	17.0	22.8	17.4	9.3	2.8	6.9	5.2	18.1
London	16.4	22.5	16.6	10.4	4.7	6.0	5.5	17.5
South East	15.9	22.9	17.4	8.9	4.0	6.9	4.8	17.2
South West	17.5	23.0	17.5	9.0	4.6	6.4	5.3	18.0
England	17.7	22.9	17.1	9.7	4.4	6.6	4.8	18.1
Wales	17.3	21.5	16.6	9.6	..	6.8	.	18.4 [6]
Scotland [8]	28.5	19.0	13.0	10.1	.	4.2	3.3	15.4
Northern Ireland	24.4	20.1	14.5	9.3	.	5.9	.	16.6

Sources: Department for Education and Skills; National Assembly for Wales; Scottish Executive; Northern Ireland Department of Education

1 Qualified teachers only for all countries.
2 Includes full-time equivalents of part-time pupils and teachers.
3 Government Office Regions in England and each UK country.
4 Includes preparatory departments attached to grammar schools in Northern Ireland.
5 From 1993/94 excludes sixth form colleges in England and Wales which were reclassified as further education colleges from 1 April 1993.
6 Excludes Pupil Referral Units as information on teachers is not collected for Wales.
7 Includes revised data.
8 Nursery schools figures for Scotland include pre-school education centres and are not therefore directly comparable with figures prior to 1999/00.
9 Nursery schools figures for Scotland refer to 2001/02.
10 Provisional.

2.8

Pupil/teacher [1] ratios [2] by type of school and Government Office Region [3] - time series

United Kingdom   Numbers

	Public sector mainstream			Non-maintained mainstream schools	Pupil Referral Units	Special schools		All schools
	Nursery Schools	Primary Schools [4]	Secondary Schools [5]			Maintained	Non-maintained	
2001/02 [5,7]								
United Kingdom	23.6	22.0	16.4	10.1	..	6.2	.	17.7 [6]
North East	18.7	22.0	16.6	11.8	5.1	7.1	5.1	18.2
North West	17.1	22.3	16.3	11.3	6.6	6.3	4.5	18.1
Yorkshire and the Humber	15.4	22.7	16.9	11.1	6.1	6.5	4.7	18.7
East Midlands	15.5	23.2	17.2	10.3	3.9	6.6	5.3	18.8
West Midlands	18.9	22.5	16.9	10.2	3.4	6.7	3.2	18.2
Eastern	15.8	22.7	17.5	10.1	2.5	6.9	5.6	18.2
London	15.6	22.4	16.6	10.7	4.8	6.0	5.4	17.5
South East	15.7	22.3	17.2	9.2	3.7	6.8	4.8	17.0
South West	17.0	22.4	17.3	9.4	4.0	6.3	5.3	17.8
England	16.6	22.5	16.9	10.1	4.4	6.5	4.8	18.0
Wales	16.4	21.0	16.4	9.7	..	6.7	.	18.1 [6]
Scotland [8]	29.8	18.9	12.9	10.0	.	4.0	3.2	15.4
Northern Ireland	24.4	19.8	14.4	8.2	.	5.9	.	16.4
2002/03 [5,7]								
United Kingdom	23.6	21.9	16.4	9.7	..	6.1	.	17.6 [6]
North East	18.3	21.9	16.7	11.5	5.2	6.8	5.0	18.1
North West	16.2	22.3	16.4	10.8	6.4	6.2	4.7	18.0
Yorkshire and the Humber	16.7	22.7	16.9	10.7	4.9	6.4	4.4	18.6
East Midlands	16.0	23.1	17.2	10.2	4.4	6.6	5.2	18.6
West Midlands	18.8	22.5	17.0	9.7	3.4	6.6	3.7	18.1
Eastern	15.6	22.8	17.5	9.5	2.3	6.8	6.3	18.1
London	16.0	23.3	16.9	10.2	4.6	5.9	5.6	17.7
South East	14.6	22.4	17.3	8.8	3.5	6.8	4.9	16.9
South West	15.5	22.4	17.2	9.1	4.3	6.3	5.1	17.6
England	16.4	22.6	17.0	9.7	4.2	6.5	4.9	17.9
Wales	16.7	20.7	16.5	9.7	..	6.6	.	18.1 [6]
Scotland [8,9]	29.8	18.0	12.7	10.0	.	3.9	3.3	14.9
Northern Ireland	24.1	19.6	14.4	8.5	.	6.0	.	16.3
2003/04 [5,10]								
United Kingdom	23.6	21.9	16.4	9.5	..	6.0	.	17.5 [6]
North East	17.5	21.8	16.4	10.7	5.1	6.8	5.0	17.8
North West	15.8	22.4	16.2	10.9	5.0	6.0	5.0	17.9
Yorkshire and the Humber	16.5	22.8	16.8	10.4	4.5	6.2	4.3	18.5
East Midlands	15.4	23.1	17.1	9.6	4.4	6.5	5.0	18.4
West Midlands	19.7	22.6	16.9	9.8	3.1	6.6	3.7	18.1
Eastern	15.3	22.9	17.7	9.3	2.6	6.9	6.5	18.1
London	15.3	23.2	17.1	10.0	4.3	6.1	5.5	17.6
South East	14.9	22.5	17.5	8.4	3.3	6.7	4.9	16.8
South West	15.9	22.6	17.3	8.8	3.4	6.2	4.9	17.6
England	16.2	22.7	17.0	9.4	3.9	6.4	4.9	17.8
Wales	16.6	21.1	16.6	9.8	..	6.5	.	18.2 [6]
Scotland [8,9]	29.8	18.2	12.8	9.9	.	3.8	3.7	15.0
Northern Ireland	25.2	19.9	14.6	7.7	.	5.9	.	16.5

Sources: Department for Education and Skills; National Assembly for Wales; Scottish Executive; Northern Ireland Department of Education

See previous page for footnotes.

2.9 SCHOOLS
Proportion of pupils reaching or exceeding expected standards, by key stage, subject and gender – time series

England, Wales and Northern Ireland

Percentages

	England				Wales				Northern Ireland			
	Tests		Teacher assessment		Tests		Teacher assessment		Tests		Teacher assessment	
	Boys	Girls	Boys	Girls	Boys	Girls	Boys	Girls	Boys	Girls	Boys	Girls
1996												
Key Stage 1 [1]												
English	.	.	74	84	.	.	73	84	..	..	..	..
Reading	73	83	73	83	72	83	72	84	..	..	..	..
Writing	74	85	71	82	72	84	70	82	..	..	..	..
Maths	81	84	80	83	80	84	78	84	..	..	..	..
Science	.	.	83	85	.	.	81	85	..	..	..	..
Key Stage 2 [2]												
English	50	65	53	68	48	65	53	68	..	..	..	..
Maths	54	54	58	62	56	56	60	64	..	..	..	..
Science	61	63	64	67	64	66	66	70	..	..	..	..
Key Stage 3 [3]												
English	48	66	51	70	47	65	48	68	..	..	..	..
Maths	56	58	60	64	53	56	58	62	..	..	..	..
Science	57	56	59	61	55	55	57	60	..	..	..	..
2000												
Key Stage 1 [1]												
English	.	.	80	88	.	.	77	88	.	.	92	97
Reading	79	88	80	88	77	87	77	87	..	..	..	..
Writing	80	89	77	87	78	88	75	87	..	..	..	..
Welsh	.	.	.	.	84	91	82	91	.	.	.	.
Reading	.	.	.	.	76	88	76	87	.	.	.	.
Writing	.	.	.	.	68	83	67	83	.	.	.	.
Maths	89	91	87	89	88	92	85	90	.	.	94	96
Science	.	.	87	89	.	.	86	90	.	.	.	.
Key Stage 2 [2]												
English	70	79	65	76	67	80	63	76	.	.	66	77
Welsh	.	.	.	.	61	75	60	74	.	.	.	.
Maths	72	71	71	73	67	71	69	73	.	.	73	78
Science	84	85	78	80	79	82	76	80	.	.	.	.
Key Stage 3 [3]												
English	55	73	56	73	51	68	54	72	59	79	65	81
Welsh	.	.	.	.	61	78	62	81	.	.	.	.
Maths	64	65	65	68	60	61	63	66	64	70	69	75
Science	61	58	60	63	60	58	60	62	64	69	67	74
2001												
Key Stage 1 [1]												
English	.	.	81	89	.	.	79	89	.	.	93	97
Reading	80	88	80	88	79	88	79	88	..	..	.	.
Writing	82	90	79	88	79	89	76	88	..	..	.	.
Welsh	.	.	.	.	82	91	82	91	.	.	.	.
Reading	.	.	.	.	75	85	74	85	.	.	.	.
Writing	.	.	.	.	69	83	68	82	.	.	.	.
Maths	90	92	87	90	90	93	87	91	.	.	94	96
Science	.	.	88	90	.	.	87	91	.	.	.	.
Key Stage 2 [2]												
English	70	80	67	78	72	82	67	79	.	.	67	79
Welsh	.	.	.	.	65	78	63	77	.	.	.	.
Maths	71	70	73	74	73	76	73	77	.	.	73	79
Science	87	88	81	83	81	83	80	83	.	.	.	.
Key Stage 3 [3]												
English	57	73	57	73	53	71	54	72	64	80	64	81
Welsh	.	.	.	.	63	79	63	78	.	.	.	.
Maths	65	67	67	70	60	63	63	67	67	71	68	75
Science	66	66	63	66	63	64	62	64	66	69	67	74

Sources: Department for Education and Skills; National Assembly for Wales; Northern Ireland Department of Education

1 Percentage of pupils achieving level 2 or above.
2 Percentage of pupils achieving level 4 or above.
3 Percentage of pupils achieving level 5 or above.
4 Key Stage 1, Key Stage 2 and Key Stage 3 Assessment results in Northern Ireland were affected by industrial action in that some schools did not submit their results.
5 From 2002, statutory assessment at the end of Key Stage 1 in Wales is by means of teacher assessment only, following the discontinuation of the National Curriculum tests/tasks.
6 Includes revised figures.
7 Figures for England are provisional.
8 England figures shown for 'Tests' are combined results, i.e. the result of combining task/test for non trial schools and teacher assessment for trial schools. More information on the coverage of the National Curriculum assessments for 7 year olds for 2004 is given in the 'Notes to Editors' section of SFR 29/2004, available on the DfES Research and Statistics gateway at 'www.dfes.gov.uk/rsgateway/DB/SFR/s000488/index.shtml'.

CONTINUED
SCHOOLS
Proportion of pupils reaching or exceeding expected standards, by key stage, subject and gender – time series

England, Wales and Northern Ireland — Percentages

	England				Wales				Northern Ireland			
	Tests		Teacher assessment		Tests		Teacher assessment		Tests		Teacher assessment	
	Boys	Girls	Boys	Girls	Boys	Girls	Boys	Girls	Boys	Girls	Boys	Girls
2002 [4]												
Key Stage 1 [1,5]												
English	.	.	81	89	.	.	79	88	.	.	92	97
Reading	81	88	81	88	.	.	78	86	..	..	..	..
Writing	82	90	79	88	.	.	76	86	..	..	..	..
Welsh	.	.	.	.	.	.	83	91	.	.	.	.
Reading	.	.	.	.	.	.	74	85	.	.	.	.
Writing	.	.	.	.	.	.	68	83	.	.	.	.
Maths	89	92	87	90	.	.	86	89	.	.	94	96
Science	.	.	88	91	.	.	87	90	.	.	.	.
Key Stage 2 [2]												
English	70	79	67	78	75	84	71	81	.	.	68	80
Welsh	.	.	.	.	68	82	66	81	.	.	.	.
Maths	73	73	74	75	72	74	73	76	.	.	74	80
Science	86	87	82	83	85	87	82	85	.	.	.	.
Key Stage 3 [3]												
English	59	76	59	75	53	70	56	73	65	80	67	81
Welsh	.	.	.	.	63	79	63	80	.	.	.	.
Maths	67	68	69	72	62	62	65	67	71	75	69	74
Science	67	67	66	69	67	67	65	68	67	69	69	74
2003 [6]												
Key Stage 1 [1,5]												
English	.	.	81	89	.	.	78	87	.	.	93	94
Reading	80	88	81	89	.	.	77	86	..	..	..	..
Writing	76	87	78	87	.	.	75	85	..	..	..	..
Welsh	.	.	.	.	.	.	82	91	.	.	.	.
Reading	.	.	.	.	.	.	75	85	.	.	.	.
Writing	.	.	.	.	.	.	70	82	.	.	.	.
Maths	89	91	87	90	.	.	85	89	.	.	97	96
Science	.	.	88	91	.	.	86	90	.	.	.	.
Key Stage 2 [2]												
English	70	81	67	78	74	84	71	82	.	.	70	81
Welsh	.	.	.	.	72	83	70	81	.	.	.	.
Maths	73	72	74	75	74	75	75	78	.	.	76	81
Science	86	87	81	83	87	88	83	86	.	.	.	.
Key Stage 3 [3]												
English	62	76	60	75	55	72	56	74	64	81	68	82
Welsh	.	.	.	.	66	81	65	81	.	.	.	.
Maths	70	72	70	74	67	69	67	71	69	73	71	77
Science	68	69	67	70	70	69	68	70	66	70	69	76
2004 [7]												
Key Stage 1 [1,5,8]												
English	.	.	.	.	.	.	78	88	.	.	..	..
Reading	81	89	81	89	.	.	77	87	..	..	..	..
Writing	76	87	78	88	.	.	74	87	..	..	..	..
Welsh	.	.	.	.	.	.	85	91	.	.	.	.
Reading	.	.	.	.	.	.	77	86	.	.	.	.
Writing	.	.	.	.	.	.	72	83	.	.	.	.
Maths	89	92	88	91	.	.	85	89	.	.	.	.
Science	.	.	88	91	.	.	87	91	.	.	.	.
Key Stage 2 [2]												
English	72	83	69	80	74	84	71	82	.	.	..	..
Welsh	.	.	.	.	72	86	70	84	.	.	.	.
Maths	74	74	75	76	77	80	76	80	.	.	..	..
Science	86	86	82	84	88	91	85	88	.	.	.	.
Key Stage 3 [3]												
English	64	77	62	77	57	74	60	74	..	..	..	..
Welsh	.	.	.	.	67	80	66	81	.	.	.	.
Maths	72	74	72	76	69	72	69	74	..	..	..	..
Science	65	67	69	72	74	74	70	73	..	..	..	..

Sources: Department for Education and Skills; National Assembly for Wales; Northern Ireland Department of Education

See previous page for footnotes

SCHOOLS
School meal arrangements: time series

2.10

United Kingdom

	Maintained Nursery and Primary schools [1,2]			Maintained Secondary schools [1]			All Special schools [3]		
	Number on roll (thousands)	Percentage known to be eligible for free meals	Percentage taking free school meals [4]	Number on roll (thousands)	Percentage known to be eligible for free meals	Percentage taking free school meals [4]	Number on roll (thousands)	Percentage known to be eligible for free meals	Percentage taking free school meals [4]
1990/91									
United Kingdom [3]	**4,838.8**	..	**14.0**	**3,316.7**	..	**8.3**	**94.6**	..	**30.7**
England	4,099.6	..	13.7	2,848.2	..	8.3	83.0	..	28.1
Wales	280.6	17.6	17.1	185.2	13.4	9.8	3.7	44.1	45.1
Scotland	458.7	19.6	17.6	283.3	13.6	9.6	8.0	63.1	62.7
Northern Ireland	..	..	..	..	..	..	..	..	..
1995/96									
United Kingdom	**5,349.1**	..	**19.2**	**3,663.6**	..	**13.3**	**101.1**	..	**39.3**
England	4,441.6	..	18.7	3,006.9	..	13.3	89.8	..	37.2
Wales	285.0	25.9	24.0	198.5	20.0	16.1	3.6	55.1	52.5
Scotland	437.1	23.7	20.5	306.6	16.9	11.5	7.8	68.2	67.0
Northern Ireland	185.4	29.4	26.8	151.6	25.0	19.3	..	..	..
2000/01 [5]									
United Kingdom	**5,336.4**	**18.2**	**14.7**	**3,899.9**	**16.2**	**11.2**	**102.8**	**40.7**	**32.9**
North East	239.5	24.0	19.8	181.7	21.1	12.9	6.0	50.9	37.1
North West	663.6	21.7	17.6	461.8	20.3	14.5	15.2	46.4	36.7
Yorkshire and the Humber	485.2	18.3	14.9	339.3	17.2	11.1	7.8	41.3	34.4
East Midlands	382.2	13.6	11.0	289.6	12.6	8.6	5.9	35.6	30.0
West Midlands	507.1	19.1	15.6	369.3	17.4	11.9	12.6	38.9	32.8
Eastern	464.0	12.4	9.7	372.0	10.5	7.4	8.6	28.6	21.6
London	647.7	25.9	20.8	406.2	25.8	18.6	12.5	45.7	35.0
South East	660.0	10.8	8.3	493.0	9.1	6.3	15.1	29.4	23.5
South West	401.9	12.0	9.8	314.1	9.7	7.1	7.3	30.3	24.5
England	4,451.2	17.6	14.2	3,227.0	15.8	11.0	91.1	38.6	30.7
Wales	288.2	20.5	19.3	210.4	17.7	14.2	3.8	49.3	46.9
Scotland	424.5	20.8	17.5	307.0	16.7	11.5	8.0	60.3	62.1
Northern Ireland	172.5	23.1	20.0	155.6	22.0	17.0	..	..	..
2001/02 [5]									
United Kingdom	**5,296.7**	**17.7**	**14.4**	**3,932.9**	**15.3**	**11.0**	**99.6**	**40.3**	**34.1**
North East	235.3	22.5	19.5	180.9	19.0	12.5	5.8	50.6	43.3
North West	650.8	21.0	17.3	464.6	19.3	14.2	14.6	46.1	39.1
Yorkshire and the Humber	478.8	17.9	14.4	343.0	16.4	10.6	7.6	41.3	34.6
East Midlands	380.6	13.2	10.9	291.9	11.8	8.5	5.7	34.8	29.4
West Midlands	499.9	18.9	15.7	372.7	16.3	11.4	12.0	40.1	33.2
Eastern	463.0	11.9	9.5	377.2	9.8	7.0	8.6	27.8	24.4
London	644.0	25.5	21.1	412.4	24.5	18.7	11.8	45.2	38.1
South East	654.0	10.4	8.0	499.6	8.7	7.2	14.8	28.3	23.2
South West	399.0	11.7	9.4	318.8	9.3	6.9	7.0	31.1	25.5
England	4,405.6	17.1	14.0	3,260.9	14.9	10.9	87.9	38.3	32.2
Wales	284.8	19.4	17.7	212.0	16.8	13.4	3.7	47.3	44.9
Scotland	421.2	20.3	16.9	304.5	15.9	10.9	7.9	59.4	58.7
Northern Ireland	185.1	22.1	18.0	155.5	21.4	16.7	..	..	..

Sources: Department for Education and Skills; National Assembly for Wales; Scottish Executive; Northern Ireland Department of Education

1 Includes middle schools as deemed.
2 Figures for Northern Ireland include reception pupils and pupils in preparatory departments of grammar schools.
3 Great Britain only.
4 Figures shown for Wales and Scotland are calculated as the percentage of the day pupils present on the census day, therefore the percentage taking free school meals may exceed the percentage known to be eligible. Figures for England, Northern Ireland and the UK, however, are percentages of the numbers of pupils on the school roll.
5 Includes revised data.
6 From 2002/03, figures for England and its GORs include boarding pupils as well as solely and dually registered pupils.
7 Provisional. Data for Wales refer to 2002/03.

32

United Kingdom

Numbers and Percentages

	Maintained Nursery and Primary schools [1,2]			Maintained Secondary schools [1]			All Special schools [3]		
	Number on roll (thousands)	Percentage known to be eligible for free meals	Percentage taking free school meals [4]	Number on roll (thousands)	Percentage known to be eligible for free meals	Percentage taking free school meals [4]	Number on roll (thousands)	Percentage known to be eligible for free meals	Percentage taking free school meals [4]
2002/03 [5,6]									
United Kingdom	**5,228.8**	*17.3*	*14.3*	**3,986.6**	*14.9*	*10.7*	**106.0**	*37.3*	*31.3*
North East	230.1	22.1	19.1	180.4	18.1	12.6	6.0	49.8	42.6
North West	636.4	20.6	17.2	470.9	18.8	13.9	15.0	43.5	36.1
Yorkshire and the Humber	470.5	17.4	14.3	347.6	16.0	10.9	8.1	36.8	30.6
East Midlands	375.9	12.7	10.5	297.5	11.2	8.3	6.1	32.9	27.6
West Midlands	493.0	18.5	15.5	378.6	15.9	11.4	12.9	36.8	31.8
Eastern	459.0	11.7	9.5	383.9	9.6	7.0	9.2	26.3	21.6
London	640.7	25.7	21.3	417.9	24.0	18.5	12.0	43.9	36.0
South East	649.7	10.1	7.9	507.3	8.4	6.0	17.7	24.4	19.2
South West	395.0	11.3	9.2	324.3	8.9	6.6	7.6	28.4	24.5
England	4,350.3	16.8	13.9	3,308.5	14.5	10.6	94.7	35.3	29.4
Wales	280.7	18.5	17.0	214.3	15.7	12.8	3.8	44.7	43.2
Scotland	414.7	20.2	16.8	308.1	16.0	10.5	7.6	58.1	59.9
Northern Ireland	183.1	21.0	17.3	155.7	20.4	16.5	..	..	..
2003/04 [6,7]									
United Kingdom	**5,161.2**	*17.7*	*14.5*	**4,005.2**	*14.8*	*10.7*	**104.1**	*37.9*	*31.3*
North East	224.3	22.5	19.3	179.2	18.0	12.5	5.9	49.8	41.5
North West	623.2	20.9	17.3	472.7	18.4	13.6	14.4	43.8	34.7
Yorkshire and the Humber	461.2	17.5	14.3	350.0	15.5	10.8	8.0	36.9	30.1
East Midlands	373.7	13.0	10.7	297.3	11.2	8.1	6.1	32.5	27.6
West Midlands	485.6	19.0	16.0	380.3	15.8	11.6	12.6	38.1	31.2
Eastern	454.7	12.1	9.7	387.0	9.7	7.1	9.1	26.7	22.0
London	635.4	26.6	22.0	421.8	24.0	18.5	11.9	43.9	36.8
South East	643.5	10.6	8.3	512.2	8.5	6.1	17.4	24.9	20.0
South West	391.7	11.7	9.4	326.3	8.7	6.6	7.5	29.7	23.7
England	4,293.2	17.3	14.2	3,326.8	14.3	10.6	92.6	35.7	29.2
Wales	280.7	18.5	17.0	214.3	15.7	12.8	3.8	44.7	43.2
Scotland	406.9	20.6	16.5	308.8	16.2	10.2	7.7	60.8	59.9
Northern Ireland	180.4	20.7	17.1	155.4	19.8	15.3	..	..	..

Sources: Department for Education and Skills; National Assembly for Wales; Scottish Executive; Northern Ireland Department of Education

For footnotes see previous page.

Chapter 3
Post Compulsory Education and Training
(a) Institutions and Staff
(b) Participation Rates
(c) Students and Learners
(d) Job Related Training

CHAPTER 3: POST-COMPULSORY EDUCATION AND TRAINING

Key Facts

(a) INSTITUTIONS AND STAFF

- There were 89 universities, 60 other higher education institutions and 465 further education colleges (of which 102 were 6th form colleges) in the UK in 2003/04. **(Table 3.1)**

- There were 78,000 full-time higher education academic staff and 59,000 full-time further education academic staff in the United Kingdom in 2002/03. **(Table 3.1)**

(b) PARTICIPATION RATES

- 72 per cent of 16 year olds and 58 per cent of 17 year olds were in post-compulsory education either at school or in full-time further education in 2001/02. **(Table 3.2)**

- In Spring 2004, 14 per cent of people of working age had received job-related training in the last four weeks. Employees were more likely to receive job-related training than the self-employed, the unemployed or the economically inactive. **(Table 3.3)**

(c) STUDENTS AND LEARNERS

- There were 4.7 million further education students in the United Kingdom during the academic year 2002/03, compared with 2.2 million in 1990/91. Four-fifths of these students in 2002/03 were part time, a similar proportion as in 1990/91. **(Tables 3.5, 3.10)**

- There were 2.4 million [988,200 part-time] higher education students in the United Kingdom in the academic year 2002/03, compared with 1.1 million in 1990/91. Of the students in 2002/03, 502,500 were known to be postgraduate students, 1.1 million were first degree students and 760,300 were on other undergraduate courses. **(Tables 3.6, 3.10)**

- Amongst popular subjects studied by full-time students were business & administrative studies (198,100), social sciences (174,200) and subjects allied to medicine (139,200). **(Table 3.6)**

- In 2002/03, there were 212,500 students from overseas in total in full-time higher education in the UK. 31,200 of these students were from China, the highest of any overseas country. **(Table 3.7)**

- There were 1.1 million new entrants to higher education in 2002/03, of which just under half were part-time. **(Table 3.11)**

Work-Based Learning for Young People (WBLYP)

Advanced Modern Apprenticeships (AMAs)

- There were 47,300 new starts on Advanced Modern Apprenticeship schemes (AMAs) in England in 2002/03. **(Table 3.12)**

- The average number of learners on AMAs in 2002/03 was 108,300, and represented almost two-fifths of the year average for the total number of learners on work-based learning for young people. **(Table 3.13)**

Foundation Modern Apprenticeships (FMAs)

- There were 115,700 new starts on Foundation Modern Apprenticeships (FMAs) in England in 2002/03. **(Table 3.12)**

- FMA learners accounted for over two-fifths of all learners on work-based learning for young people in 2002/03. **(Table 3.13)**

Ethnicity

- Of the total number in work based learning on 1 November 2003 (290,100), 92.7 per cent were White, 2.3 per cent of learners were Asian or Asian British and 1.8 per cent were Black or Black British. **(Table 3.14)**

Area of Learning

- The most popular area of learning for those in learning on 1 November 2003 was Engineering, Technology and Manufacturing, with 70,400 learners. **(Table 3.15)**

(d) JOB RELATED TRAINING

- In Spring 2004, people in the North East (15.6 per cent) were more likely to have received job-related training in the last four weeks than people in any other region. People in Northern Ireland (9.3 per cent) were least likely to receive training. **(Table 3.16)**

- 22 per cent of employees of mixed ethnic origin, 19.9 per cent of Black or Black British employees, 16.5 per cent of Chinese employees, and 14.1 per cent of employees of Asian or Asian British origin, had received job-related training compared with 16 per cent of White employees. **(Table 3.17)**

- People with high levels of qualifications were much more likely than those with low or no qualifications to have received job-related training. **(Table 3.17)**

- In Spring 2004, 7.7 per cent of employees had received only off-the-job training in the last four weeks, 5.3 per cent had received only on-the-job training and 3.2 per cent had received both types of training. **(Table 3.17)**

- Employees in public administration, education & health were more likely than employees in other industries to have received job-related training. Those employed in manufacturing were least likely to have received training. **(Table 3.18)**

- Much of the job-related training received by employees is of short duration; in Spring 2004, almost two-fifths of the training received by employees and by the self-employed lasted for less than a week. **(Table 3.21)**

- The economically inactive tend to receive job-related training of a longer duration than that received by employees. **(Table 3.21)**

- A Further Education college or university is the most common location for off-the-job training. The employer's premises are another common location for employees' off-the-job training. **(Table 3.22)**

- In Spring 2004, young employees receiving training *in the last week* spent more hours in job-related training than older employees. Males spent more hours in training than females. **(Table 3.23)**

- In Spring 2004, 32.9 per cent of employees in temporary employment had undertaken job-related training *in the last thirteen weeks* compared to 30.3 per cent of permanent employees. 31.3 per cent of full-time employees had undertaken job-related training compared with 27.6 per cent of part-time employees. **(Table 3.24)**

- In Spring 2004, 30.4 per cent of employees had received job-related training *in the last thirteen weeks*, 16.1 per cent had received job-related training *in the last four weeks*, and 8.5 per cent had received job-related training *in the last week*. 28.6 per cent of employees had never been offered training by their current employer. **(Table 3.25)**

- In Spring 2004, 27.6 per cent of employees who were classed as both DDA disabled and work-limiting disabled had received job-related training *in the last thirteen weeks*, compared with 30.4 per cent of all employees. **(Table 3.26)**

CHAPTER 3: POST-COMPULSORY EDUCATION AND TRAINING - LIST OF TABLES

POST-COMPULSORY EDUCATION AND TRAINING – INSTITUTIONS AND STAFF

3.1

Number of establishments of further and higher education by type, and full-time academic staff by gender - time series

United Kingdom (i) Number of establishments of further and higher education Numbers

		Academic years					
		1990/91	1995/96	2000/01[1]	2001/02[1]	2002/03[1]	2003/04
UNITED KINGDOM							
Universities (including Open University)[2]		48	89	89	90	89	89
Other higher education institutions	}		66	55	58	60	60
	} 588						
Further education colleges	}		543	491	483	466	465
of which 6th form colleges		.	110	103	101	103	102
ENGLAND							
Universities (including Open University)[2]		37	72	72	73	72	72
Other higher education institutions	}		50	43	45	47	47
	} 460						
Further education colleges	}		453	403	396	381	380
of which 6th form colleges		.	110	103	101	103	102
WALES							
Universities[2]		1	2	2	2	2	2
Other higher education institutions	}		5	4	4	4	4
	} 38						
Further education colleges	}		26	24	24	23	23
SCOTLAND							
Universities[2]		8	13	13	13	13	13
Other higher education institutions	}		9	6	7	7	7
	} 64						
Further education colleges	}		47	47	46	46	46
NORTHERN IRELAND							
Universities		2	2	2	2	2	2
Colleges of Education		2	2	2	2	2	2
Further education colleges		24	17	17	17	16	16

United Kingdom (ii) Number of full-time academic staff Thousands

	Academic years					
	1990/91	1995/96[3]	2000/01	2001/02	2002/03	2003/04
All						
Further and Higher Education Institutions	122	139	134	135	137	..
of which						
Further Education Institutions(FEIs)[4,5]	..	63	56	57	59	..
Higher Education Institutions(HEIs)[2,6,7]	..	76	78	78	78	..
Males						
Further and Higher Education Institutions	89	91	84	83	84	..
of which						
Further Education Institutions(FEIs)[4,5]	..	36	30	30	31	..
Higher Education Institutions(HEIs)[2,6,7]	..	55	54	54	53	..
Females						
Further and Higher Education Institutions	33	48	50	52	54	..
of which						
Further Education Institutions(FEIs)[4,5]	..	27	26	27	28	..
Higher Education Institutions(HEIs)[2,6,7]	..	21	24	25	25	..

Sources: Department for Education and Skills; National Assembly for Wales; Scottish Executive; Northern Ireland Department for Employment and Learning

1 Includes revised data.

2 From 1993/94 includes former polytechnics and colleges which became universities as a result of the Further and Higher Education Act 1992.

3 Further education institution figures include 1996/97 data for Wales.

4 Figures for England relate to staff whose primary role is teaching, and do not include other staff whose primary role is supporting teaching and learning or other.

5 Scotland figures comprise of full-time equivalent (rather than headcount) Lecturer/Instructor/Senior Lecturer staff in academic departments only.

6 Excludes the Open University.

7 Non-clinical academic staff paid wholly by the institution.

3.2 POST-COMPULSORY EDUCATION AND TRAINING – PARTICIPATION RATES

16 and 17 year olds participating in post-compulsory education[1] and Government-supported training, 2001/02[2]

United Kingdom   Percentages[3]

	16 year olds					17 year olds				
	At school	In further education[4]		Government-supported training (GST)	All in full-time education and GST[5]	At school	In further education[4]		Government-supported training (GST)	All in full-time education and GST[5]
		Full-time	Part-time[6]				Full-time	Part-time[6]		
Region of study										
All										
United Kingdom	38	34	5	..	..	30	28	7	..	..
North East	28	39	8	14	80	22	31	9	16	68
North West	24	43	5	10	76	20	35	6	12	67
Yorkshire and the Humber	31	36	7	10	77	24	29	7	12	65
East Midlands	37	31	6	8	76	31	26	7	11	67
West Midlands	32	37	6	8	76	26	31	7	11	67
Eastern	40	31	4	6	78	33	26	5	8	66
London	40	34	4	4	78	32	31	5	5	67
South East	39	35	3	5	79	32	29	5	7	68
South West	39	35	4	6	80	32	28	6	10	70
England	35	36	5	7	78	28	30	6	10	67
Wales	39	33	6	8	80	31	28	9	11	70
Scotland[7]	71	14	8	..	..	41	12	11	..	..
Northern Ireland[8]	49	29	11	..	..	40	26	12	..	..
Males										
United Kingdom	36	32	6	..	..	28	26	7	..	..
North East	27	36	8	17	79	21	29	9	18	68
North West	23	40	5	11	73	19	32	7	14	65
Yorkshire and the Humber	29	34	7	13	75	22	27	8	14	63
East Midlands	34	29	6	9	72	29	24	7	12	65
West Midlands	29	34	6	9	73	24	28	8	12	64
Eastern	39	30	5	7	75	31	24	6	9	64
London	37	33	5	4	74	29	30	6	5	64
South East	37	34	4	5	76	30	28	5	8	66
South West	37	32	5	8	77	30	26	7	12	67
England	33	34	5	9	75	26	28	7	11	65
Wales	35	33	6	9	78	28	26	10	13	68
Scotland[7]	67	15	8	..	..	39	12	13	..	..
Northern Ireland[8]	40	32	11	..	..	32	29	11	..	..
Females										
United Kingdom	41	35	5	..	..	32	30	6	..	..
North East	30	42	7	11	82	22	33	8	13	69
North West	26	46	4	8	79	21	37	6	10	69
Yorkshire and the Humber	33	38	7	8	78	25	32	7	11	67
East Midlands	40	34	5	7	81	32	28	7	9	70
West Midlands	34	40	5	7	80	27	34	7	9	70
Eastern	42	33	4	5	80	34	28	5	7	69
London	43	36	4	4	82	35	32	5	4	71
South East	40	37	3	4	82	33	31	4	6	70
South West	41	38	4	5	84	34	31	5	7	72
England	38	40	5	6	83	30	32	6	8	70
Wales	42	34	6	6	82	33	30	7	9	72
Scotland[7]	76	12	8	..	..	43	12	9	..	..
Northern Ireland[8]	59	26	12	..	..	49	24	13	..	..

Source: Department for Education and Skills; National Assembly for Wales; Scottish Executive; Northern Ireland Department of Education

1 Excluding higher education.

2 Data for Scotland refer to 2000/01.

3 As a percentage of the estimated 16 year old and 17 year old population respectively.

4 Including sixth form colleges in England, and a small element of further education in higher education institutions in Great Britain.

5 Figures for England exclude overlap between full-time education and Government-supported training.

6 Figures in the United Kingdom rows refer to Great Britain only.

7 The estimates of 16 year olds at school exclude those pupils who leave school in the Winter term at the minimum statutory school-leaving age.

8 Participation in part-time FE should not be aggregated with full-time FE or schools activity due to the unquantifiable overlap with these activities.

POST COMPULSORY EDUCATION AND TRAINING: PARTICIPATION RATES

3.3 Participation in job-related training[1] in the last four weeks - time series

United Kingdom: People of working age[2]Thousands and percentages[3]

	1991[4]	1996	2001	2002	2003[5]	2004
Numbers (thousands)						
All People						
All	4,428	4,555	5,203	5,228	4,979	5,112
Males	2,344	2,255	2,412	2,438	2,296	2,330
Females	2,084	2,301	2,791	2,790	2,683	2,781
Employees [6,7]						
All	3,228	3,190	3,832	3,891	3,678	3,791
Males	1,711	1,570	1,755	1,808	1,690	1,699
Females	1,517	1,620	2,077	2,083	1,988	2,092
Self-employed [7,8]						
All	183	207	241	242	247	248
Males	126	130	145	151	142	146
Females	57	77	96	91	105	102
ILO unemployed [9]						
All	141	191	149	169	132	139
Males	76	111	76	88	68	73
Females	65	80	73	80	64	67
Economically inactive [10]						
All	561	792	868	848	854	846
Males	249	343	367	351	356	365
Females	312	449	502	498	498	481
Percentages [3]						
All People						
All	12.7	13.0	14.5	14.5	13.8	14.1
Males	13.0	12.5	13.1	13.2	12.4	12.5
Females	12.4	13.5	16.0	15.9	15.3	15.8
Employees [6,7]						
All	14.9	14.8	16.4	16.6	15.7	16.1
Males	14.7	14.0	14.4	14.9	13.9	14.0
Females	15.1	15.7	18.6	18.5	17.6	18.4
Self-employed [7,8]						
All	5.7	6.4	7.9	7.9	7.6	7.5
Males	5.1	5.4	6.5	6.6	6.0	5.9
Females	7.5	9.4	12.2	11.6	12.2	12.0
ILO unemployed [9]						
All	6.0	8.5	11.0	11.6	9.5	10.4
Males	5.1	7.5	9.4	10.1	8.0	9.4
Females	7.5	10.2	13.5	14.0	11.8	11.8
Economically inactive [10]						
All	7.9	10.3	11.1	10.8	10.9	10.7
Males	11.1	12.3	12.1	11.4	11.7	11.6
Females	6.4	9.1	10.4	10.4	10.4	10.1

Source: Labour Force Survey, Spring of each year [11]

1   Job-related training includes both on and off-the-job training.
2   Working age is defined as males aged 16-64 and females aged 16-59.
3   Expressed as a percentage of the total number of people in each group.
4   Due to a change in the LFS questionnaire, data from Summer 1994 onwards are not comparable with earlier figures.
5   Includes revised data as a result of a LFS regrossing exercise carried out by the Office for National Statistics in 2004.
6   Employees are those in employment excluding the self-employed, unpaid family workers and those on government employment and training programmes.
7   The split into employees and self-employed is based on respondents' own assessment of their employment status.
8   Self-employed are those in employment excluding employees, unpaid family workers and those on government employment and training programmes.
9   Unemployed according to the International Labour Organization (ILO) definition.
10 Economically inactive are those who are neither in employment nor ILO unemployed.
11 Users of these data should read the LFS entry in Annex A, as it contains important information about the LFS and the concepts and definitions used.

3.4

POST COMPULSORY EDUCATION AND TRAINING: PARTICIPATION RATES
Participation in job-related training[1] in the last four weeks by economic activity and age, 2004

United Kingdom: People of working age[2]

Thousands and percentages[3]

	Thousands			Percentages[3]		
	All	Males	Females	All	Males	Females
All people						
All	5,112	2,330	2,781	14.1	12.5	15.8
16-19	664	348	316	21.8	22.4	21.2
20-24	823	386	437	22.8	21.6	23.9
25-29	595	261	334	16.8	15.1	18.4
30-39	1,245	563	682	14.2	13.1	15.2
40-49	1,071	432	639	12.9	10.5	15.2
50-64	714	341	373	7.9	6.6	9.8
Employees [4,5]						
All	3,791	1,699	2,092	16.1	14.0	18.4
16-19	318	168	150	22.6	24.4	20.9
20-24	482	221	262	20.5	18.3	22.8
25-29	471	207	264	18.3	15.7	21.0
30-39	1,020	476	544	16.4	14.8	18.2
40-49	900	356	544	15.4	12.2	18.5
50-64	600	272	329	11.7	9.7	14.2
Self-employed [5,6]						
All	248	146	102	7.5	5.9	12.0
16-19	*	*	*	*	*	*
20-24	13	*	*	10.8	*	*
25-29	19	12	*	9.3	7.5	*
30-39	71	34	37	8.3	5.6	14.7
40-49	76	47	29	7.8	6.8	10.5
50-64	64	43	22	5.7	4.8	9.0
ILO unemployed [7]						
All	139	73	67	10.4	9.4	11.8
16-19	46	27	19	16.9	17.0	16.6
20-24	27	13	14	12.6	11.3	14.3
25-29	*	*	*	*	*	*
30-39	25	14	11	8.9	8.7	9.0
40-49	19	*	12	8.8	*	11.3
50-64	12	*	*	6.2	*	*
Economically inactive [8]						
All	846	365	481	10.7	11.6	10.1
16-19	252	121	131	19.8	18.9	20.6
20-24	285	136	148	31.9	38.5	27.5
25-29	90	35	55	15.1	22.1	12.6
30-39	120	36	84	8.5	11.8	7.6
40-49	68	19	49	5.5	5.1	5.7
50-64	31	18	13	1.2	1.3	1.1

Source: Labour Force Survey, Spring 2004 [9]

1   Job-related training includes both on and off-the-job training.
2   Working age is defined as males aged 16-64 and females aged 16-59.
3   Expressed as a percentage of the total number of people in each group.
4   Employees are those in employment excluding the self-employed, unpaid family workers and those on government employment and training programmes.
5   The split into employees and self-employed is based on respondents' own assessment of their employment status.
6   Self-employed are those in employment excluding employees, unpaid family workers and those on government employment and training programmes.
7   Unemployed according to the International Labour Organization (ILO) definition.
8   Economically inactive are those who are neither in employment nor ILO unemployed.
9   Users of these data should read the LFS entry in Annex A, as it contains important information about the LFS and the concepts and definitions used.

THIS PAGE HAS BEEN LEFT BLANK

POST COMPULSORY EDUCATION AND TRAINING: STUDENTS AND LEARNERS

Students in further education [1] by country of study, mode of study [2], gender and area of learning [3], during 2002/03 [4]

United Kingdom   (i) Home and Overseas Students   Thousands

	United Kingdom		England [5]		Wales		Scotland [6]		Northern Ireland	
	Full-time	Part-time	Full-time	Part-time	Full-time	Part-time	Full-time	Part-time	Full-time	Part-time
All										
Business Administration, Management & Professional	64.0	339.8	56.3	295.6	-	-	4.6	33.2	3.1	10.9
Construction	41.0	102.6	32.6	85.0	-	-	4.5	15.2	3.9	2.4
Engineering, Technology and Manufacturing	40.7	106.0	33.3	83.7	-	0.1	5.1	18.9	2.3	3.3
English, Languages and Communications	42.5	178.9	40.5	143.7	-	0.1	2.0	35.0	-	-
Foundation programmes	77.0	281.9	76.6	278.1	-	-	0.4	3.8	-	-
Hairdressing and Beauty Therapy	44.2	87.8	38.9	78.7	-	-	3.7	6.6	1.5	2.5
Health, Social Care and Public Services	154.8	487.4	144.2	428.5	-	-	8.2	54.9	2.4	4.0
Hospitality, Sports, Leisure and Travel	59.1	237.2	52.1	203.8	-	-	4.6	31.2	2.3	2.2
Humanities	66.3	83.6	64.1	73.5	-	-	2.2	10.1	-	-
Information & Communication Technology	81.6	733.2	76.4	644.0	-	-	3.6	76.2	1.6	13.0
Land-based provision	15.8	49.2	14.4	42.1	-	-	1.3	6.8	0.1	0.2
Retailing, Customer Service and Transportation	7.1	66.2	6.8	60.0	-	-	0.3	5.4	-	0.8
Science and Mathematics	50.6	96.8	47.1	79.8	-	-	1.1	6.8	2.4	10.2
Visual and Performing Arts & Media	80.5	155.5	74.4	126.2	-	-	4.3	25.0	1.8	4.3
Other Subjects [7]	16.1	82.0	15.8	74.9	0.3	6.9	-	0.2	-	-
Unknown	185.4	613.6	141.0	407.0	44.4	206.6	-	-	-	-
All subjects	**1,026.7**	**3,701.6**	**914.5**	**3,104.7**	**44.8**	**213.7**	**46.0**	**329.3**	**21.5**	**54.0**
Males										
Business Administration, Management & Professional	28.5	102.5	25.7	88.1	-	-	1.3	11.0	1.5	3.3
Construction	39.2	94.7	31.2	79.6	-	-	4.2	12.7	3.8	2.3
Engineering, Technology and Manufacturing	36.0	90.7	28.8	72.1	-	0.1	4.9	15.5	2.3	3.1
English, Languages and Communications	16.5	69.4	15.5	55.1	-	-	1.0	14.2	-	-
Foundation programmes	39.2	118.7	39.0	117.0	-	-	0.2	1.8	-	-
Hairdressing and Beauty Therapy	2.8	15.1	2.7	14.7	-	-	0.1	0.3	-	0.1
Health, Social Care and Public Services	63.7	154.6	62.2	134.9	-	-	1.4	19.4	0.1	0.4
Hospitality, Sports, Leisure and Travel	30.1	81.9	26.2	68.3	-	-	2.6	12.8	1.2	0.8
Humanities	24.7	24.2	23.8	21.0	-	-	0.8	3.2	-	-
Information & Communication Technology	52.8	268.2	48.9	236.5	-	-	2.6	27.5	1.3	4.2
Land-based provision	8.1	21.4	7.3	17.5	-	-	0.8	3.8	-	0.1
Retailing, Customer Service and Transportation	4.7	26.2	4.5	21.9	-	-	0.2	4.0	-	0.3
Science and Mathematics	26.5	35.8	24.9	29.4	-	-	0.5	2.6	1.1	3.7
Visual and Performing Arts & Media	35.0	45.4	32.0	35.6	-	-	2.0	8.3	0.9	1.5
Other Subjects [7]	5.8	32.3	5.7	29.8	0.1	2.4	-	-	-	-
Unknown	95.9	242.9	74.2	158.0	21.7	84.9	-	-	-	-
All subjects	**509.3**	**1,423.9**	**452.6**	**1,179.4**	**21.8**	**87.4**	**22.6**	**137.3**	**12.3**	**19.8**
Females										
Business Administration, Management & Professional	35.5	237.3	30.6	207.5	-	-	3.3	22.2	1.6	7.6
Construction	1.8	7.9	1.5	5.4	-	-	0.3	2.5	0.1	0.1
Engineering, Technology and Manufacturing	4.8	15.3	4.5	11.6	-	-	0.3	3.4	-	0.3
English, Languages and Communications	26.0	109.5	25.0	88.6	-	0.1	1.0	20.8	-	-
Foundation programmes	37.7	163.2	37.6	161.2	-	-	0.2	2.0	-	-
Hairdressing and Beauty Therapy	41.3	72.7	36.2	64.0	-	-	3.7	6.3	1.5	2.4
Health, Social Care and Public Services	91.1	332.7	81.9	293.6	-	-	6.9	35.5	2.3	3.6
Hospitality, Sports, Leisure and Travel	29.0	155.2	25.9	135.5	-	-	2.0	18.3	1.1	1.4
Humanities	41.6	59.4	40.3	52.5	-	-	1.3	6.9	-	-
Information & Communication Technology	28.7	465.0	27.5	407.5	-	-	1.0	48.7	0.3	8.8
Land-based provision	7.8	27.8	7.2	24.6	-	-	0.5	3.0	0.1	0.1
Retailing, Customer Service and Transportation	2.4	40.0	2.3	38.1	-	-	-	1.4	-	0.5
Science and Mathematics	24.2	61.1	22.2	50.4	-	-	0.6	4.1	1.3	6.5
Visual and Performing Arts & Media	45.6	110.1	42.4	90.6	-	-	2.3	16.7	0.9	2.8
Other Subjects [7]	10.3	49.7	10.1	45.1	0.2	4.5	-	0.2	-	-
Unknown	89.5	370.7	66.8	249.0	22.7	121.7	-	-	-	-
All subjects	**517.5**	**2,277.7**	**462.0**	**1,925.2**	**23.0**	**126.3**	**23.3**	**192.0**	**9.2**	**34.2**

Sources: Department for Education and Skills; National Assembly for Wales; Scottish Executive; Northern Ireland Department for Employment and Learning

1 Further education (FE) institution figures are whole year counts except for Northern Ireland, which are collected on a snapshot basis. Higher education (HE) institution figures are based on the HESA July 'standard registration' count and are not directly comparable with previous years prior to 2001/02.
2 Full-time includes sandwich. Part-time comprises both day and evening, including block release.
3 Data are shown by area of learning and are not directly comparable with subject groups previously shown.
4 Provisional.
5 Further education institution figures for England include LSC funded students only. Figures are not directly comparable with previous years.
6 Figures for Scotland further education colleges are enrolments rather than headcounts.
7 For UK higher education institutions, includes the previous subject groups not allocated to specific areas of learning, i.e. medicine & dentistry, subjects allied to medicine, biological, veterinary, physical, mathematical, computing and social (inc law) sciences, creative arts & design and education.
8 Includes estimated breakdowns for further education students in UK higher education institutions, and in further education institutions in England.

POST COMPULSORY EDUCATION AND TRAINING: STUDENTS AND LEARNERS

3.5 Students in further education [1] by country of study, mode of study [2], gender and area of learning [3], during 2002/03 [4]

United Kingdom   (ii) of which Overseas Students   Thousands

	United Kingdom		England [5]		Wales		Scotland [6]		Northern Ireland	
	Full-time	Part-time	Full-time	Part-time	Full-time	Part-time	Full-time	Part-time	Full-time	Part-time
All										
Business Administration, Management & Professional	0.3	0.8	0.1	0.4	-	-	0.1	0.2	-	0.1
Construction	-	0.1	-	-	-	-	-	-	-	0.1
Engineering, Technology and Manufacturing	0.1	1.2	-	1.0	-	-	-	0.1	-	0.1
English, Languages and Communications	0.8	2.0	0.4	0.4	-	-	0.3	1.7	-	-
Foundation programmes	-	-	-	-	-	-	-	-	-	-
Hairdressing and Beauty Therapy	0.1	0.1			-	-	-	-	0.1	0.1
Health, Social Care and Public Services	0.1	0.2			-	-	-	0.1	0.1	0.1
Hospitality, Sports, Leisure and Travel	0.1	0.1			-	-	-	-	0.1	0.1
Humanities	-	-			-	-	-	-	-	-
Information & Communication Technology	0.1	0.3	-	-	-	-	-	0.1	-	0.1
Land-based provision	0.1	0.2	-	0.2	-	-	-	-	-	-
Retailing, Customer Service and Transportation	-	0.3	-	-	-	-	-	0.2	-	-
Science and Mathematics	0.1	0.1	-	-	-	-	-	-	-	0.1
Visual and Performing Arts & Media	0.1	0.1	-	-	-	-	-	0.1	0.1	-
Other Subjects [7]	2.2	3.5	2.1	2.9	-	0.6	-	-	-	-
Unknown	10.0	25.9	10.0	25.6	-	0.3	-	-	-	-
All subjects	**13.9**	**34.8**	**12.8**	**30.5**	**0.1**	**0.9**	**0.6**	**2.6**	**0.4**	**0.8**
of which European Union [8]	4.7	8.2	4.1	4.9	-	0.8	0.2	1.6	0.4	0.8
Other Europe [8]	0.6	1.8	0.6	1.6	-	-	-	0.2	-	-
Commonwealth [8]	1.5	1.6	1.5	1.3	-	-	-	0.3	-	-
Other Countries [8]	7.0	23.2	6.6	22.6	0.1	-	0.3	0.6	-	-
Males										
Business Administration, Management & Professional	0.1	0.4	0.1	0.3	-	-	0.1	0.1	-	-
Construction	-	0.1	-	-	-	-	-	-	-	0.1
Engineering, Technology and Manufacturing	0.1	1.1	-	0.9	-	-	-	0.1	-	0.1
English, Languages and Communications	0.4	0.9	0.2	0.2	-	-	0.2	0.7	-	-
Foundation programmes	-	-	-	-	-	-	-	-	-	-
Hairdressing and Beauty Therapy	-	-	-	-	-	-	-	-	-	-
Health, Social Care and Public Services	-	0.1	-	-	-	-	-	0.1	-	-
Hospitality, Sports, Leisure and Travel	-	-	-	-	-	-	-	-	-	-
Humanities	-	-	-	-	-	-	-	-	-	-
Information & Communication Technology	0.1	0.1	-	-	-	-	-	0.1	-	-
Land-based provision	-	0.1	-	0.1	-	-	-	-	-	-
Retailing, Customer Service and Transportation	-	0.2	-	-	-	-	-	0.2	-	-
Science and Mathematics	-	-	-	-	-	-	-	-	-	-
Visual and Performing Arts & Media	-	-	-	-	-	-	-	-	-	-
Other Subjects [7]	0.7	1.7	0.7	1.1	-	0.6	-	-	-	-
Unknown	5.0	11.2	5.0	11.2	-	-	-	-	-	-
All subjects	**6.6**	**16.0**	**6.1**	**13.7**	**0.1**	**0.6**	**0.3**	**1.4**	**0.1**	**0.3**
of which European Union [8]	1.9	3.5	1.6	1.9	-	0.6	0.1	0.7	0.1	0.3
Other Europe [8]	0.2	0.5	0.2	0.4	-	-	-	-	-	-
Commonwealth [8]	0.9	1.1	0.8	0.8	-	-	-	0.3	-	-
Other Countries [8]	3.7	10.9	3.4	10.6	0.1	-	0.2	0.3	-	-
Females										
Business Administration, Management & Professional	0.1	0.3	-	0.1	-	-	0.1	0.1	-	0.1
Construction	-	-	-	-	-	-	-	-	-	-
Engineering, Technology and Manufacturing	-	0.1	-	0.1	-	-	-	-	-	-
English, Languages and Communications	0.4	1.2	0.2	0.2	-	-	0.1	1.0	-	-
Foundation programmes	-	-	-	-	-	-	-	-	-	-
Hairdressing and Beauty Therapy	0.1	0.1	-	-	-	-	-	-	0.1	0.1
Health, Social Care and Public Services	0.1	0.1	-	-	-	-	-	-	0.1	0.1
Hospitality, Sports, Leisure and Travel	-	0.1	-	-	-	-	-	-	-	0.1
Humanities	-	-	-	-	-	-	-	-	-	-
Information & Communication Technology	-	0.1	-	-	-	-	-	-	-	0.1
Land-based provision	-	0.1	-	0.1	-	-	-	-	-	-
Retailing, Customer Service and Transportation	-	-	-	-	-	-	-	-	-	-
Science and Mathematics	-	0.1	-	-	-	-	-	-	-	0.1
Visual and Performing Arts & Media	0.1	0.1	-	-	-	-	-	0.1	0.1	-
Other Subjects [7]	1.5	1.8	1.5	1.8	-	-	-	-	-	-
Unknown	5.0	14.7	5.0	14.4	-	0.3	-	-	-	-
All subjects	**7.3**	**18.8**	**6.7**	**16.7**	**-**	**0.3**	**0.3**	**1.3**	**0.3**	**0.5**
of which European Union [8]	2.9	4.7	2.4	3.0	-	0.3	0.1	0.9	0.3	0.5
Other Europe [8]	0.4	1.3	0.4	1.2	-	-	-	0.1	-	-
Commonwealth [8]	0.7	0.5	0.6	0.5	-	-	-	-	-	-
Other Countries [8]	3.4	12.3	3.2	12.0	-	-	0.1	0.2	-	-

Sources: Department for Education and Skills; National Assembly for Wales; Scottish Executive; Northern Ireland Department for Employment and Learning

See previous page for footnotes.

3.6

Students in higher [1] education by level, mode of study [2], gender and subject group [3], 2002/03 [4,5]

United Kingdom   (i) Home and Overseas Students   Thousands

| | Postgraduate level | | | | | | First degree | | Other Undergraduate | | Total higher education students [6] | |
| | PhD & equivalent | | Masters and Others | | Total Postgraduate | | | | | | | |
	Full-time	Part-time	Full-time	Part-time	Full-time	Part-time	Full-time	Part-time	Full-time	Part-time	Full-time	Part-time
All												
Medicine & Dentistry	2.8	3.8	2.7	6.2	5.5	10.0	33.1	0.1	0.3	0.1	38.8	10.1
Subjects Allied to Medicine	2.2	2.8	5.1	24.4	7.3	27.2	62.7	30.0	69.2	72.4	139.2	129.6
Biological Sciences	6.6	4.6	6.1	7.9	12.7	12.6	90.1	4.7	2.4	3.6	105.3	20.8
Vet. Science, Agriculture & related	0.9	0.7	1.4	1.3	2.3	2.0	10.0	0.6	3.8	3.0	16.2	5.6
Physical Sciences	6.9	3.2	5.2	3.1	12.0	6.3	46.7	1.8	0.9	3.4	59.6	11.6
Mathematical and Computing Sciences	3.3	2.0	14.0	10.7	17.2	12.7	94.7	7.3	13.7	23.1	125.7	43.1
Engineering & Technology	6.8	4.4	13.3	12.1	20.1	16.5	71.8	8.5	11.2	24.1	103.0	49.1
Architecture, Building & Planning	0.6	0.7	4.5	7.0	5.1	7.7	19.8	6.7	3.0	11.7	27.9	26.1
Social Sciences (inc Law)	4.4	5.1	27.4	24.6	31.8	29.7	133.0	16.1	9.4	35.8	174.2	81.6
Business & Administrative Studies	1.7	2.9	33.0	58.4	34.7	61.4	135.1	15.6	28.2	74.1	198.1	151.0
Mass Communications & Documentation	0.3	0.3	4.3	4.0	4.6	4.3	28.8	1.2	2.4	2.4	35.8	7.9
Languages	2.5	2.9	6.1	4.9	8.6	7.8	73.2	4.4	4.6	32.2	86.4	44.4
Historical and Philosophical Studies	2.5	3.4	4.8	8.9	7.3	12.3	47.9	5.6	1.6	30.2	56.8	48.1
Creative Arts & Design	1.2	1.4	6.9	4.5	8.1	5.9	96.9	4.2	13.6	11.5	118.6	21.7
Education [7]	0.8	4.4	29.1	57.0	29.9	61.4	32.6	6.8	2.9	38.9	65.4	107.1
Other subjects [8]	-	0.1	0.1	16.7	0.1	16.7	7.4	2.6	4.1	184.5	11.6	203.8
Unknown [6]	-	-	0.1	0.4	0.1	0.4	6.4	1.6	16.8	21.2	24.1	26.4
All subjects	**43.5**	**42.8**	**164.0**	**252.2**	**207.5**	**295.0**	**990.3**	**117.9**	**188.1**	**572.1**	**1,386.7**	**988.2**
Males												
Medicine & Dentistry	1.1	2.1	1.1	2.8	2.3	4.9	14.2	-	0.1	-	16.5	5.0
Subjects Allied to Medicine	0.9	1.1	1.5	6.1	2.4	7.3	14.1	3.9	9.3	7.8	25.8	18.9
Biological Sciences	2.8	2.0	2.3	2.6	5.1	4.6	32.6	1.6	1.4	1.3	39.0	7.6
Vet. Science, Agriculture & related	0.5	0.4	0.7	0.6	1.2	1.0	3.4	0.2	1.6	1.3	6.2	2.5
Physical Sciences	4.6	2.2	2.9	1.7	7.5	3.9	27.8	1.1	0.5	2.0	35.8	7.0
Mathematical and Computing Sciences	2.5	1.5	10.4	7.3	12.8	8.8	71.7	5.4	11.2	11.7	95.8	25.9
Engineering & Technology	5.4	3.7	10.8	10.3	16.1	13.9	60.5	7.8	9.8	22.3	86.5	44.0
Architecture, Building & Planning	0.4	0.5	2.7	4.5	3.1	5.0	14.2	5.3	2.4	9.2	19.7	19.4
Social Sciences (inc Law)	2.3	2.7	12.2	10.0	14.5	12.7	54.0	6.1	2.0	9.1	70.6	27.8
Business & Administrative Studies	1.0	1.9	17.9	30.7	18.9	32.5	65.7	6.7	12.7	27.5	97.3	66.7
Mass Communications & Documentation	0.1	0.2	1.5	1.3	1.6	1.5	11.4	0.4	1.3	0.9	14.3	2.8
Languages	1.0	1.2	2.0	1.6	3.0	2.8	20.3	1.3	2.0	12.4	25.4	16.5
Historical and Philosophical Studies	1.4	2.0	2.2	4.0	3.7	6.0	21.4	2.1	0.5	10.1	25.6	18.3
Creative Arts & Design	0.6	0.8	2.9	1.8	3.5	2.6	38.2	1.4	5.9	3.7	47.6	7.7
Education [7]	0.3	1.9	8.8	16.4	9.1	18.4	6.1	1.5	1.1	11.1	16.3	31.0
Other subjects [8]	-	-	-	9.2	-	9.2	2.9	0.9	2.1	75.7	5.0	85.8
Unknown [6]	-	-	-	0.1	-	0.1	2.5	0.6	8.7	8.0	11.7	10.1
All subjects	**25.0**	**24.2**	**79.8**	**111.1**	**104.8**	**135.3**	**461.1**	**46.4**	**72.8**	**214.1**	**639.1**	**397.1**
Females												
Medicine & Dentistry	1.6	1.7	1.6	3.3	3.2	5.0	18.9	-	0.2	0.1	22.3	5.1
Subjects Allied to Medicine	1.2	1.7	3.6	18.3	4.9	20.0	48.6	26.2	59.9	64.6	113.4	110.7
Biological Sciences	3.9	2.6	3.8	5.3	7.7	8.0	57.5	3.1	1.1	2.2	66.3	13.3
Vet. Science, Agriculture & related	0.4	0.4	0.7	0.7	1.1	1.1	6.6	0.3	2.2	1.6	10.0	3.0
Physical Sciences	2.3	1.1	2.3	1.4	4.6	2.4	18.9	0.8	0.3	1.4	23.8	4.6
Mathematical and Computing Sciences	0.8	0.5	3.6	3.5	4.4	3.9	23.0	1.9	2.5	11.4	29.9	17.2
Engineering & Technology	1.4	0.8	2.5	1.8	3.9	2.6	11.3	0.7	1.3	1.8	16.6	5.1
Architecture, Building & Planning	0.2	0.2	1.8	2.5	2.0	2.7	5.7	1.4	0.6	2.5	8.2	6.6
Social Sciences (inc Law)	2.1	2.4	15.2	14.6	17.2	17.0	79.1	10.0	7.4	26.7	103.7	53.7
Business & Administrative Studies	0.7	1.1	15.1	27.8	15.8	28.8	69.4	8.9	15.5	46.6	100.8	84.4
Mass Communications & Documentation	0.2	0.2	2.9	2.6	3.0	2.8	17.3	0.8	1.1	1.6	21.5	5.2
Languages	1.5	1.6	4.1	3.4	5.6	5.0	52.9	3.1	2.5	19.9	61.0	28.0
Historical and Philosophical Studies	1.1	1.4	2.6	4.9	3.6	6.3	26.5	3.5	1.1	20.1	31.2	29.9
Creative Arts & Design	0.6	0.6	4.1	2.7	4.6	3.4	58.7	2.8	7.7	7.8	71.0	14.0
Education [7]	0.5	2.5	20.3	40.6	20.8	43.0	26.5	5.3	1.8	27.8	49.0	76.1
Other subjects [8]	-	-	-	7.5	-	7.5	4.5	1.8	2.0	108.7	6.6	118.0
Unknown [6]	-	-	0.1	0.3	0.1	0.3	3.9	1.0	8.1	13.2	12.4	16.3
All subjects	**18.5**	**18.6**	**84.2**	**141.1**	**102.6**	**159.7**	**529.3**	**71.5**	**115.4**	**358.0**	**747.6**	**591.1**

Sources: Department for Education and Skills; National Assembly for Wales; Scottish Executive; Northern Ireland Department for Employment and Learning

1 Higher Education Statistics Agency (HESA) higher education institutions include Open University students. Part-time figures include dormant modes, those writing up at home and on sabbaticals.
2 Full-time includes sandwich. Part-time comprises both day and evening, including block release and open/distance learning.
3 For HE students in further education institutions in England, includes those areas of learning which cannot be allocated to specific subject groups shown.
4 FE institution figures for England include Learning and Skills Council (LSC) funded students only.
5 Figures for higher education (HE) institutions are based on the HESA July 'standard registration' count and are not directly comparable with previous years prior to 2001/02. Figures for further education (FE) institutions (other than in Scotland FE colleges) are snapshots counted at a particular point in the year [November for FE institutions in England and Northern Ireland, and December for FE institutions in Wales]. Students starting courses after these dates will not therefore be counted. Figures for Scotland, however, are whole year (not snapshot) enrolments (rather than headcounts).
6 Includes data for higher education students in further education institutions in Wales which cannot be split by level.
7 Including ITT and INSET.
8 Includes Combined and general categories.
9 Numbers in grouped countries do not sum to overall student numbers due to overlaps.

POST COMPULSORY EDUCATION AND TRAINING: STUDENTS AND LEARNERS

Students in higher [1] education by level, mode of study [2], gender and subject group [3], 2002/03 [4,5]

United Kingdom (ii) of which Overseas Students Thousands

| | Postgraduate level | | | | | | First degree | | Other Undergraduate | | Total higher education students [6] | |
| | PhD & equivalent | | Masters and Others | | Total Postgraduate | | | | | | | |
	Full-time	Part-time	Full-time	Part-time	Full-time	Part-time	Full-time	Part-time	Full-time	Part-time	Full-time	Part-time
All												
Medicine & Dentistry	0.8	0.5	1.3	0.8	2.1	1.3	2.9	-	-	-	**5.0**	**1.3**
Subjects Allied to Medicine	0.7	0.5	1.6	2.0	2.3	2.5	4.1	0.9	3.8	1.8	**10.2**	**5.2**
Biological Sciences	1.6	1.0	2.1	1.0	3.8	1.9	5.1	0.2	0.1	0.1	**9.0**	**2.2**
Vet. Science, Agriculture & related	0.4	0.3	0.7	0.1	1.1	0.4	0.8	-	0.2	0.1	**2.1**	**0.5**
Physical Sciences	2.1	0.9	1.9	0.6	4.0	1.5	2.3	-	0.1	0.1	**6.4**	**1.6**
Mathematical and Computing Sciences	1.6	0.8	7.7	2.6	9.3	3.4	10.6	0.5	0.7	0.6	**20.6**	**4.5**
Engineering & Technology	3.9	1.9	9.6	2.8	13.5	4.8	14.9	1.1	1.4	1.6	**29.8**	**7.5**
Architecture, Building & Planning	0.4	0.3	2.1	0.7	2.5	1.0	2.6	0.5	0.3	0.2	**5.4**	**1.7**
Social Sciences (inc Law)	2.6	2.1	13.1	3.7	15.7	5.9	14.1	1.4	0.6	0.3	**30.4**	**7.6**
Business & Administrative Studies	1.2	1.1	24.8	8.8	26.0	9.9	22.4	1.9	2.3	1.3	**50.7**	**13.2**
Mass Communications & Documentation	0.2	0.1	2.0	0.6	2.2	0.7	2.2	0.2	-	-	**4.5**	**0.9**
Languages	1.2	1.1	3.1	1.1	4.3	2.3	4.8	0.3	4.1	5.5	**13.2**	**8.1**
Historical and Philosophical Studies	1.1	1.0	1.7	0.6	2.8	1.6	1.9	0.1	0.1	0.3	**4.9**	**2.0**
Creative Arts & Design	0.5	0.4	3.0	0.6	3.5	1.0	8.6	0.2	0.6	0.2	**12.7**	**1.4**
Education [7]	0.5	1.5	2.9	4.1	3.4	5.6	0.7	0.9	0.2	0.9	**4.2**	**7.3**
Other subjects [8]	-	-	-	0.1	-	0.1	0.7	-	1.9	1.6	**2.6**	**1.7**
Unknown [6]	-	-	-	-	-	-	0.2	-	0.8	0.4	**1.0**	**0.4**
All subjects	**18.9**	**13.5**	**77.6**	**30.3**	**96.5**	**43.8**	**98.9**	**8.5**	**17.1**	**14.9**	**212.5**	**67.2**
of which European Union [9]	5.3	4.3	19.8	11.5	25.1	15.8	38.8	2.5	3.8	5.8	**67.7**	**24.1**
Other Europe [9]	1.3	1.0	4.2	2.6	5.5	3.6	7.8	0.4	0.6	0.7	**13.9**	**4.6**
Commonwealth [9]	4.4	2.6	20.7	7.2	25.2	9.8	25.0	3.0	4.8	2.7	**54.9**	**15.5**
Other Countries [9]	8.0	5.8	33.8	9.7	41.8	15.5	30.0	2.8	8.1	5.8	**80.0**	**24.2**
Males												
Medicine & Dentistry	0.4	0.3	0.6	0.5	1.0	0.7	1.3	-	-	-	**2.3**	**0.8**
Subjects Allied to Medicine	0.3	0.2	0.6	0.7	1.0	0.9	1.2	0.2	1.0	0.3	**3.2**	**1.4**
Biological Sciences	0.8	0.5	0.9	0.4	1.7	0.8	1.6	0.1	-	0.1	**3.3**	**1.0**
Vet. Science, Agriculture & related	0.3	0.2	0.4	0.1	0.7	0.2	0.3	-	0.1	0.1	**1.1**	**0.3**
Physical Sciences	1.3	0.6	1.0	0.4	2.4	0.9	1.3	-	0.1	0.1	**3.7**	**1.0**
Mathematical and Computing Sciences	1.2	0.6	5.7	1.7	6.8	2.3	7.7	0.4	0.6	0.4	**15.1**	**3.1**
Engineering & Technology	3.1	1.6	7.9	2.4	11.0	4.0	12.3	1.0	1.3	1.5	**24.6**	**6.5**
Architecture, Building & Planning	0.2	0.2	1.2	0.5	1.5	0.7	1.5	0.4	0.2	0.1	**3.2**	**1.2**
Social Sciences (inc Law)	1.5	1.2	6.4	2.0	7.9	3.2	6.5	0.9	0.3	0.1	**14.6**	**4.2**
Business & Administrative Studies	0.7	0.8	13.3	5.4	14.0	6.2	11.0	0.9	1.2	0.7	**26.1**	**7.8**
Mass Communications & Documentation	0.1	-	0.6	0.2	0.7	0.3	0.7	-	-	-	**1.4**	**0.3**
Languages	0.5	0.5	0.9	0.3	1.3	0.8	1.3	0.2	1.9	2.2	**4.6**	**3.2**
Historical and Philosophical Studies	0.7	0.6	0.8	0.3	1.5	0.9	0.8	0.1	-	0.1	**2.3**	**1.1**
Creative Arts & Design	0.3	0.2	1.1	0.2	1.3	0.4	2.9	0.1	0.2	0.1	**4.4**	**0.6**
Education [7]	0.2	0.7	0.7	1.6	0.9	2.3	0.1	0.4	0.1	0.3	**1.1**	**3.0**
Other subjects [8]	-	-	-	0.1	-	0.1	0.3	-	0.8	0.6	**1.1**	**0.6**
Unknown [6]	-	-	-	-	-	-	0.1	-	0.4	0.1	**0.5**	**0.2**
All subjects	**11.6**	**8.1**	**42.1**	**16.7**	**53.7**	**24.8**	**50.9**	**4.7**	**8.0**	**6.6**	**112.6**	**36.2**
of which European Union [9]	3.0	2.4	10.5	6.1	13.5	8.5	19.6	1.3	1.5	2.5	**34.5**	**12.3**
Other Europe [9]	0.7	0.5	2.1	1.3	2.8	1.8	3.6	0.1	0.3	0.2	**6.7**	**2.1**
Commonwealth [9]	2.9	1.7	13.9	4.5	16.9	6.2	14.2	1.6	2.4	1.5	**33.5**	**9.3**
Other Countries [9]	5.0	3.7	16.1	5.1	21.1	8.8	15.0	1.7	4.0	2.4	**40.0**	**12.9**
Females												
Medicine & Dentistry	0.4	0.2	0.7	0.4	1.1	0.5	1.6	-	-	-	**2.7**	**0.6**
Subjects Allied to Medicine	0.4	0.3	0.9	1.3	1.3	1.6	2.9	0.7	2.8	1.5	**7.0**	**3.8**
Biological Sciences	0.8	0.5	1.3	0.6	2.1	1.1	3.5	0.1	0.1	0.1	**5.6**	**1.3**
Vet. Science, Agriculture & related	0.2	0.1	0.3	0.1	0.5	0.2	0.5	-	0.1	-	**1.0**	**0.2**
Physical Sciences	0.8	0.3	0.9	0.2	1.6	0.5	1.1	-	0.1	-	**2.7**	**0.6**
Mathematical and Computing Sciences	0.5	0.2	2.0	0.9	2.5	1.1	2.9	0.1	0.2	0.2	**5.5**	**1.4**
Engineering & Technology	0.8	0.3	1.7	0.4	2.5	0.8	2.6	0.1	0.1	0.1	**5.2**	**1.0**
Architecture, Building & Planning	0.1	0.1	0.9	0.2	1.0	0.3	1.1	0.1	0.1	-	**2.2**	**0.5**
Social Sciences (inc Law)	1.1	0.9	6.8	1.7	7.9	2.6	7.6	0.5	0.3	0.2	**15.8**	**3.4**
Business & Administrative Studies	0.5	0.4	11.5	3.4	12.0	3.7	11.5	1.1	1.1	0.6	**24.5**	**5.4**
Mass Communications & Documentation	0.1	0.1	1.4	0.4	1.5	0.4	1.5	0.1	-	-	**3.0**	**0.6**
Languages	0.7	0.7	2.2	0.8	3.0	1.4	3.5	0.2	2.2	3.3	**8.6**	**4.9**
Historical and Philosophical Studies	0.5	0.4	0.9	0.3	1.3	0.7	1.1	0.1	0.1	0.2	**2.5**	**0.9**
Creative Arts & Design	0.3	0.2	1.9	0.4	2.2	0.6	5.7	0.1	0.4	0.1	**8.3**	**0.8**
Education [7]	0.3	0.8	2.2	2.5	2.5	3.3	0.5	0.4	0.1	0.6	**3.1**	**4.3**
Other subjects [8]	-	-	-	-	-	-	0.4	-	1.1	1.0	**1.5**	**1.1**
Unknown [6]	-	-	-	-	-	-	0.1	-	0.4	0.2	**0.5**	**0.3**
All subjects	**7.3**	**5.4**	**35.5**	**13.6**	**42.8**	**18.9**	**48.0**	**3.8**	**9.1**	**8.3**	**100.0**	**31.0**
of which European Union [9]	2.3	1.9	9.3	5.4	11.6	7.3	19.2	1.2	2.3	3.3	**33.2**	**11.8**
Other Europe [9]	0.6	0.4	2.1	1.3	2.7	1.8	4.2	0.2	0.3	0.5	**7.2**	**2.5**
Commonwealth [9]	1.5	1.0	6.8	2.7	8.3	3.6	10.8	1.3	2.3	1.1	**21.4**	**6.1**
Other Countries [9]	3.0	2.2	17.8	4.5	20.8	6.7	15.1	1.1	4.2	3.4	**40.0**	**11.3**

Sources: Department for Education and Skills; National Assembly for Wales; Scottish Executive; Northern Ireland Department for Employment and Learning

See previous page for footnotes.

POST COMPULSORY EDUCATION AND TRAINING: STUDENTS AND LEARNERS

Full-time students from overseas in higher education [1], by level, gender and country, 2002/03 and time series

United Kingdom

Thousands

2002/03 RANK	2001/02 RANK	TOP FIFTY NAMED COUNTRIES	2000/01 All	2001/02[2] All	2001/02 Males	2001/02 Females	2002/03 All	2002/03 Males	2002/03 Females	Postgraduate PhD	Postgraduate Masters	Total post-graduate	First degree	Other under-graduate
1	(2)	China	9.0	17.9	8.7	9.2	31.2	14.5	16.6	1.4	14.3	15.8	11.7	3.7
2	(1)	Greece	24.6	23.3	14.1	9.1	20.5	12.4	8.2	1.3	9.1	10.4	9.8	0.3
3	(7)	India	3.5	6.6	4.9	1.7	10.9	8.4	2.5	0.7	7.5	8.1	2.2	0.6
4	(3)	Malaysia	7.9	9.3	5.3	4.0	9.5	5.3	4.2	1.2	2.2	3.3	6.0	0.2
5	(4)	Irish Republic	9.3	9.2	3.6	5.6	9.1	3.7	5.4	0.4	1.6	2.1	5.7	1.3
6	(5)	Germany	11.3	8.4	4.0	4.3	8.6	4.1	4.5	0.9	2.0	2.8	5.2	0.5
7	(6)	France	11.0	7.9	4.2	3.7	8.0	4.3	3.7	0.6	2.2	2.8	4.8	0.4
8	(8)	USA	8.8	6.6	2.8	3.8	7.9	3.3	4.6	1.1	3.7	4.8	1.9	1.2
9	(9)	Hong Kong	5.5	6.4	3.2	3.2	7.1	3.6	3.5	0.2	1.1	1.3	5.5	0.3
10	(10)	Japan	4.9	4.9	1.7	3.1	4.8	1.8	3.0	0.4	1.7	2.1	2.0	0.8
11	(12)	Taiwan	3.3	3.8	1.5	2.3	4.4	1.7	2.7	0.5	2.9	3.4	0.9	0.2
12	(11)	Spain	6.2	4.4	2.3	2.1	4.4	2.3	2.1	0.4	1.1	1.5	2.5	0.4
13	(18)	Nigeria	2.0	2.8	1.6	1.2	3.9	2.3	1.6	0.2	1.7	1.9	1.7	0.3
14	(13)	Italy	4.8	3.8	1.9	1.9	3.8	1.9	1.8	0.7	1.1	1.8	1.7	0.2
15	(14)	Singapore	3.7	3.4	2.0	1.4	3.2	1.8	1.5	0.2	0.5	0.8	2.4	-
16	(16)	Cyprus	3.2	3.2	1.7	1.5	3.2	1.7	1.5	0.1	0.8	0.9	2.2	0.1
17	(15)	Norway	3.5	3.3	1.4	1.8	3.2	1.4	1.8	0.1	0.7	0.7	2.4	0.1
18	(17)	Sweden	3.4	3.0	1.1	1.9	2.9	1.1	1.8	0.1	0.5	0.6	2.2	0.1
19	(20)	Thailand	2.2	2.5	1.0	1.4	2.8	1.2	1.6	0.4	1.6	2.0	0.6	0.1
20	(23)	Pakistan	1.5	2.2	1.8	0.3	2.6	2.2	0.4	0.2	1.3	1.5	1.0	0.1
21	(22)	Korea [3]	1.9	2.3	1.2	1.1	2.6	1.4	1.2	0.4	1.0	1.4	1.0	0.2
22	(19)	Zimbabwe	2.1	2.6	1.1	1.5	2.6	1.1	1.4	0.1	0.2	0.3	0.6	1.7
23	(21)	Kenya	2.1	2.3	1.1	1.1	2.4	1.2	1.2	0.1	0.6	0.6	1.6	0.1
24	(24)	Canada	2.1	2.1	0.9	1.2	2.3	1.0	1.3	0.5	1.2	1.7	0.5	0.1
25	(26)	Portugal	1.8	1.8	0.9	0.9	1.9	1.0	0.9	0.3	0.4	0.8	1.0	0.1
26	(27)	Belgium	2.0	1.8	0.9	0.9	1.8	0.9	0.9	0.1	0.4	0.5	1.3	-
27	(35)	Ghana	0.8	1.3	0.9	0.4	1.7	1.2	0.5	0.1	0.9	1.0	0.5	0.2
28	(25)	Finland	2.3	1.8	0.6	1.2	1.7	0.6	1.1	0.1	0.3	0.3	1.3	0.1
29	(29)	Sri Lanka	1.1	1.4	0.9	0.5	1.7	1.1	0.6	0.1	0.4	0.6	1.0	0.1
30	(28)	Netherlands	1.7	1.4	0.7	0.7	1.5	0.7	0.8	0.1	0.4	0.6	0.9	0.1
31	(32)	Mexico	1.1	1.3	0.8	0.5	1.4	0.9	0.5	0.5	0.8	1.3	0.1	-
32	(34)	Russia	1.1	1.3	0.6	0.7	1.4	0.7	0.7	0.2	0.4	0.6	0.7	0.1
33	(36)	Saudi Arabia	1.0	1.1	0.9	0.3	1.4	1.1	0.3	0.4	0.4	0.8	0.4	0.2
34	(30)	Turkey	1.3	1.3	0.8	0.6	1.3	0.8	0.6	0.1	0.7	0.8	0.4	0.1
35	(31)	Mauritius	1.0	1.3	0.7	0.6	1.3	0.7	0.6	-	0.2	0.3	0.8	0.2
36	(33)	Denmark	1.5	1.3	0.5	0.8	1.3	0.5	0.8	0.1	0.3	0.4	0.8	0.1
37	(43)	Bangladesh	0.6	0.9	0.7	0.2	1.2	1.0	0.2	0.1	0.4	0.6	0.5	0.1
38	(37)	Libya	0.5	1.1	1.0	0.1	1.1	1.0	0.1	0.2	0.7	0.9	0.1	0.1
39	(38)	Oman	0.9	1.0	0.8	0.2	1.0	0.8	0.2	0.1	0.2	0.3	0.6	0.1
40	(46)	United Arab Emirates	0.6	0.7	0.5	0.2	0.9	0.6	0.3	0.1	0.2	0.3	0.6	0.1
41	(42)	Austria	1.1	0.9	0.4	0.4	0.9	0.4	0.5	0.1	0.2	0.3	0.6	-
42	(41)	Switzerland	1.0	0.9	0.4	0.5	0.9	0.4	0.4	0.1	0.3	0.4	0.5	-
43	(40)	Indonesia	0.9	0.9	0.5	0.4	0.9	0.5	0.4	0.1	0.4	0.6	0.3	-
44	(44)	Australia	0.8	0.8	0.4	0.4	0.9	0.5	0.4	0.2	0.3	0.6	0.2	0.1
45	(45)	Iran	0.6	0.7	0.5	0.2	0.8	0.6	0.2	0.3	0.2	0.6	0.2	0.1
46	(39)	Brazil	0.8	0.9	0.5	0.4	0.8	0.4	0.4	0.2	0.4	0.6	0.2	-
47	(47)	Jordan	0.6	0.7	0.5	0.2	0.8	0.6	0.2	0.2	0.3	0.5	0.3	-
48	(-)	Tanzania	0.5	0.6	0.4	0.3	0.7	0.4	0.3	-	0.3	0.3	0.3	0.1
49	(50)	Israel	0.7	0.7	0.4	0.3	0.7	0.4	0.3	0.1	0.3	0.4	0.3	-
50	(-)	Luxembourg	0.6	0.6	0.3	0.3	0.7	0.3	0.3	-	0.1	0.1	0.5	-
		Other/unknown	16.2	18.2	9.8	8.4	19.8	10.7	9.0	2.5	6.9	9.4	8.4	2.0
		TOTAL	**181.3**	**188.4**	**99.7**	**88.7**	**212.5**	**112.6**	**100.0**	**18.9**	**77.6**	**96.5**	**98.9**	**17.1**

Full-time students from overseas
of which

			2000/01 All	2001/02 All	2001/02 Males	2001/02 Females	2002/03 All	2002/03 Males	2002/03 Females	PhD	Masters	Total post-graduate	First degree	Other under-graduate
		European Union [4,5]	82.3	70.0	36.0	34.1	67.7	34.5	33.2	5.3	19.8	25.1	38.8	3.8
		Other Europe [4]	13.4	13.5	6.5	7.1	13.9	6.7	7.2	1.3	4.2	5.5	7.8	0.6
		Commonwealth [4]	39.1	47.3	27.8	19.5	54.9	33.5	21.4	4.4	20.7	25.2	25.0	4.8
		Other Countries [6]	50.4	61.6	31.6	30.0	80.0	40.0	40.0	8.0	33.8	41.8	30.0	8.1

Sources: Department for Education and Skills; National Assembly for Wales; Scottish Executive; Northern Ireland Department for Employment and Learning

1 Figures for higher education (HE) institutions are based on the HESA July 'standard registration' count and are not directly comparable with previous years prior to 2001/02. Figures for further education (FE) institutions (other than in Scotland FE colleges) are snapshots counted at a particular point in the year [November for FE institutions in England and Northern Ireland, and December for FE institutions in Wales]. Students starting courses after these dates will not therefore be counted. Figures for Scotland, however, are whole year (not snapshot) enrolments (rather than headcounts).
2 Revised to include data for Tanzania and Luxembourg which replaced South Africa and Brunei in the top 50 named countries in 2002/03.
3 Includes North Korea and South Korea.
4 Gibraltar is included in both European Union (EU) and Commonwealth figures, and Cyprus and Malta are included in Other Europe and Commonwealth figures. Numbers in grouped countries do not sum to overall student numbers due to overlaps.
5 Consisting of the 15 member states of the EU in 2002/03.
6 Includes those students whose country of domicile is not known.

3.8 POST COMPULSORY EDUCATION AND TRAINING: STUDENTS AND LEARNERS

Students in further education [1] by country of study, mode of study [2], gender and age [3], during 2002/03 [4]

United Kingdom   Home and Overseas Students   Thousands

	United Kingdom		England [5]		Wales		Scotland [6]		Northern Ireland	
	Full-time	Part-time	Full-time	Part-time	Full-time	Part-time	Full-time	Part-time	Full-time	Part-time
All										
Age [3] <16	5.8	45.5	2.6	5.7	0.9	5.6	2.1	30.9	0.1	3.3
16	268.9	75.5	238.0	52.0	14.1	4.1	9.5	14.7	7.3	4.6
17	227.6	83.2	200.1	59.2	11.7	4.8	9.0	15.5	6.9	3.6
18	102.5	80.3	87.0	62.6	5.5	4.7	6.1	10.5	3.9	2.4
19	42.8	74.8	36.2	59.9	2.2	4.6	3.1	8.5	1.3	1.9
20	25.5	70.1	21.8	57.3	1.2	4.4	1.9	6.9	0.5	1.5
21	21.0	73.4	18.4	61.5	0.9	4.4	1.4	6.2	0.3	1.4
22	18.7	79.1	16.7	67.0	0.6	4.6	1.1	6.1	0.2	1.4
23	16.3	77.0	14.7	65.5	0.5	4.3	0.9	5.9	0.1	1.2
24	14.4	73.2	13.1	62.6	0.4	3.8	0.8	5.6	0.1	1.2
25	13.2	71.9	12.1	62.0	0.4	3.7	0.7	5.1	0.1	1.1
26	13.0	74.0	12.0	63.7	0.4	3.8	0.6	5.4	-	1.1
27	12.6	75.3	11.7	64.9	0.3	3.9	0.5	5.5	-	1.0
28	12.4	76.9	11.4	66.5	0.4	4.0	0.5	5.4	-	1.0
29	12.1	79.4	11.2	68.6	0.3	4.1	0.5	5.7	-	1.0
30+	218.5	2,565.1	205.8	2,202.0	4.9	146.0	7.3	191.5	0.5	25.7
Unknown	1.5	27.0	1.4	23.6	0.1	2.9	-	-	-	0.5
All ages	1,026.7	3,701.6	914.5	3,104.7	44.8	213.7	46.0	329.3	21.5	54.0
Males										
Age [3] <16	3.2	23.5	1.3	2.5	0.6	3.2	1.2	15.6	0.1	2.1
16	132.5	36.7	115.5	26.0	7.3	2.1	5.3	6.5	4.3	2.1
17	109.9	41.0	95.8	29.0	5.7	2.7	4.6	7.7	3.8	1.6
18	52.4	39.0	44.3	28.9	2.7	2.7	3.1	6.2	2.3	1.2
19	23.2	34.7	19.5	26.3	1.2	2.5	1.7	5.0	0.8	0.9
20	13.6	30.5	11.6	24.1	0.7	2.2	1.0	3.6	0.3	0.6
21	10.5	29.9	9.2	24.3	0.4	2.0	0.7	3.0	0.1	0.5
22	9.2	31.3	8.3	26.1	0.3	2.0	0.5	2.7	0.1	0.5
23	8.0	29.9	7.3	25.2	0.2	1.8	0.4	2.5	0.1	0.4
24	7.0	28.7	6.4	24.4	0.2	1.6	0.4	2.4	0.1	0.4
25	6.5	28.4	6.0	24.4	0.2	1.6	0.3	2.1	-	0.4
26	6.4	29.0	6.0	24.9	0.2	1.6	0.3	2.1	-	0.3
27	6.2	30.0	5.8	26.0	0.1	1.5	0.2	2.1	-	0.3
28	6.0	30.1	5.7	26.0	0.1	1.7	0.2	2.1	-	0.3
29	5.8	30.9	5.5	26.7	0.1	1.6	0.2	2.3	-	0.3
30+	107.9	940.0	103.4	805.8	1.8	55.3	2.6	71.2	0.1	7.7
Unknown	0.9	10.1	0.9	8.7	-	1.2	-	-	-	0.2
All ages	509.3	1,423.9	452.6	1,179.4	21.8	87.4	22.6	137.3	12.3	19.8
Females										
Age [3] <16	2.6	22.0	1.3	3.1	0.3	2.4	0.9	15.3	0.1	1.2
16	136.5	38.8	122.5	26.0	6.8	2.0	4.2	8.2	3.0	2.5
17	117.7	42.1	104.4	30.2	6.0	2.1	4.3	7.9	3.1	2.0
18	50.1	41.2	42.7	33.7	2.7	2.0	3.1	4.3	1.6	1.2
19	19.6	40.1	16.7	33.6	1.0	2.1	1.4	3.5	0.5	0.9
20	11.9	39.5	10.3	33.2	0.6	2.2	0.9	3.3	0.2	0.9
21	10.5	43.5	9.2	37.1	0.5	2.4	0.7	3.2	0.1	0.9
22	9.4	47.8	8.4	40.9	0.3	2.6	0.6	3.4	0.1	0.9
23	8.3	47.0	7.4	40.4	0.3	2.5	0.5	3.4	0.1	0.9
24	7.4	44.5	6.7	38.3	0.2	2.2	0.5	3.2	0.1	0.8
25	6.7	43.5	6.1	37.6	0.2	2.1	0.4	3.0	-	0.8
26	6.5	45.0	6.0	38.7	0.2	2.3	0.3	3.2	-	0.8
27	6.4	45.4	5.9	38.9	0.2	2.4	0.3	3.4	-	0.7
28	6.3	46.8	5.7	40.5	0.2	2.4	0.3	3.2	-	0.7
29	6.2	48.6	5.7	41.9	0.2	2.5	0.3	3.4	-	0.7
30+	110.6	1,625.1	102.4	1,396.2	3.1	90.7	4.7	120.3	0.3	18.0
Unknown	0.6	16.9	0.6	14.9	-	1.7	-	-	-	0.3
All ages	517.5	2,277.7	462.0	1,925.2	23.0	126.3	23.3	192.0	9.2	34.2

Sources: Department for Education and Skills; National Assembly for Wales; Scottish Executive; Northern Ireland Department for Employment and Learning

1 Further education (FE) institution figures are whole year counts except for Northern Ireland, which are collected on a snapshot basis. Higher education (HE) institution figures are based on the HESA July 'standard registration' count and are not directly comparable with previous years prior to 2001/02.
2 Full-time includes sandwich. Part-time comprises both day and evening, including block release and open/distance learning.
3 Ages as at 31 August 2002 (1 July for Northern Ireland and 31 December for Scotland).
4 Provisional.
5 Further education institution figures for England include LSC funded students only. Figures are not directly comparable with previous years.
6 Figures for Scotland further education colleges are enrolments rather than headcounts.

3.9

Students in higher [1] education by level, mode of study [2], gender and age [3], 2002/03 [4,5]

United Kingdom Home and Overseas Students Thousands

Age [3]	PhD & equivalent Full-time	PhD & equivalent Part-time	Masters and Others Full-time	Masters and Others Part-time	Total Postgraduate Full-time	Total Postgraduate Part-time	First degree Full-time	First degree Part-time	Other Undergraduate Full-time	Other Undergraduate Part-time	Total higher education students [6] Full-time	Total higher education students [6] Part-time
All												
<16	-	-	-	-	-	-	-	-	-	0.3	-	0.3
16	-	-	-	-	-	-	0.3	-	0.8	1.9	1.2	1.9
17	-	-	-	-	-	-	10.5	0.1	4.7	1.8	15.2	1.9
18	-	-	0.1	-	0.1	-	160.2	0.6	20.5	6.2	180.9	6.8
19	-	-	0.1	-	0.1	-	214.4	2.4	29.0	11.0	243.7	13.5
20	-	-	1.4	0.2	1.4	0.2	217.9	4.3	22.8	13.0	242.2	17.6
21	0.8	-	15.3	1.4	16.1	1.5	149.3	6.2	15.7	14.0	181.3	21.8
22	3.1	0.2	24.7	5.2	27.8	5.4	71.6	6.9	11.0	15.6	110.4	27.9
23	5.0	0.3	23.0	8.4	28.0	8.7	35.9	5.8	8.5	15.8	72.4	30.4
24	5.4	1.2	17.1	9.3	22.5	10.5	20.5	4.6	6.5	15.3	49.4	30.5
25	4.3	2.5	12.8	9.4	17.1	11.9	13.9	4.1	5.2	15.0	36.2	31.1
26	3.4	2.5	10.0	9.8	13.4	12.3	10.4	3.8	4.8	15.1	28.5	31.3
27	3.0	2.3	8.2	9.8	11.2	12.0	8.4	3.7	4.3	15.0	23.9	30.8
28	2.5	2.0	6.8	9.9	9.3	12.0	7.0	3.6	4.0	15.4	20.3	31.1
29	2.1	2.0	5.7	10.1	7.8	12.1	6.3	3.7	3.6	15.8	17.7	31.7
30+	13.8	29.7	38.6	176.1	52.4	205.8	63.6	67.8	46.5	386.4	162.7	662.0
Unknown	0.1	0.1	0.2	2.5	0.3	2.6	0.3	0.3	0.2	14.5	0.7	17.4
All ages	**43.5**	**42.8**	**164.0**	**252.2**	**207.5**	**295.0**	**990.3**	**117.9**	**188.1**	**572.2**	**1,386.7**	**988.2**
Males												
<16	-	-	-	-	-	-	-	-	-	0.2	-	0.2
16	-	-	-	-	-	-	0.1	-	0.2	0.8	0.4	0.8
17	-	-	-	-	-	-	4.6	0.1	1.9	0.8	6.6	0.9
18	-	-	-	-	-	-	71.9	0.3	9.1	3.4	81.0	3.7
19	-	-	0.1	-	0.1	-	98.2	1.4	13.7	6.0	112.1	7.4
20	-	-	0.7	0.1	0.7	0.1	100.5	2.5	10.3	6.5	111.5	9.2
21	0.4	-	6.4	0.5	6.8	0.5	73.1	3.4	7.0	6.6	86.9	10.6
22	1.8	0.1	11.2	2.0	13.0	2.1	37.6	3.6	4.8	6.4	55.4	12.2
23	3.0	0.2	10.8	3.3	13.8	3.4	19.2	2.9	3.4	6.0	36.4	12.3
24	3.1	0.6	8.2	3.6	11.3	4.2	10.9	2.2	2.5	5.7	24.6	12.2
25	2.4	1.5	6.3	3.7	8.7	5.2	7.1	1.8	1.9	5.4	17.8	12.4
26	1.9	1.4	4.9	4.0	6.8	5.4	5.2	1.5	1.7	5.5	13.7	12.5
27	1.6	1.2	4.2	4.0	5.8	5.2	4.0	1.4	1.4	5.6	11.2	12.3
28	1.3	1.1	3.5	4.3	4.8	5.4	3.2	1.4	1.3	5.7	9.4	12.5
29	1.2	1.1	3.0	4.5	4.1	5.6	2.8	1.5	1.2	6.1	8.2	13.3
30+	8.2	16.9	20.6	80.2	28.8	97.1	22.3	22.2	12.3	138.2	63.5	258.3
Unknown	-	0.1	0.1	1.0	0.2	1.1	0.2	0.1	0.1	5.2	0.4	6.3
All ages	**25.0**	**24.2**	**79.8**	**111.1**	**104.8**	**135.3**	**461.1**	**46.4**	**72.8**	**214.1**	**639.1**	**397.1**
Females												
<16	-	-	-	-	-	-	-	-	-	0.2	-	0.2
16	-	-	-	-	-	-	0.2	-	0.6	1.1	0.8	1.1
17	-	-	-	-	-	-	5.9	-	2.8	1.0	8.7	1.0
18	-	-	0.1	-	0.1	-	88.3	0.3	11.5	2.8	99.9	3.1
19	-	-	0.1	-	0.1	-	116.1	1.1	15.3	5.0	131.6	6.1
20	-	-	0.7	0.1	0.7	0.1	117.4	1.8	12.5	6.4	130.7	8.4
21	0.3	-	9.0	0.9	9.3	0.9	76.3	2.8	8.7	7.4	94.3	11.2
22	1.3	0.1	13.5	3.2	14.8	3.3	34.0	3.3	6.2	9.1	55.0	15.8
23	2.1	0.1	12.2	5.1	14.2	5.3	16.7	2.9	5.1	9.8	36.0	18.0
24	2.3	0.6	8.9	5.7	11.2	6.3	9.6	2.4	4.0	9.6	24.8	18.3
25	1.9	1.0	6.5	5.7	8.4	6.7	6.8	2.3	3.3	9.6	18.5	18.7
26	1.6	1.1	5.0	5.8	6.6	6.9	5.1	2.3	3.1	9.6	14.8	18.9
27	1.4	1.1	4.1	5.8	5.4	6.8	4.3	2.2	2.9	9.4	12.6	18.5
28	1.1	0.9	3.3	5.7	4.5	6.6	3.8	2.2	2.6	9.7	10.9	18.6
29	0.9	0.9	2.8	5.6	3.6	6.5	3.4	2.1	2.4	9.7	9.5	18.4
30+	5.6	12.8	18.0	95.9	23.6	108.7	41.3	45.6	34.2	248.1	99.2	403.8
Unknown	-	-	0.1	1.5	0.1	1.5	0.1	0.2	0.1	9.4	0.3	11.1
All ages	**18.5**	**18.6**	**84.2**	**141.1**	**102.6**	**159.7**	**529.3**	**71.5**	**115.4**	**358.0**	**747.6**	**591.1**

Sources: Department for Education and Skills; National Assembly for Wales; Scottish Executive; Northern Ireland Department for Employment and Learning

1 Higher Education Statistics Agency (HESA) higher education institutions include Open University students. Part-time figures include dormant modes, those writing up at home and on sabbaticals.

2 Full-time includes sandwich. Part-time comprises both day and evening, including block release and open/distance learning.

3 Ages as at 31 August 2002 (1 July for Northern Ireland and 31 December for Scotland).

4 Figures for higher education (HE) institutions are based on the HESA July 'standard registration' count and are not directly comparable with previous years prior to 2001/02. Figures for further education (FE) institutions (other than in Scotland FE colleges) are snapshots counted at a particular point in the year [November for FE institutions in England and Northern Ireland, and December for FE institutions in Wales]. Students starting courses after these dates will not therefore be counted. Figures for Scotland, however, are whole year (not snapshot) enrolments (rather than headcounts).

5 FE institution figures for England include Learning and Skills Council (LSC) funded students only.

6 Includes data for HE students in FE institutions in Wales which cannot be split by level.

3.10

Students [1] in further and higher [2] education - time series

United Kingdom (i) Further education students Thousands

	United Kingdom		England		Wales		Scotland		Northern Ireland	
	Full-time [3]	Part-time [3]	Full-time [3]	Part-time [3]	Full-time [3]	Part-time [3]	Full-time [3]	Part-time [3]	Full-time [3]	Part-time [3]
1990/91 [4]										
All[5]	480.4	1,758.5	..	..	..	..	..	..	..	..
Males	218.8	767.5	..	..	..	..	..	..	..	..
Females	260.9	986.1	..	..	..	..	..	..	..	..
1995/96 [4,6]										
All	815.1	1,710.3	..	..	..	..	..	..	..	..
Males	394.8	686.4	..	..	..	..	..	..	..	..
Females	419.0	1,020.8	..	..	..	..	..	..	..	..
2000/01 [7,8]										
All	974.6	3,161.4	867.6	2,603.0	44.6	186.2	41.3	313.8	21.0	58.3
Males	477.7	1,227.4	424.5	999.3	20.8	75.2	20.6	132.1	11.8	20.8
Females	496.8	1,933.9	443.1	1,603.7	23.8	111.0	20.7	181.8	9.2	37.5
2001/02 [7,8]										
All	1,024.6	3,673.2	913.2	3,059.7	45.0	210.0	45.1	345.0	21.4	58.4
Males	507.3	1,424.3	451.6	1,174.3	21.6	85.5	22.1	143.1	12.1	21.4
Females	517.3	2,249.0	461.6	1,885.4	23.4	124.5	22.9	202.0	9.3	37.0
2002/03 [7]										
All	1,026.7	3,701.6	914.5	3,104.7	44.8	213.7	46.0	329.3	21.5	54.0
Males	509.3	1,423.9	452.6	1,179.4	21.8	87.4	22.6	137.3	12.3	19.8
Females	517.5	2,277.7	462.0	1,925.2	23.0	126.3	23.3	192.0	9.2	34.2

United Kingdom (ii) Higher education students Thousands

	Postgraduate level						First degree		Other Undergraduate		Total higher education students [9]	
	PhD & equivalent		Masters and Others		Total Postgraduate							
	Full-time [3]	Part-time [3]	Full-time [3]	Part-time [3]	Full-time [3]	Part-time [3]	Full-time [3]	Part-time [3]	Full-time [3]	Part-time [3]	Full-time [3]	Part-time [3]
1990/91												
All	..	..	..	..	83.9	78.6	553.2	45.2	111.5	209.1	748.6	332.9
Males	..	..	..	..	50.1	45.9	286.1	23.8	58.5	123.8	394.7	193.4
Females	..	..	..	..	33.8	32.8	266.9	21.4	52.1	84.2	352.8	138.4
1995/96 [10]												
All	..	..	..	..	135.4	186.2	872.1	177.8	175.1	353.1	1,182.6	717.1
Males	..	..	..	..	75.6	97.7	432.8	83.9	85.7	137.2	594.0	318.7
Females	..	..	..	..	59.8	88.6	439.3	94.0	89.4	215.8	588.6	398.4
2000/01 [11]												
All	38.1	37.2	124.4	203.4	162.5	240.6	920.1	100.2	191.7	443.4	1,275.0	785.5
Males	22.1	21.6	59.7	95.9	81.9	117.5	431.2	40.0	78.7	183.6	592.1	341.6
Females	15.9	15.6	64.7	107.5	80.6	123.1	488.9	60.2	113.0	259.9	682.8	443.9
2001/02 [12]												
All	42.6	42.4	144.0	243.4	186.6	285.8	948.7	117.0	190.2	557.6	1,326.2	961.7
Males	24.4	24.1	69.4	108.9	93.8	133.0	442.8	45.1	75.7	217.4	612.7	396.2
Females	18.2	18.3	74.6	134.5	92.8	152.9	505.9	71.8	114.5	340.2	713.5	565.5
2002/03 [12]												
All	43.5	42.8	164.0	252.2	207.5	295.0	990.3	117.9	188.1	572.2	1,386.7	988.2
Males	25.0	24.2	79.8	111.1	104.8	135.3	461.1	46.4	72.8	214.1	639.1	397.1
Females	18.5	18.6	84.2	141.1	102.6	159.7	529.3	71.5	115.4	358.0	747.6	591.1

Sources: Department for Education and Skills; National Assembly for Wales; Scottish Executive; Northern Ireland Department for Employment and Learning

1 Home and overseas students.
2 Higher education (HE) figures include Open University students. Part-time figures include dormant modes, those writing up at home and on sabbaticals.
3 Full-time includes sandwich. Part-time comprises both day and evening, including block release and open/distance learning.
4 Further education (FE) figures are enrolments and are not comparable with later figures (other than for Scotland further education colleges) which are headcounts.
5 Includes students in Scotland whose gender is not recorded.
6 Estimated.
7 FE institution figures are whole year counts except for Northern Ireland, which are collected on a snapshot basis.
8 Figures for FE institutions in England for 2000/01 and 2001/02 have been revised to show Learning and Skills Council (LSC) funded students only, and are comparable with those for 2002/03.
9 Figures for 2000/01, 2001/02 and 2002/03 include data for FE institutions in Wales which cannot be split by level.
10 Includes 1994/95 higher education in further education institution data for England and for Wales.
11 Figures for students (other than in Scotland further education colleges) are snapshots counted at a particular point in the year [December for UK HE institutions and FE institutions in Wales, November for FE institutions in England and Northern Ireland]. Students starting courses after these dates will not therefore be counted. Figures for Scotland, however, are whole year (not snapshot) enrolments (rather than headcounts).
12 Figures for higher education (HE) institutions are based on the HESA July 'standard registration' count and are not directly comparable with years prior to 2001/02.

3.11 POST COMPULSORY EDUCATION AND TRAINING: STUDENTS AND LEARNERS
New entrants to higher education [1] by level, mode of study [2], gender and age [3], 2002/03 [4,5]

United Kingdom · Home and Overseas Students · Thousands

| | Postgraduate level | | | | | | First degree | | Other Undergraduate | | Total higher education students [6] | |
| | PhD & equivalent | | Masters and Others | | Total Postgraduate | | | | | | | |
	Full-time	Part-time	Full-time	Part-time	Full-time	Part-time	Full-time	Part-time	Full-time	Part-time	Full-time	Part-time
All												
Age[3] <16	-	-	-	-	-	-	-	-	-	0.3	-	0.3
16	-	-	-	-	-	-	0.3	-	0.8	1.8	1.2	1.9
17	-	-	-	-	-	-	10.2	0.1	4.5	1.8	14.7	1.8
18	-	-	0.1	-	0.1	-	151.5	0.4	18.7	5.8	170.3	6.3
19	-	-	0.1	-	0.1	-	78.8	0.6	15.9	7.9	94.9	8.6
20	-	-	1.3	0.2	1.4	0.2	31.4	1.3	9.7	9.2	42.5	10.7
21	0.7	-	14.9	1.2	15.6	1.2	20.7	1.9	6.9	9.9	43.3	13.0
22	2.1	0.1	21.5	2.8	23.5	2.9	14.3	2.2	5.4	11.2	43.2	16.4
23	1.6	0.1	17.9	3.9	19.5	4.1	8.9	1.9	4.3	11.4	32.6	17.4
24	1.1	0.1	12.8	4.1	14.0	4.2	6.1	1.6	3.2	10.8	23.2	16.7
25	0.9	0.1	9.4	4.2	10.4	4.3	4.6	1.5	2.6	10.5	17.5	16.3
26	0.8	0.2	7.2	4.3	8.0	4.5	3.6	1.4	2.4	10.2	14.0	16.1
27	0.7	0.2	6.0	4.3	6.7	4.5	3.0	1.4	2.1	9.9	11.8	15.7
28	0.5	0.2	5.0	4.3	5.5	4.4	2.5	1.3	2.0	10.3	10.0	16.0
29	0.5	0.1	4.1	4.3	4.6	4.4	2.3	1.4	1.8	10.1	8.7	15.9
30+	3.2	3.5	27.7	72.4	30.8	76.0	24.4	24.3	23.3	220.1	78.6	320.4
Unknown	-	-	0.1	1.7	0.2	1.8	0.2	0.2	0.1	12.3	0.5	14.2
All ages	**12.1**	**4.7**	**128.3**	**107.8**	**140.4**	**112.4**	**362.9**	**41.6**	**103.8**	**353.4**	**607.3**	**507.8**
Males												
Age[3] <16	-	-	-	-	-	-	-	-	-	0.1	-	0.2
16	-	-	-	-	-	-	0.1	-	0.2	0.8	0.4	0.8
17	-	-	-	-	-	-	4.5	-	1.8	0.8	6.3	0.8
18	-	-	0.5	0.1	0.5	0.1	68.1	0.2	8.4	3.2	76.6	3.4
19	-	-	0.5	0.1	0.5	0.1	38.1	0.3	8.0	4.1	46.2	4.4
20	-	-	1.0	0.1	1.0	0.1	16.2	0.7	4.8	4.4	21.8	5.1
21	0.4	-	6.4	0.4	6.8	0.5	11.2	0.9	3.5	4.4	21.3	5.6
22	1.3	0.1	9.7	0.9	11.1	1.0	7.7	1.0	2.6	4.5	21.1	6.5
23	0.9	0.2	8.4	1.3	9.3	1.4	4.8	0.8	1.9	4.2	15.8	6.3
24	0.6	0.1	6.1	1.4	6.7	1.5	3.2	0.7	1.4	4.0	11.3	6.1
25	0.5	0.2	4.6	1.5	5.2	1.7	2.3	0.6	1.1	3.8	8.5	5.9
26	0.5	0.2	3.6	1.6	4.0	1.7	1.9	0.5	0.9	3.7	6.8	5.8
27	0.4	0.2	3.1	1.6	3.5	1.8	1.5	0.5	0.8	3.6	5.7	5.9
28	0.3	0.2	2.6	1.8	2.9	1.9	1.2	0.5	0.8	3.7	4.8	6.1
29	0.3	0.1	2.2	1.8	2.4	1.9	1.1	0.5	0.7	3.9	4.1	6.3
30+	2.2	3.0	15.1	30.1	17.3	33.2	8.4	7.7	7.0	74.7	31.9	114.6
Unknown	-	-	0.1	0.6	0.1	0.7	0.1	0.1	0.1	4.4	0.3	5.1
All ages	**7.4**	**4.3**	**63.8**	**43.2**	**71.2**	**47.5**	**170.2**	**15.0**	**44.1**	**128.2**	**282.8**	**189.0**
Females												
Age[3] <16	-	-	-	-	-	-	-	-	-	0.1	-	0.2
16	-	-	-	-	-	-	0.2	-	0.6	1.1	0.8	1.1
17	-	-	-	-	-	-	5.7	-	2.7	1.0	8.4	1.0
18	-	-	0.1	-	0.1	-	83.4	0.2	10.3	2.6	93.7	2.8
19	-	-	0.1	-	0.1	-	40.7	0.3	7.9	3.8	48.7	4.2
20	-	-	0.7	0.1	0.7	0.1	15.2	0.6	4.9	4.8	20.7	5.6
21	0.3	-	8.7	0.8	9.0	0.8	9.5	1.0	3.4	5.5	22.0	7.4
22	0.8	-	11.9	1.9	12.7	1.9	6.6	1.2	2.8	6.8	22.1	9.9
23	0.7	0.1	9.6	2.7	10.3	2.7	4.1	1.1	2.4	7.2	16.8	11.1
24	0.5	0.1	6.8	2.7	7.3	2.8	2.8	1.0	1.8	6.8	12.0	10.6
25	0.4	0.1	4.8	2.7	5.3	2.7	2.3	0.9	1.5	6.7	9.0	10.4
26	0.4	0.1	3.7	2.8	4.1	2.8	1.8	0.9	1.4	6.6	7.3	10.3
27	0.3	0.1	3.0	2.7	3.3	2.8	1.5	0.9	1.3	6.2	6.1	9.9
28	0.2	0.1	2.4	2.5	2.7	2.6	1.4	0.8	1.2	6.5	5.3	9.9
29	0.2	0.1	2.0	2.5	2.2	2.6	1.3	0.8	1.1	6.2	4.6	9.6
30+	1.3	1.6	13.1	42.2	14.3	43.9	16.1	16.5	16.3	145.4	46.7	205.8
Unknown	-	-	0.1	1.1	0.1	1.1	0.1	0.1	0.1	7.8	0.2	9.1
All ages	**5.1**	**2.1**	**67.0**	**64.7**	**72.1**	**66.8**	**192.7**	**26.5**	**59.7**	**225.3**	**324.5**	**318.8**

Sources: Department for Education and Skills; National Assembly for Wales; Scottish Executive; Northern Ireland Department for Employment and Learning

1 Figures reflect those on a first year of study, i.e. not necessarily brand new entrants to higher education. Higher Education Statistics Agency (HESA) institution figures include Open University students.

2 Full-time includes sandwich. Part-time comprises both day and evening, including block release and open/distance learning.

3 Ages as at 31 August 2002 (1 July for Northern Ireland and 31 December for Scotland).

4 Figures for higher education (HE) institutions are based on the HESA July 'standard registration' count and are not directly comparable with previous years prior to 2001/02. Figures for further education (FE) institutions (other than in Scotland FE colleges) are snapshots counted at a particular point in the year [November for FE institutions in England and Northern Ireland, and December for FE institutions in Wales]. Students starting courses after these dates will not therefore be counted. Figures for Scotland, however, are whole year (not snapshot) enrolments (rather than headcounts).

5 FE institution figures for England include Learning and Skills Council (LSC) funded students only.

6 Includes data for HE students in FE institutions in Wales which cannot be split by level.

POST COMPULSORY EDUCATION AND TRAINING: STUDENTS AND LEARNERS

3.12

Starts [1] on Work-Based Learning [2] provision by academic period and programme strand - time series

England

Thousands

	Programme				Total
	Advanced Modern Apprenticeships (AMA)	Foundation Modern Apprenticeships (FMA)	NVQ Learning	Entry to Employment (E2E) [3]	Work Based Learning for Young People
1999/00					
02 Aug 1999 - 31 Oct 1999	28.1	29.3	26.9	0.7	85.1
01 Nov 1999 - 30 Jan 2000	17.3	17.4	14.6	2.8	52.0
31 Jan 2000 - 30 Apr 2000	15.4	19.0	13.5	3.7	51.6
01 May 2000 - 30 Jul 2000	16.0	22.6	13.8	5.4	57.9
Total	**76.8**	**88.3**	**68.8**	**12.6**	**246.6**
2000/01					
31 Jul 2000 - 29 Oct 2000	28.2	33.5	18.5	6.9	87.2
30 Oct 2000 - 28 Jan 2001	16.1	20.2	9.6	6.0	51.9
29 Jan 2001 - 29 Apr 2001	14.2	23.9	10.4	6.4	54.9
30 Apr 2001 - 29 Jul 2001	13.8	26.5	11.7	7.1	59.0
Total	**72.4**	**104.1**	**50.1**	**26.3**	**252.9**
2001/02					
30 Jul 2001 - 28 Oct 2001	23.7	38.3	14.5	9.0	85.5
29 Oct 2001 - 27 Jan 2002	11.2	21.6	10.2	6.7	49.7
28 Jan 2002 - 28 Apr 2002	9.8	22.8	13.1	7.2	52.8
29 Apr 2002 - 28 Jul 2002	9.4	25.6	16.3	8.3	59.6
Total	**54.0**	**108.3**	**54.1**	**31.1**	**247.6**
2002/03					
29 Jul 2002 - 27 Oct 2002	21.7	41.0	12.9	9.2	84.8
28 Oct 2002 - 26 Jan 2003	9.8	23.5	8.7	7.4	49.3
27 Jan 2003 - 27 Apr 2003	8.2	24.6	9.1	8.3	50.1
28 Apr 2003 - 27 Jul 2003	7.6	26.7	10.0	10.8	55.1
Total	**47.3**	**115.7**	**40.6**	**35.7**	**239.3**

Source: Learning and Skills Council (LSC) Individualised Learner Record (ILR)

1   The figures in this table are under review and an updated table, inclusive of November 2003 figures, will be published by the LSC as soon as it is made available.

2   Work-Based Learning for Young People.

3   Includes former Life skills and preparatory training programmes.

POST COMPULSORY EDUCATION AND TRAINING: STUDENTS AND LEARNERS

Learners on Work-Based Learning [1] provision by academic period and programme strand - time series

England

Thousands

	Programme				Total Work Based Learning for Young People
	Advanced Modern Apprenticeships (AMA)	Foundation Modern Apprenticeships (FMA)	NVQ Learning	Entry to Employment (E2E) [2]	
In-learning at end of academic period					
1999/00					
31 Oct 1999	132.2	59.6	85.3	0.7	**277.8**
30 Jan 2000	132.4	66.4	76.9	2.6	**278.3**
30 Apr 2000	128.8	70.6	64.3	4.0	**267.7**
30 Jul 2000	127.3	77.7	59.1	5.9	**270.1**
Year average	**130.0**	**65.4**	**74.3**	**2.6**	**272.4**
2000/01					
29 Oct 2000	133.6	89.4	57.0	6.8	**286.7**
28 Jan 2001	131.7	90.7	50.9	7.4	**280.6**
29 Apr 2001	118.4	79.6	42.5	6.4	**246.9**
29 Jul 2001	115.0	87.0	43.1	8.0	**253.1**
Year average	**125.7**	**86.6**	**49.5**	**7.0**	**268.8**
2001/02					
28 Oct 2001	117.6	101.2	47.2	7.8	**273.8**
27 Jan 2002	113.7	102.7	49.1	7.8	**273.3**
28 Apr 2002	108.7	103.2	50.8	7.8	**270.5**
28 Jul 2002	102.7	106.1	54.7	10.1	**273.6**
Year average	**111.8**	**101.7**	**49.3**	**8.0**	**270.8**
2002/03					
27 Oct 2002	114.2	116.0	41.4	10.1	**281.7**
26 Jan 2003	111.6	117.6	41.4	10.8	**281.4**
27 Apr 2003	106.8	118.9	40.8	11.3	**277.9**
27 Jul 2003	98.3	115.8	38.7	13.0	**265.7**
Year average	**108.3**	**115.4**	**40.6**	**10.9**	**275.2**
2003/04					
26 Oct 2003	102.7	135.3	27.4	24.7	**290.1**

Source: Learning and Skills Council (LSC) Individualised Learner Record (ILR)

1   Work-Based Learning for Young People.
2   Includes former Life skills and preparatory training programmes.

3.14 POST COMPULSORY EDUCATION AND TRAINING: STUDENTS AND LEARNERS
Work-Based Learning for Young People [1]: ethnicity of learners on 1st November - time series

England

Thousands and Percentages

	2002	2003	change from 2002
All			
Total number of learners	281.7	290.1	3.0 (%)
of which (%)			(% point)
Asian or Asian British - Bangladeshi	0.4	0.5	0.03
Asian or Asian British - Indian	0.7	0.7	-0.07
Asian or Asian British - Pakistani	1.0	1.0	-0.04
Asian or Asian British - any other Asian background	0.2	0.2	-0.01
Black or Black British - African	0.4	0.4	0.02
Black or Black British - Caribbean	0.8	1.0	0.16
Black or Black British - any other Black background	0.5	0.4	-0.09
Chinese	0.1	0.1	-
Mixed - White and Asian	0.1	0.1	0.07
Mixed - White and Black African	0.1	0.1	0.07
Mixed - White and Black Caribbean	0.2	0.5	0.27
Mixed - any other Mixed background	0.1	0.3	0.13
White	93.5	92.7	-0.83
any other	0.9	0.6	-0.32
Not known/not provided	1.0	1.6	0.61
Males			
Total number of learners	162.3	170.1	4.8 (%)
of which (%)			(% point)
Asian or Asian British - Bangladeshi	0.3	0.4	0.06
Asian or Asian British - Indian	0.6	0.5	-0.07
Asian or Asian British - Pakistani	0.7	0.7	-0.04
Asian or Asian British - any other Asian background	0.2	0.2	0.02
Black or Black British - African	0.4	0.4	0.02
Black or Black British - Caribbean	0.8	1.0	0.17
Black or Black British - any other Black background	0.4	0.4	-0.07
Chinese	0.1	0.1	-
Mixed - White and Asian	-	0.1	0.08
Mixed - White and Black African	0.1	0.1	0.05
Mixed - White and Black Caribbean	0.2	0.4	0.23
Mixed - any other Mixed background	0.1	0.2	0.12
White	94.4	93.4	-1.04
any other	0.8	0.6	-0.21
Not known/not provided	0.9	1.6	0.70
Females			
Total number of learners	119.4	120.0	0.5 (%)
of which (%)			(% point)
Asian or Asian British - Bangladeshi	0.6	0.6	-0.01
Asian or Asian British - Indian	0.9	0.8	-0.07
Asian or Asian British - Pakistani	1.4	1.4	-0.03
Asian or Asian British - any other Asian background	0.2	0.2	-0.04
Black or Black British - African	0.4	0.5	0.02
Black or Black British - Caribbean	0.9	1.1	0.15
Black or Black British - any other Black background	0.5	0.4	-0.12
Chinese	0.1	0.1	0.01
Mixed - White and Asian	0.1	0.1	0.07
Mixed - White and Black African	0.1	0.1	0.09
Mixed - White and Black Caribbean	0.2	0.5	0.34
Mixed - any other Mixed background	0.2	0.3	0.15
White	92.3	91.8	-0.52
any other	1.0	0.5	-0.47
Not known/not provided	1.1	1.6	0.48

Source: Learning and Skills Council (LSC) Individualised Learner Record (ILR)

1 Comprising Advanced Modern Apprenticeships (AMA), Foundation Modern Apprenticeships (FMA), NVQ Learning and Entry to Employment (E2E).

3.15

POST COMPULSORY EDUCATION AND TRAINING: STUDENTS AND LEARNERS
Work-Based Learning for Young People [1]: learners by areas of learning on 1st November - time series

England

Thousands and Percentages

	2002	% of total	2003	% of total	Change from 2002 (000s)
All					
Business Administration, Management & Professional	34.9	12.4	31.2	10.7	-3.7
Construction	33.1	11.7	33.9	11.7	0.8
Engineering, Technology and Manufacturing	67.0	23.8	70.4	24.3	3.4
Hairdressing and Beauty Therapy	20.7	7.3	22.4	7.7	1.7
Health, Social Care and Public Services	30.1	10.7	32.2	11.1	2.1
Hospitality, Sports, Leisure and Travel	26.1	9.3	25.0	8.6	-1.1
Information & Communication Technology	9.5	3.4	7.6	2.6	-1.9
Land-based provision	6.0	2.1	7.0	2.4	1.0
Retailing, Customer Service and Transportation	36.1	12.8	33.6	11.6	-2.5
Science and Mathematics	0.4	0.1	0.3	0.1	-0.1
Visual and Performing Arts and Media	1.1	0.4	0.8	0.3	-0.3
Not known	16.8	6.0	25.8	8.9	9.0
Total	**281.7**	**100.0**	**290.1**	**100.0**	**8.4**
Males					
Business Administration, Management & Professional	9.1	5.6	8.2	4.8	-0.9
Construction	32.8	20.2	33.6	19.8	0.8
Engineering, Technology and Manufacturing	65.4	40.3	68.6	40.3	3.2
Hairdressing and Beauty Therapy	1.1	0.7	1.4	0.8	0.3
Health, Social Care and Public Services	2.9	1.8	3.4	2.0	0.5
Hospitality, Sports, Leisure and Travel	13.0	8.0	12.4	7.3	-0.6
Information & Communication Technology	8.0	4.9	6.4	3.8	-1.6
Land-based provision	3.5	2.1	4.1	2.4	0.7
Retailing, Customer Service and Transportation	15.3	9.5	14.5	8.5	-0.9
Science and Mathematics	0.2	0.1	0.2	0.1	-
Visual and Performing Arts and Media	1.0	0.6	0.7	0.4	-0.3
Not known	10.1	6.2	16.5	9.7	6.5
Total	**162.3**	**100.0**	**170.1**	**100.0**	**7.8**
Females					
Business Administration, Management & Professional	25.8	21.6	22.9	19.1	-2.9
Construction	0.3	0.2	0.3	0.2	-
Engineering, Technology and Manufacturing	1.6	1.3	1.8	1.5	0.2
Hairdressing and Beauty Therapy	19.6	16.4	21.0	17.5	1.4
Health, Social Care and Public Services	27.2	22.8	28.8	24.0	1.6
Hospitality, Sports, Leisure and Travel	13.2	11.0	12.6	10.5	-0.6
Information & Communication Technology	1.5	1.3	1.2	1.0	-0.3
Land-based provision	2.6	2.1	2.9	2.4	0.3
Retailing, Customer Service and Transportation	20.7	17.4	19.1	15.9	-1.6
Science and Mathematics	0.1	0.1	0.1	0.1	-
Visual and Performing Arts and Media	0.1	0.1	0.1	0.1	-
Not known	6.7	5.7	9.2	7.7	2.5
Total	**119.4**	**100.0**	**120.0**	**100.0**	**0.5**

Source: Learning and Skills Council (LSC) Individualised Learner Record (ILR)

1 Comprising Advanced Modern Apprenticeships (AMA), Foundation Modern Apprenticeships (FMA), NVQ Learning and Entry to Employment (E2E).

THIS PAGE HAS BEEN LEFT BLANK

3.16 POST COMPULSORY EDUCATION AND TRAINING: JOB-RELATED TRAINING

Participation in job-related training[1] in the last four weeks by economic activity and region[2], 2004

United Kingdom: People of working age[3]

Thousands and percentages[4]

	Thousands			Percentages[4]		
	All	Males	Females	All	Males	Females
All people						
United Kingdom	5,112	2,330	2,781	14.1	12.5	15.8
North East	238	110	128	15.6	14.1	17.2
North West	571	271	300	14.0	12.9	15.1
Yorkshire and the Humber	435	194	241	14.3	12.4	16.4
East Midlands	369	166	203	14.3	12.6	16.2
West Midlands	427	190	237	13.4	11.5	15.4
Eastern	412	188	224	12.5	11.1	13.8
London	699	325	374	14.7	13.2	16.2
South East	717	330	386	14.6	13.1	16.1
South West	425	183	242	14.4	12.1	16.9
England	4,292	1,957	2,335	14.1	12.5	15.8
Wales	270	126	144	15.5	14.1	16.9
Scotland	452	203	250	14.5	12.7	16.3
Northern Ireland	97	44	52	9.3	8.3	10.3
Employees [5,6]						
United Kingdom	3,791	1,699	2,092	16.1	14.0	18.4
North East	183	81	102	19.2	16.7	21.7
North West	422	200	221	16.0	14.7	17.3
Yorkshire and the Humber	330	140	190	16.5	13.5	19.7
East Midlands	296	133	163	17.0	14.7	19.4
West Midlands	319	139	180	15.3	12.7	18.0
Eastern	325	144	180	14.5	12.5	16.5
London	459	208	251	16.3	13.9	19.1
South East	542	251	291	16.5	14.8	18.4
South West	315	128	187	16.1	12.9	19.4
England	3,190	1,425	1,766	16.2	13.9	18.6
Wales	202	96	107	18.2	16.5	20.0
Scotland	337	152	185	16.2	14.4	18.0
Northern Ireland	61	27	35	10.6	9.3	12.0
Self-employed [6,7]						
United Kingdom	248	146	102	7.5	5.9	12.0
North East	*	*	*	*	*	*
North West	26	15	10	7.8	6.4	11.5
Yorkshire and the Humber	18	12	*	7.3	6.6	*
East Midlands	10	*	*	4.8	*	*
West Midlands	18	*	*	7.6	*	*
Eastern	26	16	10	7.3	6.1	10.9
London	42	23	19	8.4	6.3	13.7
South East	44	25	19	8.2	6.4	13.0
South West	25	13	11	7.4	5.4	13.3
England	217	125	92	7.6	6.0	12.4
Wales	*	*	*	*	*	*
Scotland	18	13	*	8.1	8.1	*
Northern Ireland	*	*	*	*	*	*

Source: Labour Force Survey, Spring 2004 [10]

1 Job-related training includes both on and off-the-job training.
2 Government Office Regions in England and each UK country.
3 Working age is defined as males aged 16-64 and females aged 16-59.
4 Expressed as a percentage of the total number of people in each group.
5 Employees are those in employment excluding the self-employed, unpaid family workers and those on government employment and training programmes.
6 The split into employees and self-employed is based on respondents' own assessment of their employment status.
7 Self-employed are those in employment excluding employees, unpaid family workers and those on government employment and training programmes.
8 Unemployed according to the International Labour Organization (ILO) definition.
9 Economically inactive are those who are neither in employment nor ILO unemployed.
10 Users of these data should read the LFS entry in Annex A, as it contains important information about the LFS and the concepts and definitions used.

3.16 POST COMPULSORY EDUCATION AND TRAINING: JOB-RELATED TRAINING
Participation in job-related training[1] in the last four weeks by economic activity and region[2], 2004

United Kingdom: People of working age[3]

Thousands and percentages[4]

	Thousands			Percentages[4]		
	All	Males	Females	All	Males	Females
ILO unemployed [8]						
United Kingdom	139	73	67	10.4	9.4	11.8
North East	*	*	*	*	*	*
North West	14	*	*	10.0	*	*
Yorkshire and the Humber	11	*	*	11.0	*	*
East Midlands	*	*	*	*	*	*
West Midlands	13	*	*	9.8	*	*
Eastern	*	*	*	*	*	*
London	25	15	10	10.6	11.3	9.6
South East	21	10	10	13.4	12.3	14.9
South West	10	*	*	13.3	*	*
England	116	64	52	10.6	10.1	11.2
Wales	*	*	*	*	*	*
Scotland	14	*	*	9.1	*	*
Northern Ireland	*	*	*	*	*	*
Economically inactive [9]						
United Kingdom	846	365	481	10.7	11.6	10.1
North East	37	20	18	9.0	10.7	7.7
North West	102	44	58	10.6	10.5	10.6
Yorkshire and the Humber	70	32	37	10.3	11.7	9.3
East Midlands	49	19	30	9.5	9.0	9.8
West Midlands	68	32	36	9.6	11.1	8.6
Eastern	44	19	25	7.5	8.7	6.8
London	162	72	90	13.7	16.4	12.1
South East	100	38	61	10.8	11.7	10.4
South West	67	31	36	11.8	14.0	10.4
England	698	306	392	10.7	11.9	9.9
Wales	45	19	26	10.7	11.0	10.5
Scotland	80	30	50	12.1	10.9	13.1
Northern Ireland	23	10	13	7.4	7.9	7.1

Source: Labour Force Survey, Spring 2004 [10]

See previous page for footnotes.

3.17 POST COMPULSORY EDUCATION AND TRAINING: JOB-RELATED TRAINING

Participation by employees[1] in job-related training[2] in the last four weeks by type of training and a range of personal characteristics, 2004

United Kingdom: Employees[1] of working age[3]

Thousands and percentages[4]

	Total number of employees (thousands)	of which: receiving off-the-job training only (%)	receiving on-the-job training only (%)	receiving both on and off-the-job training (%)	receiving any training (%)
All employees	23,510	7.7	5.3	3.2	16.1
By gender					
Males	12,144	6.6	4.7	2.7	14.0
Females	11,365	8.8	5.9	3.7	18.4
By age					
16-19	1,406	9.9	6.6	6.1	22.6
20-24	2,357	9.6	6.4	4.5	20.5
25-29	2,570	8.3	6.1	3.9	18.3
30-39	6,207	7.9	5.2	3.4	16.4
40-49	5,845	7.4	5.3	2.7	15.4
50-64	5,125	5.9	4.1	1.6	11.7
By ethnic origin					
White	21,856	7.6	5.2	3.2	16.0
Non-white	1,653	7.8	6.2	3.3	17.3
of which:					
Mixed	147	9.3	8.7	*	22.4
Asian or Asian British	774	6.4	5.1	2.6	14.1
Black or Black British	453	8.5	7.3	4.1	19.9
Chinese	73	*	*	*	16.5
Other ethnic group	199	9.2	7.3	3.3	19.7
By highest qualification held [5]					
Degree or equivalent	4,829	11.9	6.3	4.4	22.6
Higher Education qualification (below degree level)	2,393	12.0	6.9	4.7	23.6
GCE A level or equivalent	5,690	7.7	5.1	3.2	16.0
GCSE grades A* to C, or equivalent	5,236	6.0	5.3	2.9	14.2
Other	3,018	4.9	4.8	2.1	11.8
None	2,217	1.5	2.7	1.0	5.1
By region					
United Kingdom	23,510	7.7	5.3	3.2	16.1
North East	952	8.5	6.3	4.3	19.2
North West	2,642	7.5	5.6	2.8	16.0
Yorkshire and the Humber	2,000	7.6	5.5	3.3	16.5
East Midlands	1,747	7.3	5.9	3.8	17.0
West Midlands	2,090	7.2	4.8	3.3	15.3
Eastern	2,241	7.1	4.2	3.1	14.5
London	2,821	7.9	5.3	3.1	16.3
South East	3,284	7.7	5.6	3.2	16.5
South West	1,957	7.9	5.2	3.0	16.1
England	19,734	7.6	5.3	3.2	16.2
Wales	1,113	8.7	5.8	3.6	18.2
Scotland	2,085	8.0	5.3	2.9	16.2
Northern Ireland	577	6.2	2.9	*	10.6

Source: Labour Force Survey, Spring 2004 [6]

1 Employees are those in employment excluding the self-employed, unpaid family workers and those on government employment and training programmes.
2 Job-related training includes both on and off-the-job training.
3 Working age is defined as males aged 16-64 and females aged 16-59.
4 Expressed as a percentage of the total number of people in each group.
5 Apart from rounding, figures may not sum to grand totals because of questions in the LFS which were unanswered or did not apply.
6 Users of these data should read the LFS entry in Annex A, as it contains important information about the LFS and the concepts and definitions used.

3.18 POST COMPULSORY EDUCATION AND TRAINING: JOB-RELATED TRAINING

Participation by employees[1] in job-related training[2] in the last four weeks by a range of economic characteristics, 2004

United Kingdom: Employees[1] of working age[3]

Thousands and percentages[4]

	Thousands			Percentages[4]		
	All	Males	Females	All	Males	Females
All employees	3,791	1,699	2,092	16.1	14.0	18.4
By industry						
Agriculture, forestry & fishing	17	14	*	11.7	12.1	*
Energy and water supply	43	34	*	16.5	17.4	*
Manufacturing	329	239	90	9.5	9.2	10.4
Construction	172	150	22	13.0	13.1	12.4
Distribution, hotels & restaurants	570	260	310	12.0	11.6	12.3
Transport	185	131	54	11.4	10.9	13.1
Banking, finance & insurance	550	273	276	15.5	14.5	16.6
Public administration, education & health	1,729	500	1,228	24.1	23.0	24.6
Other services	196	96	100	16.2	16.7	15.7
By occupation						
Managers and senior officials	516	318	198	15.3	14.1	17.9
Professional occupations	721	342	379	24.3	20.7	28.8
Associate professional and technical	769	331	439	23.6	20.0	27.2
Administrative and secretarial	460	101	359	14.3	15.2	14.1
Skilled trades	211	194	17	10.4	10.5	9.6
Personal service occupations	436	61	374	23.2	20.2	23.8
Sales and customer service occupations	276	91	185	13.2	14.2	12.7
Process, plant and machine operatives	128	111	17	7.2	7.4	6.4
Elementary occupations	273	150	123	9.4	9.4	9.4
By full-time/part-time work [5]						
Full-time	2,842	1,513	1,329	16.1	13.7	20.2
Part-time	947	185	763	16.1	16.9	16.0
of which [6]:						
students	324	125	200	28.2	25.9	29.9
could not find full-time job	50	17	33	10.9	8.5	12.7
did not want full-time job	560	40	520	13.7	11.0	13.9
ill or disability	11	*	*	8.0	*	*
By employment status [6]						
Permanent job	3,534	1,600	1,934	15.9	13.9	18.1
Temporary job	256	98	158	19.6	15.7	23.0
of which:						
seasonal / casual work	55	25	30	17.3	15.1	19.6
contract for fixed term or task	140	46	95	22.3	16.6	26.8
agency temping	28	13	16	12.8	10.5	15.5
other	32	15	18	23.2	23.8	22.7

Source: Labour Force Survey, Spring 2004 [7]

1 Employees are those in employment excluding the self-employed, unpaid family workers and those on government employment and training programmes.
2 Job-related training includes both on and off-the-job training.
3 Working age is defined as males aged 16-64 and females aged 16-59.
4 Expressed as a percentage of the total number of people in each group.
5 The split between employees working full-time and part-time is based on respondents' own assessment.
6 Apart from rounding, figures may not sum to grand totals because of questions in the LFS which were unanswered or did not apply.
7 Users of these data should read the LFS entry in Annex A, as it contains important information about the LFS and the concepts and definitions used.

3.19 POST COMPULSORY EDUCATION AND TRAINING: JOB-RELATED TRAINING

Participation by employees[1] in job-related training[2] in the last four weeks by type of training and a range of economic characteristics, 2004

United Kingdom: Employees[1] of working age[3]

Thousands and percentages[4]

	Total number of employees (thousands)	of which: receiving off-the-job training only (%)	receiving on-the-job training only (%)	receiving both on and off-the-job training (%)	receiving any training (%)
All employees	23,510	7.7	5.3	3.2	16.1
By industry [5]					
Agriculture, forestry & fishing	149	*	*	*	11.7
Energy & water supply	258	8.9	4.8	*	16.5
Manufacturing	3,461	4.2	3.5	1.8	9.5
Construction	1,320	5.9	3.5	3.6	13.0
Distribution, hotels & restaurants	4,769	6.3	3.7	2.0	12.0
Transport	1,619	5.0	5.0	1.5	11.4
Banking, finance & insurance	3,540	7.6	5.3	2.6	15.5
Public administration, education & health	7,169	11.2	7.7	5.2	24.1
Other services	1,212	7.8	5.0	3.4	16.2
By occupation [5]					
Managers and senior officials	3,368	7.9	4.6	2.8	15.3
Professional occupations	2,968	11.9	6.9	5.5	24.3
Associate professional and technical	3,264	10.9	7.9	4.8	23.6
Administrative and secretarial	3,218	7.4	4.8	2.1	14.3
Skilled trades	2,029	3.9	3.1	3.4	10.4
Personal service occupations	1,875	8.4	8.5	6.2	23.2
Sales and customer service occupations	2,095	7.1	4.7	1.3	13.2
Process, plant and machine operatives	1,775	2.5	3.7	1.0	7.2
Elementary occupations	2,905	5.3	3.0	1.1	9.4
By full-time/part-time work [5,6]					
Full-time	17,635	7.1	5.6	3.4	16.1
Part-time	5,868	9.3	4.3	2.6	16.1
of which:					
students	1,149	21.7	2.6	3.9	28.1
could not find full-time job	459	4.7	3.7	2.5	10.9
did not want full-time job	4,099	6.5	4.9	2.3	13.7
ill or disability	137	4.1	2.6	1.3	8.0
By employment status [5]					
Permanent	22,193	7.5	5.3	3.2	15.9
Temporary	1,309	10.3	5.9	3.3	19.6
of which:					
seasonal / casual work	318	11.7	3.7	*	17.3
contract for fixed term or task	630	11.0	7.4	3.8	22.3
agency temping	221	6.9	4.8	*	12.8
other	140	9.4	*	7.9	23.2

Source: Labour Force Survey, Spring 2004 [7]

1   Employees are those in employment excluding the self-employed, unpaid family workers and those on government employment and training programmes.

2   Job-related training includes both on and off-the-job training.

3   Working age is defined as males aged 16-64 and females aged 16-59.

4   Expressed as a percentage of the total number of people in each group.

5   Apart from rounding, figures may not sum to grand totals because of questions in the LFS which were unanswered or did not apply.

6   The split between employees working full-time and part-time is based on respondents' own assessment.

7   Users of these data should read the LFS entry in Annex A, as it contains important information about the LFS and the concepts and definitions used.

THIS PAGE HAS BEEN LEFT BLANK

POST COMPULSORY EDUCATION AND TRAINING: JOB-RELATED TRAINING

3.20

Participation by employees[1] in job-related training[2] in the last four weeks by region[3] and a range of personal and economic characteristics, 2004

United Kingdom: Employees[1] of working age[4]

Thousands and percentages[5]

				Region[3]			
	United Kingdom	North East	North West	Yorkshire and the Humber	East Midlands	West Midlands	Eastern
All employees	3,791	183	422	330	296	319	325
By gender							
Males	1,699	81	200	140	133	139	144
Females	2,092	102	221	190	163	180	180
By age							
16-19	318	21	36	26	24	31	28
20-24	482	17	46	46	39	37	37
25-29	471	19	53	40	34	37	36
30-39	1,020	56	115	87	67	88	90
40-49	900	44	103	82	82	75	75
50-64	600	26	70	49	49	50	58
By highest qualification held [6]							
Degree or equivalent	1,092	44	118	91	76	78	97
Higher Education qualification (below degree level)	564	29	60	43	47	45	45
GCE A level or equivalent	908	40	105	83	76	85	68
GCSE grades A* to C, or equivalent	743	50	88	67	61	69	78
Other	357	13	35	34	23	26	28
None	114	*	15	11	13	14	*
By industry							
Agriculture & fishing	17	*	*	*	*	*	*
Energy & water	43	*	*	*	*	*	*
Manufacturing	329	14	48	34	36	37	21
Construction	172	10	21	14	17	16	15
Distribution, hotels & restaurants	570	30	56	41	49	45	47
Transport & communication	185	*	18	15	*	17	22
Banking, finance & insurance etc	550	18	56	45	30	32	47
Public admin, education & health	1,729	89	192	158	138	152	151
Other services	196	*	23	16	14	14	18
By occupation							
Managers and senior officials	516	20	61	39	40	32	53
Professional occupations	721	30	74	59	53	56	63
Associate professional and technical	769	39	79	65	65	59	68
Administrative and secretarial	460	23	61	39	23	41	37
Skilled trades	211	12	33	14	21	19	19
Personal service occupations	436	23	45	49	32	41	37
Sales and customer service occupations	276	13	29	20	22	26	21
Process, plant and machine operatives	128	*	12	17	16	17	*
Elementary occupations	273	18	28	30	25	28	17
Percentages [5]							
All employees	16.1	19.2	16.0	16.5	17.0	15.3	14.5
By gender							
Males	14.0	16.7	14.7	13.5	14.7	12.7	12.5
Females	18.4	21.7	17.3	19.7	19.4	18.0	16.5
By age							
16-19	22.6	33.9	22.4	19.9	20.9	25.2	20.4
20-24	20.5	17.2	16.9	23.8	22.2	17.3	18.1
25-29	18.3	19.7	19.1	19.7	19.4	18.5	14.9
30-39	16.4	22.4	16.2	16.8	15.1	16.0	15.2
40-49	15.4	17.1	15.7	15.9	19.0	14.5	13.9
50-64	11.7	13.8	12.2	11.1	12.3	10.4	11.2
By highest qualification held							
Degree or equivalent	22.6	28.7	25.7	24.6	23.3	21.1	22.9
Higher Education qualification (below degree level)	23.6	29.6	21.6	23.1	28.2	22.2	22.3
GCE A level or equivalent	16.0	17.0	15.3	17.2	17.4	17.2	12.9
GCSE grades A* to C, or equivalent	14.2	19.6	13.4	13.9	15.0	14.4	13.8
Other	11.8	11.0	12.8	11.8	10.7	9.4	9.0
None	5.1	*	5.4	6.2	6.8	5.6	*
By industry							
Agriculture & fishing	11.7	*	*	*	*	*	*
Energy & water	16.5	*	*	*	*	*	*
Manufacturing	9.5	8.4	10.9	10.1	10.6	8.5	6.5
Construction	13.0	17.6	15.2	11.5	16.4	14.8	12.7
Distribution, hotels & restaurants	12.0	16.2	10.4	10.4	13.1	10.8	10.8
Transport & communication	11.4	*	10.5	11.0	*	11.4	13.0
Banking, finance & insurance etc	15.5	19.3	15.5	19.1	15.8	13.2	11.9
Public admin, education & health	24.1	28.0	23.5	24.0	26.9	25.0	23.1
Other services	16.2	*	16.7	19.5	16.9	13.9	16.3
By occupation							
Managers and senior officials	15.3	19.4	17.3	15.3	16.4	12.3	14.9
Professional occupations	24.3	29.7	25.2	25.9	26.0	22.5	21.4
Associate professional and technical	23.6	30.5	21.9	24.4	28.0	23.7	21.5
Administrative and secretarial	14.3	18.8	16.1	15.0	10.9	14.7	11.9
Skilled trades	10.4	12.4	13.4	7.9	12.9	9.5	10.1
Personal service occupations	23.2	28.4	20.7	28.6	25.6	24.6	20.7
Sales and customer service occupations	13.2	13.3	11.8	10.8	13.9	13.3	11.7
Process, plant and machine operatives	7.2	*	5.3	9.2	9.3	8.0	*
Elementary occupations	9.4	13.5	8.7	10.4	10.2	10.1	6.6

Source: Labour Force Survey, Spring 2004 [7]

1 Employees are those in employment excluding the self-employed, unpaid family workers and those on government employment and training programmes.
2 Job-related training includes both on and off-the-job training.
3 Government Office Regions in England and each UK country.
4 Working age is defined as males aged 16-64 and females aged 16-59.
5 Expressed as a percentage of the total number of people in each group.
6 Apart from rounding, figures may not sum to grand totals because of questions in the LFS which were unanswered or did not apply.
7 Users of these data should read the LFS entry in Annex A, as it contains important information about the LFS and the concepts and definitions used.

3.20 POST COMPULSORY EDUCATION AND TRAINING: JOB-RELATED TRAINING

Participation by employees[1] in job-related training[2] in the last four weeks by region[3] and a range of personal and economic characteristics, 2004

United Kingdom: Employees[1] of working age[4]

Thousands and percentages[5]

	Region[3]						
	London	South East	South West	England	Wales	Scotland	Northern Ireland
All employees	459	542	315	3,190	202	337	61
By gender							
Males	208	251	128	1,425	96	152	27
Females	251	291	187	1,766	107	185	35
By age							
16-19	19	38	31	255	21	34	*
20-24	64	70	41	397	30	46	*
25-29	82	66	36	403	23	35	10
30-39	133	155	74	865	43	92	19
40-49	103	121	77	763	49	78	10
50-64	58	91	56	507	36	52	*
By highest qualification held [6]							
Degree or equivalent	182	169	80	936	51	87	18
Higher Education qualification (below degree level)	51	76	46	442	34	79	*
GCE A level or equivalent	88	122	82	748	51	95	13
GCSE grades A* to C, or equivalent	55	108	67	643	41	45	13
Other	72	53	34	318	15	19	*
None	*	13	*	93	*	*	*
By industry							
Agriculture & fishing	*	*	*	14	*	*	*
Energy & water	*	*	*	31	*	11	*
Manufacturing	15	43	27	276	22	25	*
Construction	14	21	10	139	13	18	*
Distribution, hotels & restaurants	64	83	60	475	32	52	12
Transport & communication	27	33	15	165	*	11	*
Banking, finance & insurance etc	111	89	41	469	23	55	*
Public admin, education & health	198	241	140	1,459	93	146	31
Other services	28	25	17	164	13	17	*
By occupation							
Managers and senior officials	72	88	43	449	20	41	*
Professional occupations	117	111	51	614	34	65	*
Associate professional and technical	93	115	63	645	40	72	11
Administrative and secretarial	58	65	41	388	25	36	12
Skilled trades	17	26	11	171	15	21	*
Personal service occupations	45	55	41	368	25	35	*
Sales and customer service occupations	25	37	33	225	15	30	*
Process, plant and machine operatives	*	14	*	105	13	*	*
Elementary occupations	25	30	24	225	15	29	*
Percentages [5]							
All employees	16.3	16.5	16.1	16.2	18.2	16.2	10.6
By gender							
Males	13.9	14.8	12.9	13.9	16.5	14.4	9.3
Females	19.1	18.4	19.4	18.6	20.0	18.0	12.0
By age							
16-19	19.9	19.0	23.5	22.0	24.3	26.5	*
20-24	21.3	22.4	22.6	20.3	25.7	21.0	*
25-29	18.2	19.9	18.0	18.5	21.2	16.5	13.5
30-39	16.4	17.7	15.6	16.5	15.9	17.0	11.7
40-49	15.3	15.1	15.5	15.6	17.7	14.5	7.2
50-64	11.8	12.0	11.8	11.7	14.3	11.6	*
By highest qualification held							
Degree or equivalent	20.6	22.4	22.2	22.8	24.5	22.8	13.8
Higher Education qualification (below degree level)	23.7	22.7	23.3	23.5	29.7	23.1	15.8
GCE A level or equivalent	16.3	15.5	16.4	16.0	19.3	15.9	9.9
GCSE grades A* to C, or equivalent	12.1	14.7	14.1	14.3	15.5	13.4	10.3
Other	14.5	13.1	12.8	12.0	12.2	9.3	*
None	*	5.3	*	3.7	*	*	*
By industry							
Agriculture & fishing	*	*	*	11.3	*	*	*
Energy & water	*	*	*	16.9	*	18.2	*
Manufacturing	7.4	10.5	9.5	9.4	12.6	9.6	*
Construction	10.8	12.2	9.7	13.1	18.0	12.1	*
Distribution, hotels & restaurants	12.3	12.7	13.2	11.9	12.8	11.9	11.0
Transport & communication	11.8	12.6	13.1	11.8	*	9.0	*
Banking, finance & insurance etc	15.2	14.7	16.7	15.1	18.7	19.8	*
Public admin, education & health	25.1	25.2	22.6	24.6	25.9	22.5	13.4
Other services	14.0	15.5	17.8	16.1	22.5	14.8	*
By occupation							
Managers and senior officials	13.9	15.1	16.0	15.2	15.8	17.4	*
Professional occupations	25.4	24.0	23.1	24.4	26.1	26.3	*
Associate professional and technical	20.2	23.6	24.0	23.4	30.4	24.4	15.0
Administrative and secretarial	13.7	14.1	15.2	14.3	18.4	13.0	12.6
Skilled trades	10.1	10.3	6.7	10.4	14.0	9.7	*
Personal service occupations	22.6	21.7	23.4	23.5	28.3	20.3	*
Sales and customer service occupations	11.8	13.8	17.2	13.1	12.5	14.9	*
Process, plant and machine operatives	*	8.4	*	7.2	12.0	*	*
Elementary occupations	9.5	8.8	9.1	9.4	9.0	10.0	*

Source: Labour Force Survey, Spring 2004 [7]

See previous page for footnotes.

3.21

POST COMPULSORY EDUCATION AND TRAINING: JOB-RELATED TRAINING

Length of job-related training[1], 2004

United Kingdom: People of working age[2]

Thousands and percentages[3]

	Total receiving training[6] (thousands)	Length of training[4,5]							
		Under 1 week	1 week < 1 month	1 month < 6 months	6 months < 1 year	1 year < 2 years	2 years < 3 years	3 years or more	Ongoing or no definite limit
All people	5,112	30.4	3.2	5.7	6.1	8.4	8.5	13.8	15.0
Economic activity									
Employees [7,8]	3,791	38.0	3.8	5.5	5.1	7.3	6.5	8.4	16.6
Self-employed [8,9]	248	38.5	*	6.5	6.9	6.8	6.0	5.8	18.9
ILO unemployed [10]	139	*	*	12.0	11.3	13.1	13.1	17.5	13.9
Economically inactive [11]	846	*	*	4.4	8.7	12.6	16.5	39.3	7.0
All employees	3,791	38.0	3.8	5.5	5.1	7.3	6.5	8.4	16.6
By gender									
Males	1,699	37.7	4.6	4.8	3.9	6.0	6.4	9.1	17.3
Females	2,092	38.2	3.1	6.1	6.1	8.3	6.6	7.9	16.0
By age									
16-19	318	8.4	*	*	6.0	14.8	21.7	21.7	10.9
20-24	482	18.6	4.4	5.1	5.4	9.3	8.1	21.2	15.1
25-29	471	33.0	4.6	5.4	4.0	8.1	7.3	8.7	17.7
30-39	1,020	41.7	4.6	5.6	5.6	6.7	4.9	6.4	17.3
40-49	900	46.4	2.9	6.5	5.3	5.9	4.4	3.5	17.3
50-64	600	54.5	3.4	6.1	4.1	4.2	2.5	1.9	17.8
By highest qualification held [5]									
Degree or equivalent	1,092	49.3	3.5	4.5	4.0	6.0	5.1	5.7	14.9
Higher Education qualification (below degree level)	564	44.6	2.8	6.5	4.7	5.5	4.9	8.3	16.0
GCE A level or equivalent	908	32.0	4.2	5.5	5.3	7.5	7.0	13.7	14.9
GCSE grades A* to C, or equivalent	743	31.1	3.7	6.1	6.7	9.9	9.8	8.5	18.9
Other qualification	357	27.1	4.8	5.0	5.1	8.2	5.9	4.3	20.3
No qualification	114	27.7	*	9.0	*	*	*	*	22.0
By industry									
Agriculture, forestry & fishing	17	*	*	*	*	*	*	*	*
Energy & water supply	43	47.5	*	*	*	*	*	*	*
Manufacturing	329	34.3	6.1	6.5	5.3	6.6	6.5	6.6	18.1
Construction	172	31.3	*	*	*	*	12.7	15.5	13.3
Distribution, hotels & restaurants	570	23.0	2.8	4.2	5.7	10.7	9.0	16.6	16.5
Transport	185	43.7	7.4	*	*	*	*	*	19.3
Banking, finance & insurance	550	40.0	3.7	5.0	4.0	4.7	4.6	8.2	20.9
Public administration, education & health	1,729	43.8	3.2	6.1	5.8	7.8	5.2	5.5	15.5
Other services	196	31.1	*	5.2	*	7.8	13.1	11.0	13.3
By occupation									
Managers and senior officials	516	51.9	4.0	4.7	4.9	5.1	2.8	3.0	15.2
Professional occupations	721	48.9	3.0	3.2	2.5	5.7	6.0	6.3	16.5
Associate professional and technical	769	41.6	4.4	6.8	4.8	5.6	6.0	6.3	16.3
Administrative and secretarial	460	34.4	4.7	7.8	6.2	6.9	5.3	9.4	18.8
Skilled trades	211	23.2	*	*	*	5.8	11.3	18.8	15.5
Personal service occupations	436	30.6	3.1	5.8	9.4	11.9	8.2	7.1	15.4
Sales and customer service occupations	276	21.9	*	5.1	5.3	10.9	9.4	17.5	17.5
Process, plant and machine operatives	128	33.7	*	*	*	*	*	*	22.9
Elementary occupations	273	20.6	*	6.6	6.7	11.8	10.4	15.4	15.7
By region [12]									
United Kingdom	3,791	38.0	3.8	5.5	5.1	7.3	6.5	8.4	16.6
North East	183	33.2	*	6.4	*	6.3	6.4	10.4	18.3
North West	422	35.3	3.7	5.8	4.1	8.8	7.2	7.3	20.1
Yorkshire and the Humber	330	36.7	3.8	8.3	4.8	7.4	6.4	8.0	15.5
East Midlands	296	39.9	4.2	5.4	6.4	7.2	5.6	8.0	15.9
West Midlands	319	37.3	4.7	5.6	5.9	6.1	7.3	6.7	19.0
Eastern	325	38.2	3.5	4.9	4.9	7.9	6.6	7.3	17.3
London	459	39.0	4.1	4.0	3.9	7.9	6.9	7.5	14.6
South East	542	41.6	3.8	5.8	5.8	7.1	5.1	7.6	14.8
South West	315	40.0	*	5.5	6.2	6.5	6.5	8.3	16.1
England	3,190	38.3	3.9	5.6	5.1	7.4	6.4	7.8	16.6
Wales	202	32.1	*	5.2	5.1	7.9	7.2	11.4	19.3
Scotland	337	41.3	3.7	4.7	4.1	5.3	6.5	11.6	15.6
Northern Ireland	61	24.2	*	*	*	*	*	16.6	*

Source: Labour Force Survey, Spring 2004 [13]

1 Job-related training includes both on and off-the-job training.
2 Working age is defined as males aged 16-64 and females aged 16-59. These figures include unpaid family workers, those on government employment and training programmes, or those who did not answer, who are excluded from the Economic activity analyses below.
3 Expressed as a percentage of those in the group who received training in the last four weeks.
4 The total length of the course was recorded not just the part completed. For people engaged on day or block release, the total length of training is given. For people who dropped out of a course the time spent on the course, not the total length is recorded.
5 Apart from rounding, figures may not sum to grand totals because of questions in the LFS which were unanswered or did not apply.
6 People of working age who received on or off-the-job training in the last four weeks.
7 Employees are those in employment excluding the self-employed, unpaid family workers and those on government employment and training programmes.
8 The split into employees and self-employed is based on respondents' own assessment of their employment status.
9 Self-employed are those in employment excluding employees, unpaid family workers and those on government employment and training programmes.
10 Unemployed according to the International Labour Organization (ILO) definition.
11 Economically inactive are those who are neither in employment nor ILO unemployed.
12 Government Office Regions in England and each UK country.
13 Users of these data should read the LFS entry in Annex A, as it contains important information about the LFS and the concepts and definitions used.

POST COMPULSORY EDUCATION AND TRAINING: JOB-RELATED TRAINING

3.22

Location of off-the-job training[1], 2004

United Kingdom: People of working age[2]

Thousands and percentages[3]

	Total receiving training[1] (thousands)	Main place of training (percentages)[4]						
		Employer's premises	Another employer's premises	Private training centre	At home[5]	Further Education college or University	Other educational institution	Others
All people [2]	3,803	21.7	3.6	7.7	6.5	38.9	3.3	9.8
Economic activity								
Employees [6,7]	2,543	30.8	4.5	9.1	7.0	28.0	2.5	9.6
Self-employed [7,8]	205	5.9	6.8	19.0	10.2	23.8	5.4	22.1
ILO unemployed [9]	139	*	*	*	7.5	53.3	*	13.7
Economically inactive [10]	846	1.9	*	*	3.9	73.5	4.8	5.1
All employees	2,543	30.8	4.5	9.1	7.0	28.0	2.5	9.6
By gender								
Males	1,124	29.9	4.6	10.7	7.2	26.4	2.0	9.0
Females	1,419	31.6	4.5	7.9	6.8	29.3	3.0	10.2
By age								
16-19	225	14.0	*	*	*	62.7	*	*
20-24	332	18.9	*	5.3	5.6	48.0	*	5.9
25-29	313	30.6	4.3	9.5	9.6	25.5	*	7.6
30-39	699	33.6	4.7	10.1	8.1	23.3	2.8	10.5
40-49	588	35.7	5.8	9.6	8.2	19.5	2.6	11.7
50-64	386	38.5	6.2	13.4	5.5	14.0	3.1	14.0
By highest qualification held [4]								
Degree or equivalent	788	32.9	4.6	12.3	7.6	21.1	3.0	11.6
Higher Education qualification (below degree level)	399	32.1	6.8	8.7	7.6	25.4	*	11.5
GCE A level or equivalent	617	27.5	3.8	8.1	5.8	35.3	1.8	7.0
GCSE grades A* to C, or equivalent	402	32.2	4.5	7.0	5.8	34.4	2.9	9.3
Other qualification	275	26.3	*	7.0	9.1	27.4	*	8.1
No qualification	55	43.0	*	*	*	18.4	*	*
By industry [4]								
Agriculture, forestry & fishing	12	*	*	*	*	*	*	*
Energy & water supply	30	42.5	*	*	*	*	*	*
Manufacturing	206	33.2	*	10.7	8.1	26.8	*	8.5
Construction	126	16.9	*	15.8	*	41.0	*	*
Distribution, hotels & restaurants	395	18.4	2.7	6.5	5.0	46.9	2.6	6.5
Transport	104	43.3	*	9.7	*	14.9	*	11.8
Banking, finance & insurance	361	29.2	4.8	11.8	12.5	20.1	*	10.6
Public administration, education & health	1,174	36.5	5.2	8.4	6.4	22.8	3.1	11.0
Other services	135	20.2	*	*	*	37.3	*	8.9
By occupation								
Managers and senior officials	361	33.9	5.3	13.6	7.8	14.4	*	14.7
Professional occupations	517	33.6	5.1	12.0	6.8	19.4	3.6	12.4
Associate professional and technical	510	35.4	6.6	10.0	6.5	23.8	*	8.8
Administrative and secretarial	307	32.7	*	5.8	10.3	30.3	*	8.8
Skilled trades	148	24.1	*	8.5	*	35.6	*	*
Personal service occupations	275	34.4	4.3	5.5	6.4	30.1	3.9	8.5
Sales and customer service occupations	177	15.6	*	*	*	54.4	*	*
Process, plant and machine operatives	62	34.9	*	*	*	22.0	*	*
Elementary occupations	186	14.8	*	*	5.6	53.7	*	*
By region [11]								
United Kingdom	2,543	30.8	4.5	9.1	7.0	28.0	2.5	9.6
North East	122	26.3	*	9.6	*	28.1	*	11.7
North West	273	33.2	5.7	9.9	6.1	29.6	*	7.3
Yorkshire and the Humber	219	31.6	*	7.6	*	27.9	*	13.3
East Midlands	193	34.2	*	10.1	8.5	26.7	*	6.8
West Midlands	218	32.5	*	6.5	7.0	29.3	*	11.6
Eastern	230	32.2	5.6	10.3	7.3	22.9	*	10.3
London	308	27.0	3.7	8.7	7.5	29.9	*	8.2
South East	358	31.3	5.5	10.2	7.0	25.2	*	9.2
South West	213	31.5	*	10.9	7.0	25.5	*	11.6
England	2,134	31.2	4.7	9.3	6.9	27.2	2.5	9.8
Wales	137	27.0	*	7.3	*	32.7	*	10.1
Scotland	227	31.1	*	9.0	7.9	27.6	*	9.2
Northern Ireland	45	25.2	*	*	*	52.8	*	*

Source: Labour Force Survey, Spring 2004 [12]

1 Excludes those receiving on-the-job training only.
2 Working age is defined as males aged 16-64 and females aged 16-59. These figures include unpaid family workers, those on government employment and training programmes, or those who did not answer, who are excluded from the Economic activity analyses below.
3 Expressed as a percentage of those in the group who received training in the last four weeks.
4 Apart from rounding, figures may not sum to grand totals because of questions in the LFS which were unanswered or did not apply.
5 Includes open university, open tech, correspondence course and college.
6 Employees are those in employment excluding the self-employed, unpaid family workers and those on government employment and training programmes.
7 The split into employees and self-employed is based on respondents' own assessment of their employment status.
8 Self-employed are those in employment excluding employees, unpaid family workers and those on government employment and training programmes.
9 Unemployed according to the International Labour Organization (ILO) definition.
10 Economically inactive are those who are neither in employment nor ILO unemployed.
11 Government Office Regions in England and each UK country.
12 Users of these data should read the LFS entry in Annex A, as it contains important information about the LFS and the concepts and definitions used.

3.23

POST COMPULSORY EDUCATION AND TRAINING: JOB-RELATED TRAINING
Hours spent on job-related training[1] in the last week, 2004

United Kingdom: People of working age[2]

Thousands and percentages[3]

	Total receiving training[5] (thousands)	Hours spent on training [4]						
		Less than 7.5 hours	7.5 to <15 hours	15 to < 22.5 hours	22.5 to < 30 hours	30 to < 37.5 hours	37.5 hours or more	Average number of hours per week
All people[2]	2,585	39.3	18.8	13.1	6.0	10.0	12.9	16.8
Economic activity								
Employees [6,7]	1,736	48.4	22.0	11.6	3.7	6.1	8.2	12.9
Self-employed [7,8]	117	55.0	21.3	11.3	*	*	*	11.0
ILO unemployed [9]	85	21.9	15.6	21.1	*	18.5	11.9	21.0
Economically inactive [10]	583	12.6	9.5	17.0	11.9	21.0	28.0	28.4
All employees	1,736	48.4	22.0	11.6	3.7	6.1	8.2	12.9
By gender								
Males	742	42.9	23.9	12.6	3.7	6.6	10.2	14.1
Females	994	52.5	20.5	10.9	3.6	5.7	6.7	12.0
By age								
16-19	184	21.5	17.9	15.6	7.0	18.1	19.9	22.1
20-24	256	36.6	18.9	12.9	6.4	10.0	15.2	17.7
25-29	226	43.8	20.7	16.5	*	7.8	8.6	14.3
30-39	446	51.2	24.4	11.5	3.2	4.5	5.2	11.2
40-49	380	57.9	23.7	9.7	3.0	*	4.2	9.5
50-64	243	65.5	22.2	5.9	*	*	*	8.0
By highest qualification held [4]								
Degree or equivalent	453	52.3	23.5	10.5	2.9	4.4	6.5	11.6
Higher Education qualification (below degree level)	275	51.3	25.4	11.2	*	3.9	4.8	10.9
GCE A level or equivalent	425	42.4	20.3	13.4	6.0	8.3	9.7	14.9
GCSE grades A* to C, or equivalent	383	47.2	20.8	11.6	*	8.4	9.5	13.6
Other qualification	141	48.2	22.3	11.9	*	*	10.7	13.1
No qualification	53	58.6	*	*	*	*	*	11.6
By industry [4]								
Agriculture, forestry & fishing	*	*	*	*	*	*	*	21.7
Energy & water supply	18	*	*	*	*	*	*	14.8
Manufacturing	137	43.8	25.7	11.2	*	*	10.3	13.8
Construction	88	44.5	29.5	*	*	*	11.5	13.2
Distribution, hotels & restaurants	281	33.7	17.3	15.8	8.8	12.1	12.3	17.6
Transport	77	43.1	25.7	*	*	*	10.5	13.7
Banking, finance & insurance	235	54.6	20.4	11.9	*	5.8	4.8	11.1
Public administration, education & health	788	54.9	22.7	9.6	2.2	4.2	6.2	11.1
Other services	103	39.8	19.5	18.2	*	*	10.8	15.2
By occupation								
Managers and senior officials	203	49.5	29.2	11.2	*	*	*	10.8
Professional occupations	308	56.0	22.0	9.7	3.5	4.0	4.8	10.6
Associate professional and technical	348	48.3	25.3	11.3	*	5.3	7.4	12.3
Administrative and secretarial	221	56.8	20.1	12.4	*	4.5	5.1	10.8
Skilled trades	109	38.1	22.4	8.1	*	*	17.2	16.4
Personal service occupations	212	50.8	20.4	12.1	*	5.0	9.8	12.8
Sales and customer service occupations	142	38.5	14.5	14.5	*	13.2	12.5	16.9
Process, plant and machine operatives	46	40.7	24.1	6.7	*	*	*	17.7
Elementary occupations	147	35.0	15.3	16.6	9.7	12.2	11.2	17.5
By region[11]								
United Kingdom	1,736	48.4	22.0	11.6	3.7	6.1	8.2	12.9
North East	83	49.6	23.8	*	*	*	*	12.1
North West	200	53.5	22.3	10.5	*	*	6.0	11.2
Yorkshire and the Humber	143	47.8	23.3	11.7	*	*	8.2	12.8
East Midlands	135	50.7	24.0	11.0	*	*	8.2	12.1
West Midlands	143	51.5	22.0	11.7	*	*	7.8	11.8
Eastern	154	46.7	20.9	14.2	*	*	7.9	13.1
London	195	44.3	19.8	15.4	*	7.6	8.6	14.1
South East	242	45.2	24.9	10.7	4.2	5.9	9.1	13.4
South West	149	51.2	18.0	12.4	*	*	8.6	12.8
England	1,443	48.7	22.1	12.0	3.5	5.7	8.0	12.7
Wales	93	49.9	18.3	11.3	*	*	*	12.7
Scotland	165	49.5	21.0	7.3	*	7.8	8.9	13.5
Northern Ireland	35	29.0	29.2	*	*	*	*	19.8

Source: Labour Force Survey, Spring 2004 [12]

1 Job-related training includes both on and off-the-job training.
2 Working age is defined as males aged 16-64 and females aged 16-59. These figures include unpaid family workers, those on government employment and training programmes, or those who did not answer, who are excluded from the Economic activity analyses below.
3 Expressed as a percentage of those in the group who received training in the last week, who specified a valid length of training.
4 Apart from rounding, figures may not sum to grand totals because of questions in the LFS which were unanswered or did not apply.
5 Those who specified a valid length of training.
6 Employees are those in employment excluding the self-employed, unpaid family workers and those on government employment and training programmes.
7 The split into employees and self-employed is based on respondents' own assessment of their employment status.
8 Self-employed are those in employment excluding employees, unpaid family workers and those on government employment and training programmes.
9 Unemployed according to the International Labour Organization (ILO) definition.
10 Economically inactive are those who are neither in employment nor ILO unemployed.
11 Government Office Regions in England and each UK country.
12 Users of these data should read the LFS entry in Annex A, as it contains important information about the LFS and the concepts and definitions used.

THIS PAGE HAS BEEN LEFT BLANK

POST COMPULSORY EDUCATION AND TRAINING: JOB-RELATED TRAINING

3.24

Participation by employees[1] in job-related training[2] in the last thirteen weeks by a range of personal and economic characteristics - time series

United Kingdom: Employees[1] of working age[3]

Thousands

	1995[4]			1999[4]			2004		
	All	Males	Females	All	Males	Females	All	Males	Females
All employees [1]	5,440	2,752	2,689	6,536	3,229	3,307	7,147	3,350	3,797
By age									
16-19	284	146	138	459	237	222	448	234	214
20-24	676	330	346	773	383	390	799	378	421
25-29	895	464	431	966	482	484	896	419	477
30-39	1,571	821	751	1,867	961	906	1,952	939	1,014
40-49	1,368	652	716	1,528	698	830	1,801	793	1,008
50-64	646	339	307	943	468	475	1,250	588	662
By highest qualification held [5,6]									
Degree or equivalent	1,266	723	543	1,658	886	772	2,047	991	1,056
Higher Education qualification (below degree level)	885	364	521	982	381	601	1,056	396	661
GCE A level or equivalent	1,279	822	456	1,573	947	626	1,656	925	731
GCSE grades A* to C, or equivalent	1,142	453	689	1,434	601	833	1,409	575	834
Other	583	269	314	640	311	329	702	337	365
None	277	115	162	214	86	127	244	104	140
By industry [5]									
Agriculture, forestry & fishing	29	19	10	34	25	*	35	29	*
Energy & water supply	108	86	23	89	65	24	85	67	18
Manufacturing	820	616	204	929	694	235	664	501	163
Construction	185	155	29	246	216	30	334	299	36
Distribution, hotels & restaurants	769	362	407	962	464	497	1,003	472	531
Transport	305	213	91	352	238	114	392	283	109
Banking, finance & insurance	873	492	381	1,095	578	517	1,069	570	499
Public administration, education & health	2,117	697	1,420	2,546	824	1,722	3,219	956	2,263
Other services	227	106	121	279	121	158	342	171	171
By occupation [5]									
Managers and senior officials	949	598	351	1,055	648	407	1,057	662	395
Professional occupations	1,012	527	485	1,199	605	594	1,358	662	696
Associate professional and technical	815	349	467	983	398	585	1,413	624	789
Administrative and secretarial	873	233	640	1,037	278	759	840	190	651
Skilled trades	375	351	24	454	430	24	426	394	32
Personal service occupations	622	243	379	826	309	517	775	112	662
Sales and customer service occupations	359	142	217	460	179	281	490	166	323
Process, plant and machine operatives	252	215	37	313	262	51	286	253	33
Elementary occupations	174	88	85	209	121	88	500	286	215
By full-time/part-time work [7]									
Full-time	4,425	2,595	1,830	5,182	2,983	2,199	5,523	3,067	2,456
Part-time	1,015	157	859	1,354	246	1,108	1,623	282	1,341
of which:									
students	243	102	140	377	160	217	403	157	246
could not find full-time job	124	34	90	117	36	81	109	39	69
did not want full-time job	636	19	617	839	46	792	1,079	76	1,003
By employment status [5]									
Permanent	5,044	2,585	2,459	6,038	3,018	3,020	6,714	3,176	3,538
Temporary	395	165	230	496	210	285	431	173	258
of which:									
seasonal/casual work	59	26	33	89	32	57	78	37	41
contract for fixed term or task	270	112	157	308	134	174	253	89	163
agency temping	27	11	16	52	22	29	51	25	26
other	39	16	23	47	22	25	50	22	28

Source: Labour Force Survey, Spring 1995, 1999, 2004 [8]

1 Employees are those in employment excluding the self-employed, unpaid family workers and those on government employment and training programmes.
2 Job-related training includes both on and off-the-job training.
3 Working age is defined as males aged 16-64 and females aged 16-59.
4 Includes revised data as a result of a LFS regrossing exercise carried out by the Office for National Statistics in 2004.
5 Apart from rounding, figures may not sum to grand totals because of questions in the LFS which were unanswered or did not apply.
6 Highest qualifications held figures for 1995 are not directly comparable with later years due to changes in the level of detail collected for qualifications from the 1996 LFS onwards.
7 The split between employees working full-time and part-time is based on respondents' own assessment.
8 Users of these data should read the LFS entry in Annex A, as it contains important information about the LFS and the concepts and definitions used.
9 Expressed as a percentage of the total number of people in each group.

CONTINUED
POST COMPULSORY EDUCATION AND TRAINING: JOB-RELATED TRAINING
Participation by employees [1] in job-related training [2] in the last thirteen weeks by a range of personal and economic characteristics
- time series

United Kingdom: Employees [1] of working age [3]

Percentages [9]

	1995[4]			1999[4]			2004		
	All	Males	Females	All	Males	Females	All	Males	Females
All employees [1]	25.8	25.0	26.6	28.8	27.3	30.4	30.4	27.6	33.4
By age									
16-19	25.6	27.5	23.9	33.8	35.3	32.4	31.8	33.9	29.8
20-24	29.0	27.9	30.2	35.6	34.7	36.6	33.9	31.3	36.6
25-29	29.9	29.7	30.0	32.6	31.2	34.1	34.9	31.8	38.1
30-39	27.7	27.3	28.3	29.7	29.3	30.2	31.5	29.2	33.9
40-49	26.4	25.2	27.6	28.6	26.2	30.9	30.8	27.3	34.3
50-64	16.9	15.9	18.2	20.6	18.3	23.6	24.4	20.9	28.6
By highest qualification held [6]									
Degree or equivalent	42.9	39.8	47.8	44.2	41.1	48.4	42.4	38.0	47.6
Higher Education qualification (below degree level)	42.9	38.6	46.5	43.3	37.5	48.0	44.1	36.9	50.0
GCE A level or equivalent	26.1	24.4	29.9	29.2	26.6	34.3	29.1	25.9	34.5
GCSE grades A* to C, or equivalent	24.9	25.1	24.7	27.1	27.8	26.6	26.9	26.4	27.3
Other	17.9	16.6	19.3	19.9	18.9	21.0	23.3	21.5	25.3
None	8.4	8.2	8.6	8.3	7.4	9.0	11.0	9.8	12.1
By industry									
Agriculture, forestry & fishing	13.9	12.5	17.4	18.2	17.7	*	23.3	25.4	*
Energy & water supply	33.8	33.3	35.7	32.5	31.2	37.0	33.0	34.1	29.6
Manufacturing	18.4	19.3	16.2	21.1	21.6	19.7	19.2	19.3	19.0
Construction	19.8	19.6	20.8	21.5	21.6	21.1	25.3	26.2	20.0
Distribution, hotels & restaurants	18.4	19.7	17.3	21.4	23.1	19.9	21.0	21.1	21.0
Transport	22.1	20.4	27.6	23.0	21.3	27.6	24.2	23.5	26.5
Banking, finance & insurance	30.2	34.0	26.4	32.5	33.7	31.3	30.2	30.3	30.1
Public administration, education & health	37.5	39.3	36.7	41.4	43.1	40.6	44.9	43.9	45.4
Other services	21.2	21.3	21.1	24.8	24.2	25.3	28.4	30.1	26.9
By occupation									
Managers and senior officials	30.6	29.2	33.4	31.5	29.5	35.2	31.4	29.3	35.7
Professional occupations	46.2	42.7	50.8	48.8	44.1	54.7	45.8	40.0	52.9
Associate professional and technical	41.5	36.6	46.0	43.7	37.8	48.9	43.3	37.7	49.0
Administrative and secretarial	24.5	26.3	23.9	27.2	29.0	26.6	26.1	28.5	25.5
Skilled trades	17.2	18.5	8.7	20.0	21.0	11.0	21.0	21.3	18.1
Personal service occupations	26.4	29.3	24.8	30.7	34.6	28.8	41.3	37.0	42.1
Sales and customer service occupations	20.4	24.4	18.3	23.4	27.3	21.5	23.4	25.8	22.3
Process, plant and machine operatives	11.7	12.7	8.1	14.5	15.1	11.8	16.1	16.8	12.2
Elementary occupations	9.6	10.3	9.0	12.0	13.2	10.7	17.2	17.9	16.4
By full-time/part-time work [7]									
Full-time	27.4	25.1	31.4	30.1	27.3	35.1	31.3	27.8	37.3
Part-time	20.5	23.2	20.1	24.6	27.3	24.1	27.6	25.8	28.1
of which:									
students	33.0	31.4	34.3	38.7	38.4	38.9	35.1	32.6	36.8
could not find full-time job	17.9	16.6	18.4	20.1	17.2	21.8	23.7	20.0	26.4
did not want full-time job	18.4	14.4	18.6	21.8	18.9	22.0	26.3	21.0	26.8
By employment status [5]									
Permanent	25.7	25.0	26.4	28.5	27.2	30.0	30.3	27.6	33.1
Temporary	26.8	24.4	28.8	32.4	29.2	35.2	32.9	27.8	37.7
of which:									
seasonal/casual work	16.8	17.0	16.6	23.7	20.3	26.2	24.4	22.4	26.6
contract for fixed term or task	33.6	29.9	36.8	39.5	35.7	43.1	40.2	32.3	46.3
agency temping	17.1	14.2	19.8	21.0	17.5	24.7	23.1	21.0	25.5
other	24.4	22.1	26.2	36.2	37.5	35.2	35.7	35.0	36.2

Source: Labour Force Survey, Spring 1995, 1999, 2004 [8]

See previous page for footnotes.

POST COMPULSORY EDUCATION AND TRAINING: JOB-RELATED TRAINING

3.25

Employees[1] of working age[2] in the UK – summary of job-related training[3] received, 2004

United Kingdom: Employees[1] of working age[2]

Thousands and percentages

	Total number of employees (thousands)	Number who received training in the last			Never offered training by current employer (thousands)	Percentage who received training in the last			Never offered training by current employer (percentage)
		13 weeks	4 weeks	1 week		13 weeks	4 weeks	1 week	
All employees[1]	23,510	7,147	3,791	1,997	6,726	30.4	16.1	8.5	28.6
By gender									
Males	12,144	3,350	1,699	880	3,653	27.6	14.0	7.2	30.1
Females	11,365	3,797	2,092	1,118	3,073	33.4	18.4	9.8	27.0
By age									
16-19	1,406	448	318	230	416	31.8	22.6	16.4	29.6
20-24	2,357	799	482	311	755	33.9	20.5	13.2	32.0
25-29	2,570	896	471	265	681	34.9	18.3	10.3	26.5
30-39	6,207	1,952	1,020	500	1,620	31.5	16.4	8.1	26.1
40-49	5,845	1,801	900	428	1,559	30.8	15.4	7.3	26.7
50-64	5,125	1,250	600	264	1,694	24.4	11.7	5.2	33.1
By ethnic origin									
White	21,856	6,623	3,505	1,827	6,191	30.3	16.0	8.4	28.3
Non-white	1,653	524	286	170	535	31.7	17.3	10.3	32.4
Mixed	147	58	33	18	43	39.9	22.4	12.4	29.1
Asian or Asian British	774	219	109	62	273	28.3	14.1	8.1	35.3
Black or Black British	453	160	90	54	122	35.4	19.9	11.9	27.0
Chinese	73	22	12	*	27	29.6	16.5	*	37.4
Other Ethnic Group	199	61	39	26	70	30.7	19.7	13.1	35.1
By highest qualification held [4]									
Degree or equivalent	4,829	2,047	1,092	504	806	42.4	22.6	10.4	16.7
Higher Education qualification (below degree level)	2,393	1,056	564	305	407	44.1	23.6	12.7	17.0
GCE A level or equivalent	5,690	1,656	908	496	1,628	29.1	16.0	8.7	28.6
GCSE grades A* to C, or equivalent	5,236	1,409	743	421	1,584	26.9	14.2	8.0	30.2
Other qualification	3,018	702	357	198	1,082	23.3	11.8	6.6	35.9
No qualification	2,217	244	114	64	1,172	11.0	5.1	2.9	52.9
By industry [4]									
Agriculture, forestry & fishing	149	35	17	12	58	23.3	11.7	7.9	38.9
Energy & water supply	258	85	43	19	50	33.0	16.5	7.5	19.3
Manufacturing	3,461	664	329	164	1,275	19.2	9.5	4.7	36.8
Construction	1,320	334	172	105	496	25.3	13.0	8.0	37.5
Distribution, hotels & restaurants	4,769	1,003	570	342	1,935	21.0	12.0	7.2	40.6
Transport	1,619	392	185	86	529	24.2	11.4	5.3	32.7
Banking, finance & insurance	3,540	1,069	550	273	978	30.2	15.5	7.7	27.6
Public administration, education & health	7,169	3,219	1,729	879	996	44.9	24.1	12.3	13.9
Other services	1,212	342	196	117	403	28.4	16.2	9.7	33.4
By occupation [4]									
Managers and senior officials	3,368	1,057	516	228	804	31.4	15.3	6.8	23.9
Professional occupations	2,968	1,358	721	347	372	45.8	24.3	11.7	12.5
Associate professional and technical	3,264	1,413	769	390	499	43.3	23.6	11.9	15.3
Administrative and secretarial	3,218	840	460	245	946	26.1	14.3	7.6	29.4
Skilled trades	2,029	426	211	137	751	21.0	10.4	6.8	37.0
Personal service occupations	1,875	775	436	244	349	41.3	23.2	13.0	18.6
Sales and customer service occupations	2,095	490	276	172	801	23.4	13.2	8.2	38.2
Process, plant and machine operatives	1,775	286	128	54	817	16.1	7.2	3.1	46.0
Elementary occupations	2,905	500	273	180	1,386	17.2	9.4	6.2	47.7
By region [5]									
United Kingdom	23,510	7,147	3,791	1,997	6,726	30.4	16.1	8.5	28.6
North East	952	334	183	98	268	35.1	19.2	10.3	28.1
North West	2,642	777	422	223	727	29.4	16.0	8.4	27.5
Yorkshire and the Humber	2,000	610	330	162	566	30.5	16.5	8.1	28.3
East Midlands	1,747	539	296	153	504	30.8	17.0	8.1	28.3
West Midlands	2,090	585	319	168	673	28.0	15.3	8.7	28.9
Eastern	2,241	664	325	173	602	29.6	14.5	7.7	26.9
London	2,821	892	459	236	794	31.6	16.3	8.4	28.2
South East	3,284	1,044	542	279	880	31.8	16.5	8.5	26.8
South West	1,957	575	315	170	577	29.4	16.1	8.7	29.5
England	19,734	6,020	3,190	1,661	5,590	30.5	16.2	8.4	28.3
Wales	1,113	360	202	112	302	32.3	18.2	10.0	27.1
Scotland	2,085	629	337	185	636	30.2	16.2	8.9	30.5
Northern Ireland	577	138	61	39	199	24.0	10.6	6.7	34.4

Source: Labour Force Survey, Spring 2004 [6]

1 Employees are those in employment excluding the self-employed, unpaid family workers and those on government employment and training programmes.
2 Working age is defined as males aged 16-64 and females aged 16-59.
3 Job-related training includes both on and off-the-job training.
4 Apart from rounding, figures may not sum to grand totals because of questions in the LFS which were unanswered or did not apply.
5 Government Office Regions in England and each UK country.
6 Users of these data should read the LFS entry in Annex A, as it contains important information about the LFS and the concepts and definitions used.

3.26 POST COMPULSORY EDUCATION AND TRAINING: JOB-RELATED TRAINING

Participation by employees in job-related training[1] in the last thirteen weeks by disability status and a range of personal characteristics, 2004

United Kingdom: Employees[2] of working age[3]

Thousands and percentages[4]

	Total number of employees by disability status (thousands)					Percentage receiving job-related training in the last thirteen weeks				
	Total number of employees (thousands)	Both DDA disabled and work-limiting disabled	DDA disabled only	Work-limiting disabled only	Not disabled	All employees	Both DDA disabled and work-limiting disabled	DDA disabled only	Work-limiting disabled only	Not disabled
All employees	23,510	1,183	1,069	678	20,580	30.4	27.6	31.5	30.3	30.5
By gender										
Males	12,144	582	519	386	10,657	27.6	23.1	26.6	27.2	27.9
Females	11,365	601	550	292	9,923	33.4	31.9	36.2	34.4	33.3
By age										
16-19	1,406	37	27	41	1,301	31.8	29.5	36.5	42.0	31.5
20-24	2,357	73	52	51	2,180	33.9	32.9	36.6	34.8	33.9
25-29	2,570	74	66	55	2,375	34.9	25.8	39.2	43.0	34.8
30-39	6,207	227	189	152	5,639	31.5	31.9	37.2	32.0	31.2
40-49	5,845	338	288	171	5,049	30.8	28.5	33.6	31.2	30.8
50-64	5,125	434	447	208	4,036	24.4	23.9	25.7	21.6	24.4
By highest qualification held [5]										
Degree or equivalent	4,829	160	179	93	4,398	42.4	37.8	46.3	45.5	42.3
Higher Education qualification (below degree level)	2,393	129	113	69	2,082	44.1	49.5	47.0	48.8	43.5
GCE A level or equivalent	5,690	273	271	173	4,973	29.1	26.5	30.1	29.8	29.2
GCSE grades A* to C, or equivalent	5,236	264	221	149	4,602	26.9	28.3	31.0	27.3	26.6
Other qualification	3,018	183	155	102	2,578	23.3	19.7	22.0	24.0	23.6
No qualification	2,217	170	125	87	1,835	11.0	10.4	12.2	12.4	10.9
By industry [5]										
Agriculture, forestry & fishing	149	*	*	*	129	23.3	*	*	*	23.9
Energy & water supply	258	11	17	*	224	33.0	30.4	52.5	*	32.0
Manufacturing	3,461	167	160	103	3,031	19.2	17.0	17.3	16.4	19.5
Construction	1,320	59	56	43	1,162	25.3	19.2	24.4	19.8	25.9
Distribution, hotels & restaurants	4,769	249	192	142	4,187	21.0	17.4	23.6	27.7	20.9
Transport	1,619	86	66	54	1,413	24.2	27.5	20.2	23.6	24.3
Banking, finance & insurance	3,540	151	140	79	3,170	30.2	22.8	29.3	29.9	30.6
Public administration, education & health	7,169	382	374	206	6,207	44.9	43.2	45.3	45.6	45.0
Other services	1,212	68	59	39	1,045	28.4	21.7	29.6	18.9	29.1
By occupation [5]										
Managers and senior officials	3,368	122	156	76	3,014	31.4	35.2	36.2	37.2	30.8
Professional occupations	2,968	102	124	69	2,673	45.8	43.8	48.6	47.0	45.7
Associate professional and technical	3,264	153	128	78	2,906	43.3	41.7	41.5	46.0	43.4
Administrative and secretarial	3,218	169	168	89	2,793	26.1	28.3	27.3	31.6	25.7
Skilled trades	2,029	100	87	70	1,772	21.0	16.7	22.4	16.1	21.4
Personal service occupations	1,875	107	97	58	1,613	41.3	36.6	45.5	38.2	41.5
Sales and customer service occupations	2,095	120	78	62	1,835	23.4	21.0	26.6	27.7	23.2
Process, plant and machine operatives	1,775	107	97	59	1,511	16.1	14.7	14.6	14.9	16.4
Elementary occupations	2,905	202	134	116	2,453	17.2	14.8	16.9	18.2	17.4
By full-time/part-time work [5]										
Full-time	17,635	761	802	485	15,586	31.3	28.9	32.5	29.9	31.4
Part-time	5,868	422	266	192	4,988	27.6	25.1	28.5	31.2	27.7
of which:										
Males										
Full-time	11,051	480	474	339	9,757	27.8	24.0	26.5	26.8	28.0
Part-time	1,091	102	45	46	898	25.8	19.1	27.7	30.1	26.3
Females										
Full-time	6,584	280	329	146	5,829	37.3	37.4	41.2	37.3	37.1
Part-time	4,778	320	221	146	4,090	28.1	27.1	28.7	31.6	28.0

Source: Labour Force Survey, Spring 2004 [6]

1 Job-related training includes both on and off-the-job training.
2 Employees are those in employment excluding the self-employed, unpaid family workers and those on government employment and training programmes.
3 Working age is defined as males aged 16-64 and females aged 16-59.
4 Expressed as a percentage of those in the group who received training in the last thirteen weeks.
5 Apart from rounding, figures may not sum to grand totals because of questions in the LFS which were unanswered or did not apply.
6 Users of these data should read the LFS entry in Annex A, as it contains important information about the LFS and the concepts and definitions used.

Chapter 4
Qualifications and Destinations

CHAPTER 4: QUALIFICATIONS AND DESTINATIONS

Key Facts

GCE, GCSE, SCE and Vocational Qualifications

- In 2002/03, 38.5 per cent of young people in the United Kingdom achieved 2 or more GCE A level passes or equivalent in schools and FE colleges. At GCSE/Standard Grade level, of pupils in their last year of compulsory schooling:

    - 53.5 per cent gained 5 or more passes at grades A*-C/1-3

    - 23.1 per cent gained 1-4 passes at grades A*-C/1-3

    - 18.2 per cent gained no passes at grades A*-C/1-3 but gained at least one grade D-G

    - 5.2 per cent had no graded results. **(Table 4.1)**

- Almost 6 million entries were made for GCSE/Standard Grade examinations by pupils in their last year of compulsory education in schools in the United Kingdom in 2002/03. 59 per cent of all entries achieved passes at grades A*-C. **(Table 4.2)**

- A total of 873,800 entries were made by young people for GCE A level/Higher Grade examinations in the United Kingdom in 2002/03. 69 per cent of all entries achieved grades A-C. **(Table 4.3)**

- Of the 138,400 Intermediate and Foundation GNVQ entries in England, Wales and Northern Ireland in 2002/03, 42 per cent achieved GNVQ Part One, and 27 per cent achieved a Full GNVQ. Of the VCE A/AS and Double Award passes in 2002/03, 33,100 were Double Awards, 31,600 were A level and 12,500 were AS passes. **(Table 4.4)**

Subject Choice

- Most frequently studied subjects at GCE A level/Higher Grade were English (105,300 entries - English Language 41,800, English Literature 63,500), Social Studies (83,600), Mathematics (72,900), Biological Sciences (57,600) and General Studies (57,200). **(Table 4.3)**

- Of the 77,200 VCE A/AS and Double Award qualifications obtained in England, Wales and Northern Ireland in 2002/03, the most frequent subject areas were Information Technology (24,000) and Business (19,200). **(Table 4.4)**

Full Vocational Awards

- There were 432,000 NVQs awarded in the United Kingdom in 2002/03. Almost three-fifths (57 per cent) were awarded at level 2. Some 217,000 vocationally related qualifications were awarded in

2002/03, with 45 per cent of these awarded at level 1. **(Table 4.5)**

National Learning Targets

- In Summer 2004, progress towards selected targets in England was:

    - 77 per cent of 11-year-olds achieving level 4 or above in *English* (target 85%)

    - 74 per cent of 11-year-olds achieving level 4 or above in *mathematics* (target 85%)

    - 73 per cent of 14-year-olds achieving level 5 or above in *mathematics* (target 75%)

    - 66 per cent of 14-year-olds achieving level 5 or above in *science* (target 70%)

    - 53 per cent of 16-year-olds gaining at least five GCSEs at grades A*-C (target: on average, a 2 percentage point increase each year between 2002 and 2006)

    - 86 per cent of 16-year-olds gaining at least five GCSEs at grades A*-G (target 92%). **(Table 4.7)**

- In Summer 2004, progress towards selected targets in Wales was:

    - 79 per cent of 11-year-olds achieving level 4 or above in *English*, 79 per cent in *Welsh (first language)*, 78 per cent in *mathematics*, and 89 per cent in *science* (target 80-85 per cent)

    - 65 per cent of 14-year-olds achieving level 5 or above in *English*, 73 per cent in *Welsh (first language)*, 71 per cent in *mathematics*, and 74 per cent in *science* (target 80-85 per cent)

    - 51 per cent of 15-year-olds gaining at least five GCSEs at grades A*-C (target 58%)

    - 85 per cent of 15-year-olds gaining at least five GCSEs at grades A*-G (target 95%). **(Table 4.7)**

Higher Education Qualifications

- A total of 511,500 higher education qualifications were awarded in higher education institutions in the United Kingdom in 2002/03. Of these, 94,400 were sub-degree qualifications, 273,400 were first degrees, 11,800 were PhD or equivalents and 131,900 were at Masters / other postgraduate level. 57 per cent of all higher education qualifications were awarded to women. **(Table 4.8)**

Highest Qualification Held

- 45 per cent of people of working age were qualified to NVQ level 3 equivalent or above in Spring 2004, with 26 per cent of people of working age qualified to NVQ level 4 equivalent or above, and 15 per cent having no qualification. (**Table 4.9**)

- Attainment levels vary by Government Office region, with London having a higher proportion of highly qualified people (i.e. qualified to NVQ level 4 and 5 or equivalent) than any other UK region in Spring 2004. (**Table 4.9**)

- Attainment levels varied greatly by economic activity with 31 per cent of the economically inactive and 20 per cent of the unemployed having no qualifications, compared to 9 per cent of employees and 13 per cent of the self-employed. (**Table 4.9**)

- 91 per cent of employees in professional occupations held two or more A levels, or a higher level qualification, compared with 65 per cent of managers and senior officials, 22 per cent of process, plant and machine operatives and 21 per cent of those in elementary occupations. (**Table 4.9**)

People Working Towards a Qualification

- In 2002/03, of the 214,200 LSC Work-based learning provision programme leavers in England, 40 per cent met the requirements of their Modern Apprenticeship Framework or NVQ. The proportion for those aged 16-18 meeting the requirements was 41 per cent, and for those aged 19 and over, it was 37 per cent. (**Table 4.6**)

- 18 per cent of all people of working age were studying towards a qualification in Spring 2004. Young people aged 16-24 were far more likely to be working towards a qualification than people in any other age group. (**Table 4.10**)

- People of non-white ethnic origin were far more likely to be studying towards a qualification than people of white ethnic origin - 28 per cent compared to 17 per cent. (**Table 4.10**)

Destinations of School Leavers

- The number of school leavers in the United Kingdom increased by 18,500 between 2002 and 2003, to 730,100. The proportion of pupils at the end of compulsory education continuing their education in England remained at 72 per cent - 11 percentage points higher than in 1991. In Northern Ireland, the proportion increased to 70 per cent in 2003 - 12 percentage points higher than in 1991. In Scotland the percentage of all school leavers continuing their education remained at 52 per cent in 2003, 20 percentage points higher than in 1991. The percentage of school leavers continuing their education in Wales in 2003 increased to 74 per cent - 12 percentage points higher than in 1991. (**Table 4.11**)

Destinations of Higher Education Graduates

- Of the 227,900 full-time home and EU first-degree graduates from the academic year 2002/03, 109,600 were known to go into UK employment only, 4,800 went into overseas employment only, 14,500 went into a combination of employment and study, 29,100 went into further study only, 9,600 were not available for employment, 12,900 were believed to be unemployed and 1,800 had other known destinations. Some 45,600 graduates had unknown destinations. (**Table 4.12**)

CHAPTER 4: QUALIFICATIONS AND DESTINATIONS - LIST OF TABLES

4.1 QUALIFICATIONS AND DESTINATIONS

GCE, GCSE, SCE[1] and vocational qualifications obtained by pupils and students at a typical age[2,3], and students of any age — time series

United Kingdom   (i) Students at a typical age   Percentages and thousands

| | Pupils in their last year of compulsory education[2] | | | | | Pupils/students in education[3] | | | |
| | | | | | | % Achieving GCE A Levels and equivalent | | | |
	5 or more grades A*-C[4] (%)	1-4 grades A*-C[4] (%)	Grades D-G[5] only (%)	No graded results (%)	Total (=100%) (thousands)	2 or more passes[6,7]	1 pass[8]	1 or more passes	population aged 17 (thousands)
1995/96									
All	45.5	25.9	21.2	7.4	722.8	29.6	7.8	37.4	672.1
Males	40.6	25.5	25.3	8.6	369.0	26.7	7.1	33.8	345.8
Females	50.5	26.4	16.9	6.2	353.7	32.7	8.6	41.2	326.3
2000/01 [1,9]									
All	51.0	24.1	19.4	5.5	729.7	36.5	4.8	41.3	735.4
Males	45.7	24.6	23.1	6.5	372.1	32.3	4.5	36.9	378.5
Females	56.5	23.6	15.5	4.4	357.6	41.0	5.0	46.0	356.9
2001/02 [1,9]									
All	52.5	23.7	18.4	5.4	732.5	37.6	4.7	42.3	735.2
Males	47.2	24.3	22.0	6.4	374.0	33.2	4.5	37.8	377.0
Females	58.0	23.1	14.6	4.3	358.5	42.1	5.0	47.1	358.2
2002/03 [1]									
All	53.5	23.1	18.2	5.2	750.2	38.5	3.8	42.3	769.0
Males	48.3	23.6	21.8	6.3	382.7	34.1	3.8	37.9	395.1
Females	58.8	22.7	14.4	4.1	367.6	43.2	3.8	47.0	373.9

United Kingdom   (ii) Students of any age achieving   Thousands

| | GCSE and SCE S Grade/Standard Grade (SG) | | | | GCE A Level and SCE/NQ Higher Grade | | |
	5 or more grades A*-C[4,10]	1-4 grades A*-C[4,10]	Grades D-G[5,11] only	No graded results[12]	2 or more passes[6,7]	1 pass[8]	Total 1 or more passes
1995/96							
All	331.4	371.7	236.5	40.0	204.5	78.2	282.6
Males	151.3	175.3	130.9	20.0	95.2	33.8	129.0
Females	180.1	196.4	105.6	20.0	109.3	44.3	153.6
2000/01 [1]							
All	375.1	335.0	227.3	31.8	280.8	64.2	345.1
Males	171.8	164.1	127.3	16.0	128.4	29.1	157.5
Females	203.3	170.9	100.1	15.8	152.4	35.2	187.6
2001/02 [1]							
All	394.9	381.1	234.2	50.6	286.7	67.8	354.5
Males	182.4	188.7	131.1	27.9	130.0	31.6	161.6
Females	212.4	192.3	103.1	22.7	156.7	36.2	192.9
2002/03 [1]							
All	409.4	340.9	234.2	51.7	309.1	60.8	369.9
Males	189.6	168.1	131.2	28.3	140.5	28.7	169.3
Females	219.9	172.9	103.0	23.4	168.6	32.0	200.6

Source: Department for Education and Skills; National Assembly for Wales; Scottish Executive; Northern Ireland Department of Education

1 From 1999/00 National Qualifications (NQ) were introduced in Scotland but are not all shown until 2000/01. NQs include Standard Grades, Intermediate 1 & 2 and Higher Grades. The figures for Higher Grades combine the new NQ Higher and the old SCE Higher and include Advanced Highers.

2 Pupils aged 15 at the start of the academic year, pupils in Year S4 in Scotland.

3 Pupils in schools and students in further education institutions generally aged 16-18 at the start of the academic year in England, Wales and Northern Ireland as a percentage of the 17 year old population. Data for 2002/03 for Wales and Northern Ireland, however, relate to schools only. Pupils in Scotland generally sit Highers one year earlier than their A level counterparts and the figures relate to the results of pupils in Year S5/S6.

4 Standard Grades 1-3/Intermediate 2 A-C/Intermediate 1 A-B in Scotland.

5 Grades D-G at GCSE and Scottish Standard Grades 4-6/Intermediate 1(C)/Access 3 (pass).

6 3 or more SCE/NQ Higher Grades/2 or more Advanced Highers/1 Advanced Higher with more than 2 Higher Passes in Scotland.

7 Includes Vocational Certificates of Education (VCE) and, previously, Advanced level GNVQ/GSVQ, which is equivalent to 2 GCE A levels or AS equivalents/3 SCE/NQ Higher grades.

8 2 AS levels or 2 Highers/1 Advanced Higher or 1 each in Scotland, count as 1 A level pass. Includes those with 1.5 A level passes.

9 Includes revised data.

10 Includes GNVQ/GSVQ Intermediate Part 1, Full and Language unit which are equivalent to 2, 4 and 0.5 GCSE grades A*-C/SCE Standard grades 1-3 respectively. Figures include those with 4.5 GCSEs.

11 Includes GNVQ/GSVQ Foundation Part 1, Full and Language unit which are equivalent to 2, 4 and 0.5 GCSE grades D-G/SCE Standard grades 4-6 respectively.

12 Figures for Scotland include students in Year S4 only.

QUALIFICATIONS AND DESTINATIONS

4.2 GCSE and SCE Standard grade[1] entries and achievements[2] for pupils in their last year of compulsory education[3], in all schools by subject and gender by the end of 2002/03

United Kingdom

Thousands and percentages

Subject group	Number of entries (000s)			Percentage achieving grade A*–C			Percentage achieving grade D–G		
	All	Males	Females	All	Males	Females	All	Males	Females
Biological Science	71.2	34.2	37.0	85	87	83	14	12	16
Chemistry	68.8	38.3	30.5	88	88	88	11	11	11
Physics	64.5	40.8	23.7	87	86	87	12	13	12
Science Single Award [4]	77.8	39.9	37.9	20	18	21	72	72	71
Science Double Award	526.8	260.8	266.1	55	53	56	43	45	42
Other Science [5]	5.5	3.6	1.9	50	50	50	45	44	45
Mathematics [6]	732.7	370.5	362.2	52	51	53	44	45	43
Information Technology [7]	117.4	70.1	47.3	60	57	64	36	38	33
Design and Technology [8]	467.3	252.3	215.0	54	47	63	42	48	34
Business Studies	116.6	60.9	55.7	58	55	61	38	40	35
Home Economics	50.8	4.3	46.5	52	38	53	44	54	43
Art and Design	228.2	96.3	131.9	69	58	77	29	39	21
Geography	244.8	137.5	107.3	62	59	66	35	38	32
History	237.5	118.7	118.8	64	61	68	33	35	30
Economics	4.6	3.4	1.3	71	71	70	26	26	27
Humanities [5]	19.1	9.1	10.0	44	38	49	50	53	46
Religious Studies	134.1	56.5	77.6	63	55	68	33	38	28
Social Studies	17.5	4.9	12.6	54	44	58	39	47	36
English	695.6	348.1	347.5	62	54	69	37	44	29
Welsh [9]	4.9	2.3	2.5	75	67	82	25	33	18
English Literature [5]	555.4	268.8	286.6	66	58	73	32	39	26
Welsh Literature	3.9	1.7	2.1	74	66	80	26	33	19
Drama	104.4	37.4	67.0	68	58	74	30	39	25
Communication Studies [5]	51.7	19.0	32.7	55	48	59	41	47	38
Modern Languages									
French	364.8	171.1	193.6	52	43	59	46	54	39
German	138.0	66.5	71.5	56	49	62	42	49	36
Spanish	58.1	24.1	34.0	57	49	63	40	47	35
Other languages [10]	37.4	17.0	20.4	71	63	77	27	34	22
Classical Studies	16.2	8.5	7.7	87	85	89	12	13	10
Physical Education	139.0	93.4	45.5	60	58	62	39	40	37
Vocational Studies	34.5	16.2	18.3	53	49	57	41	45	38
Modern Studies [11]	14.6	6.0	8.6	65	59	68	34	39	30
Music	62.7	27.9	34.8	71	67	75	24	27	22
Other subjects [12]	0.6	0.3	0.3	82	73	91	16	24	8
All entries [13]	**5,995.9**	**2,972.2**	**3,023.6**	**59**	**54**	**63**	**38**	**42**	**34**
English and Mathematics [14,15,16]	685.9	343.1	342.8	48	44	51	49	51	46
English, Maths and a Science [14,15,16]	665.6	332.4	333.3	44	42	47	51	54	49
English, Maths, Science and Modern Languages [16,17]	509.1	241.9	267.2	41	36	46	54	58	50
Mathematics and Science [16,17]	642.9	323.0	319.9	46	45	47	49	50	48
Any Subject	719.2	363.5	355.7	77	72	81	23	28	19

Source: Department for Education and Skills; National Assembly for Wales; Scottish Executive; Northern Ireland Department of Education

1 Or equivalent.
2 Where a candidate attempted an examination in the same subject more than once, only the highest value pass has been counted. However, some double counting may occur if a student enters for more than one subject within a subject category.
3 Those in all schools who were 15 at the start of the academic year, i.e. 31 August 2002. Pupils in Year S4 in Scotland.
4 Standard Grade in General Science in Scotland.
5 England and Wales only.
6 Includes related subjects such as Statistics.
7 Includes Computer Studies, Information Systems and any combined syllabus where Information Technology is the major part.
8 Craft and Design, Graphic Communications and Technological Studies in Scotland.
9 Welsh as a first language.
10 Includes Welsh as a second language (approximately 11,500 entries).
11 Scotland only.
12 Includes combined syllabuses, Gaelic and General Studies.
13 Science Double Award are counted twice in this row.
14 English or Welsh as a first language in Wales.
15 Only includes *successful* entries (grade A*-G) in Wales so the number of entries is an underestimate.
16 Percentages are those achieving grades A*-C or D-G respectively in all these subjects.
17 England and Scotland only.

QUALIFICATIONS AND DESTINATIONS

4.3 GCE A level/SCE Higher grade[1] entries and achievements for young people[2] in all Schools and Further Education Sector Colleges[3] by subject and gender, 2002/03

United Kingdom

Thousands and percentages

	Number of entries(000s)			Percentage achieving grades A–C			Percentage achieving grades D–E[4]			Percentage with no graded results		
	All	Males	Females	All	Males	Females	All	Males	Females	All	Males	Females
Subject group												
Biological Sciences	57.6	21.6	36.0	64	61	67	28	30	26	8	9	8
Chemistry	43.3	21.1	22.3	73	70	75	21	22	19	7	7	6
Physics	38.3	29.0	9.2	69	67	76	23	24	18	8	9	6
Other Science	7.1	3.8	3.3	63	62	65	25	29	20	12	9	15
Mathematics	72.9	43.7	29.2	74	72	77	17	18	14	9	10	9
Computer Studies [5]	31.9	23.5	8.4	52	51	55	39	39	38	9	10	8
Design and Technology [6]	23.5	15.4	8.1	65	61	72	27	29	23	8	10	5
Business Studies [7]	50.0	26.9	23.1	67	65	70	25	28	22	7	7	8
Home Economics	2.1	0.1	2.0	75	59	76	20	33	19	5	8	5
Art and Design	43.0	13.2	29.8	75	67	78	21	27	19	4	6	3
Geography	42.9	23.1	19.7	74	70	79	22	25	18	4	5	3
History	48.4	23.2	25.3	75	74	76	21	23	20	3	4	3
Economics	15.4	10.7	4.7	78	77	81	19	20	17	3	3	3
Religious Studies	14.0	3.9	10.1	76	75	77	20	20	19	4	5	4
Social Studies [8]	83.6	25.4	58.2	66	60	69	29	34	27	5	7	4
English	41.8	16.1	25.7	65	62	66	20	19	20	16	19	14
Welsh Second Language [9]	0.4	0.1	0.3	73	66	76	25	30	23	2	4	1
Gaelic	0.2	0.1	0.1	94	97	93	3	2	3	3	2	4
English Literature [8]	63.5	18.8	44.8	73	72	74	26	27	25	1	2	1
Welsh [9]	0.3	0.1	0.2	83	88	82	16	12	17	1	-	1
Drama	16.2	4.4	11.8	75	69	77	23	28	21	2	3	2
Communication studies [8]	27.9	11.2	16.7	70	64	74	28	33	25	2	3	1
Modern Languages	38.2	12.1	26.1	80	80	80	16	16	16	4	4	4
of which												
French	19.3	5.7	13.6	79	79	80	17	17	17	4	4	4
German	8.4	2.7	5.7	76	76	76	20	20	19	5	4	5
Spanish	5.9	1.7	4.2	81	82	80	16	16	17	3	2	3
Other Languages	4.6	1.9	2.7	88	87	89	8	9	8	4	4	4
Classical Studies [10]	6.4	2.7	3.7	82	78	84	15	19	13	3	3	3
Creative Arts [11]	11.9	5.4	6.4	77	73	80	20	23	18	3	4	3
Physical Education	24.1	15.0	9.1	61	56	68	34	37	28	6	7	5
Vocational Studies [8]	2.4	1.5	0.9	47	46	49	41	42	41	11	12	11
General Studies [8]	57.2	26.9	30.2	52	50	55	40	41	38	8	9	7
Modern Studies [12]	7.5	3.0	4.5	76	74	77	9	10	8	16	17	15
Other subjects	2.0	0.8	1.2	69	64	72	9	9	9	22	27	19
All entries	**873.8**	**402.6**	**471.2**	**69**	**65**	**72**	**25**	**27**	**23**	**6**	**7**	**5**

Sources: Department for Education and Skills; National Assembly for Wales; Scottish Executive; Northern Ireland Department of Education

1 Includes the new Scottish qualification framework from 1999/00 which contains different subject categories to those previously used. The new Intermediate 1 and 2 qualifications (which overlap with Standard Grades and Highers) are not included in the table.

2 Pupils in schools, and students in further education institutions (other than in Wales) aged 16-18 at the start of the academic year in England, Wales and Northern Ireland. Pupils in Scotland generally sit Highers one year earlier and the figures relate to the result of pupils in Year S5/S6.

3 Schools only for Wales.

4 Compensatory Award in Scotland.

5 Includes Information Systems.

6 Craft and Design, Graphic Communication and Technological Studies in Scotland and Northern Ireland.

7 Includes Accounting, Management and Information Studies and Secretarial Studies in Scotland. Includes Business Studies and Accounting in Northern Ireland.

8 England and Wales only.

9 Wales only.

10 Includes Classical Greek and Latin.

11 Includes music.

12 Scotland only.

QUALIFICATIONS AND DESTINATIONS
GNVQ entries and results, and VCE A/AS and Double Awards qualifications obtained, by subject and gender, 2002/03[1]

England, Wales and Northern Ireland   Thousands

| | Intermediate and Foundation GNVQ Pupils aged 15 in all schools[2] | | | | | | | | VCE A/AS and Double Award passes for young people[3] in schools and colleges[4] | | |
| | Total Entries | | GNVQ Part One | | Full GNVQ[5] | | GNVQ Language Unit[6] | | Qualification obtained | | |
	Interm-ediate	Found-ation	Interm-ediate	Found-ation	Interm-ediate	Found-ation	Interm-ediate	Found-ation	Double Award	A Level	AS
All											
Art & Design	2.9	0.6	1.5	0.3	0.9	0.1	-	-	2.9	1.0	-
Business	11.3	2.6	7.1	1.3	1.9	0.2	-	-	8.2	7.6	3.4
Health & Social Care	9.2	4.4	6.2	2.5	1.2	0.6	-	-	5.7	4.9	2.0
Leisure and Recreation	7.3	3.7	4.8	2.0	0.9	0.4	-	-	2.1	1.7	-
Manufacturing	2.0	1.1	1.3	0.5	0.2	0.1	-	-	-	-	-
Construction	-	0.2	-	-	-	0.1	-	-	0.3	0.1	-
Hospitality and Catering	0.2	0.1	-	-	0.1	0.1	-	-	0.5	0.2	-
Science	4.4	0.6	-	-	3.4	0.4	-	-	0.9	0.4	-
Engineering	1.7	0.7	1.0	0.3	0.2	0.1	-	-	0.7	0.4	0.1
Information Technology	75.9	7.8	27.3	2.6	24.9	0.5	-	-	6.2	10.8	7.0
Media: Communication and Production	0.2	-	-	-	0.2	-	-	-	1.0	0.7	-
Retail and Distribution	-	-	-	-	-	-	-	-	-	0.2	-
Performing Arts	0.8	0.1	-	-	0.7	0.1	-	-	0.5	0.7	-
Other subjects[7]	-	0.2	-	-	-	0.1	-	0.1	4.0	3.3	-
Total	**116.2**	**22.2**	**49.2**	**9.5**	**34.7**	**2.7**	**-**	**0.1**	**33.1**	**31.6**	**12.5**
Males											
Art & Design	1.3	0.4	0.6	0.2	0.4	0.1	-	-	1.0	0.4	-
Business	6.2	1.5	3.8	0.7	0.9	0.1	-	-	4.2	4.0	1.8
Health & Social Care	0.5	0.5	0.3	0.2	0.1	0.1	-	-	0.2	0.2	0.1
Leisure and Recreation	2.9	2.1	1.7	1.1	0.4	0.2	-	-	1.4	1.1	-
Manufacturing	1.5	0.9	0.9	0.4	0.1	0.1	-	-	-	-	-
Construction	-	0.2	-	-	-	0.1	-	-	0.3	0.1	-
Hospitality and Catering	0.1	0.1	-	-	0.1	-	-	-	0.2	-	-
Science	2.3	0.3	-	-	1.7	0.2	-	-	0.5	0.2	-
Engineering	1.6	0.7	1.0	0.3	0.2	0.1	-	-	0.7	0.3	0.1
Information Technology	42.7	4.9	14.3	1.6	14.5	0.3	-	-	5.2	7.0	3.9
Media: Communication and Production	0.1	-	-	-	0.1	-	-	-	0.5	0.3	-
Retail and Distribution	-	-	-	-	-	-	-	-	-	0.1	-
Performing Arts	0.3	-	-	-	0.2	-	-	-	0.1	0.2	-
Other subjects[7]	-	0.1	-	-	-	-	-	0.1	0.6	0.7	-
Total	**59.5**	**11.8**	**22.6**	**4.5**	**18.6**	**1.3**	**-**	**0.1**	**14.8**	**14.7**	**5.9**
Females											
Art & Design	1.6	0.2	0.9	0.1	0.5	-	-	-	2.0	0.6	-
Business	5.2	1.0	3.3	0.6	0.9	0.1	-	-	3.9	3.5	1.6
Health & Social Care	8.7	4.0	6.0	2.3	1.2	0.5	-	-	5.5	4.7	1.9
Leisure and Recreation	4.4	1.6	3.0	0.9	0.6	0.2	-	-	0.7	0.6	-
Manufacturing	0.6	0.2	0.4	0.1	0.1	-	-	-	-	-	-
Construction	-	-	-	-	-	-	-	-	-	-	-
Hospitality and Catering	0.1	0.1	-	-	0.1	0.1	-	-	0.3	0.1	-
Science	2.1	0.3	-	-	1.7	0.2	-	-	0.4	0.2	-
Engineering	0.1	-	-	-	-	-	-	-	-	-	-
Information Technology	33.2	2.9	13.0	1.1	10.4	0.2	-	-	1.1	3.8	3.2
Media: Communication and Production	0.1	-	-	-	0.1	-	-	-	0.5	0.3	-
Retail and Distribution	-	-	-	-	-	-	-	-	-	0.1	-
Performing Arts	0.6	0.1	-	-	0.5	-	-	-	0.4	0.5	-
Other subjects[7]	-	0.1	-	-	-	-	-	0.1	3.4	2.6	-
Total	**56.7**	**10.4**	**26.6**	**5.1**	**16.1**	**1.4**	**-**	**0.1**	**18.2**	**17.0**	**6.7**

Source: Department for Education and Skills; National Assembly for Wales; Northern Ireland Department of Education

1 Including attempts and achievements by these students in previous years.
2 Those in all schools who were 15 at the start of the academic year, i.e. 31 August 2002.
3 Those aged 16-18 at the start of the academic year (i.e. 31 August 2002).
4 Data for Wales do not include FE colleges.
5 In Northern Ireland, Full Intermediate and Foundation GNVQ figures relate to pupils aged 16 and 17 in schools and FE colleges at the start of the academic year.
6 England and Wales only. GNVQ Language Units include French, German and Spanish, in England, but only include Welsh as a Second Language in Wales.
7 Includes subjects which are not specified in the table (e.g. Travel & Tourism), and Language Units in Wales.

QUALIFICATIONS AND DESTINATIONS
4.5
Full vocational awards by type of qualification, equivalent level and gender[1] - time series

United Kingdom

Thousands and percentages

	Year[2]				
	1995/96	1999/00	2000/01	2001/02	2002/03
All (thousands)					
Full vocational awards:					
By qualification & level					
NVQs/SVQs					
Level 1	62	65	50	47	52
Level 2	218	262	231	231	247
Level 3	65	113	103	114	116
Level 4 and 5	9	15	15	17	18
Total [3,4]	**354**	**454**	**428**	**408**	**432**
Vocationally Related Qualifications (VRQs) [5]					
Level 1	.	.	.	3	97
Level 2	.	.	.	6	62
Level 3	.	.	.	14	54
Level 4 and 5	.	.	.	2	4
Total [3]	**.**	**.**	**.**	**25**	**217**
Males (percentages)					
Full vocational awards:					
By qualification					
NVQs/SVQs [6,7]	*41*	*48*	*47*	*45*	*44*
VRQs [8]	*.*	*.*	*.*	*69*	*48*
Females (percentages)					
Full vocational awards:					
By qualification					
NVQs/SVQs [6,7]	*59*	*52*	*53*	*55*	*56*
VRQs [8]	*.*	*.*	*.*	*31*	*52*

Source: National Information System for Vocational Qualifications/Qualifications & Curriculum Authority (QCA)

1 Based on all awards where the gender of the candidate is identified.
2 Academic years from October to September.
3 Numbers may not add to column totals due to rounding.
4 For 2000/01, numbers do not add to column totals because SVQ data are excluded from the respective individual levels.
5 For 2001/02, the number of VRQ awards are for ASDAN, OCR and City & Guilds only. 2002/03 are full UK estimates.
6 Prior to 1997/98 data available on gender for NVQs/SVQs was limited therefore this table may not be representative of the gender split for all NVQs/SVQs awarded nationally for these years.
7 Percentage figures for 2000/01 are calculated excluding SVQ data.
8 Due to limited data available for 2001/02, awards for VRQs in this table may not be representative of the gender split for all other vocational qualifications awarded nationally.

4.6 QUALIFICATIONS AND DESTINATIONS

Success rates [1] in Learning and Skills Council funded Work-Based Learning provision: by programme type and age group, 2001/02 [2] and 2002/03 [3]

England   Percentages and thousands

| | | 2001/02 | | | | 2002/03 | | | |
| | | Work-Based Learning Provision | | | | Work-Based Learning Provision | | | |
	Age at start of learning	Framework [4] (x%)	NVQ Only [5] (y%)	Framework or NVQ (x% + y%)	Total Leavers [6] (000s)	Framework [4] (x%)	NVQ Only [5] (y%)	Framework or NVQ (x% + y%)	Total Leavers [6] (000s)
Programme Type									
Advanced Apprenticeships									
	16 - 18	31	10	41	33.5	38	10	49	29.4
	19+	21	10	31	31.8	27	12	39	31.4
	All	26	10	36	65.4	32	11	44	60.8
Apprenticeships (at level 2)									
	16 - 18	24	11	35	60.3	25	13	38	65.8
	19+	19	12	31	31.5	21	14	35	39.4
	All	22	11	34	91.8	24	13	37	105.2
All Apprenticeships									
	16 - 18	27	11	37	93.9	29	12	41	95.2
	19+	20	11	31	63.3	24	13	37	70.8
	All	24	11	35	157.2	27	13	40	166.0
NVQ Training - level 1									
	16 - 18	-	31	31	14.5	-	33	33	13.6
	19+	-	35	35	0.7	-	42	42	0.8
	All	-	31	31	15.2	-	33	33	14.4
NVQ Training - level 2									
	16 - 18	-	41	41	19.6	-	43	43	16.9
	19+	-	48	48	8.1	-	57	57	10.2
	All	-	43	43	27.7	-	49	49	27.1
NVQ Training - level 3									
	16 - 18	-	52	52	3.0	-	51	51	2.0
	19+	-	36	36	2.7	-	46	46	3.4
	All	-	45	45	5.7	-	48	48	5.4
NVQ Training - level 4									
	16 - 18	-	63	63	0.2	-	66	66	0.1
	19+	-	48	48	0.8	-	57	57	1.1
	All	-	51	51	1.0	-	58	58	1.2
All Frameworks or NVQs									
	16 - 18	-	-	37	131.1	-	-	41	127.8
	19+	-	-	33	75.6	-	-	40	86.4
	All	-	-	36	206.7	-	-	41	214.2

Source: Learning and Skills Council (LSC)

1   For Apprenticeships: the proportion who either meet all the requirements of their apprenticeship framework, or achieve an NVQ required by the framework. For NVQ learning: the proportion of learners who achieved the NVQ.

2   1st August 2001 to 31st July 2002.

3   1st August 2002 to 31st July 2003.

4   A set of requirements drawn up by a National Training Organisation (NTO) which need to be fulfilled for the recognition of training as a modern apprenticeship in the sector concerned.

5   Early apprenticeship leavers who achieved an NVQ but no framework.

6   Total leavers have been rounded to the nearest 100.

THIS PAGE HAS BEEN LEFT BLANK

QUALIFICATIONS AND DESTINATIONS
Progress towards selected National Targets [1] - time series

4.7

	(i) England										Percentages	
	2001			**2002**			**2003** [2]			**2004** [3]		
	All	Males	Females	All	Males	Females	All	Males	Females	All	Males	Females
Targets for 11-year-olds [Key Stage 2 tests]												
By 2006												
85% of 11-year-olds to achieve **level 4 or above** in												
English	75	70	80	75	70	79	75	70	81	77	72	83
85% of 11-year-olds to achieve **level 4 or above** in												
mathematics	71	71	70	73	73	73	73	73	72	74	74	74
Targets for 14-year-olds [Key Stage 3 tests]												
By 2004												
75% of 14-year olds to achieve **level 5 or above** in:												
English	65	57	73	67	59	76	69	62	76	71	64	77
mathematics	66	65	67	67	67	68	71	70	72	73	72	74
ICT (teacher assessment)	65	61	69	66	62	70	67	63	71	67	63	71
70% of 14-year-olds to achieve **level 5 or above** in												
science	66	66	66	67	67	67	68	68	69	66	65	67
Targets for 16-year-olds [Key Stage 4]												
Between 2002 and 2006, the proportion of those aged 16 who get qualifications equivalent to **5 GCSEs at Grades A*-C to rise by 2 percentage points each year** on average	50	45	55	52	46	57	53	48	58	53	48	58
By 2004												
92% of 16-year-olds to achieve **5+ GCSE/GNVQ Grades A*-G** (including *English* and *mathematics*)	87	85	89	87	85	89	87	84	89	86	84	89
Targets for Young people												
Proportion of 19 year olds [4] who achieve **5 GCSEs at Grades A*-C**, or equivalent, **should rise by 3 percentage points** between 2002 and 2004, **with a further increase of 3 percentage points** by 2006	76	74	78	75	72	77	76	73	78	..	..	..
By 2004												
55% of 19-year-olds [4] to attain a **NVQ "level 3"** or equivalent qualification [5]	53	52	53	50	48	53	51	50	53	..	..	..
Targets for Adults [6]												
Reduce by at least 40% the number of adults **who lack "level 2"** by 2010, working towards this, 1 million adults already in the workforce to achieve "level 2" between 2003 and 2006 [7,8]	69	72	65	70	72	67	70	72	68	..	..	..
By 2004												
52% of adults to attain a **NVQ "level 3"** or equivalent qualification [5]	47	51	43	48	51	44	49	52	45	..	..	..

Source: Department for Education and Skills; Labour Force Survey, Spring Quarter of each year (in England); National Assembly for Wales; Welsh Local Labour Force Survey [9]

1 There are further Public Service Agreement/Spending Review 2002 targets in England, and BEST/ETAP/Lifelong learning targets in Wales which are not included in this table.
2 Includes revised data.
3 Provisional.
4 The attainment of those aged 19-21 is used as a proxy for achievement at age 19.
5 "level 3" is 2 A levels, an NVQ level 3, an Advanced GNVQ or equivalent.
6 Adults, in England, consist of males aged 18-64 and females aged 18-59, who are in employment or actively seeking employment. In Wales, they consist of all working age adults aged 18-59 (females) and 18-64 (males).
7 "level 2" is defined here as 5 GCSEs at grades A*-C, an NVQ level 2, an Intermediate GNVQ or equivalent.
8 The percentage figures are those who have achieved "level 2".
9 More up-to-date information may be available through the DfES Research and Statistics Gateway 'www.dfes.gov.uk/rsgateway', or the National Assembly for Wales 'www.wales.gov.uk'.
10 Age at the start of the academic year.
11 The corresponding figure for 1999 was 1,322 pupils and the target for 2004 is to reduce to 992 pupils.

QUALIFICATIONS AND DESTINATIONS

4.7

Progress towards selected National Targets[1] – time series

(ii) Wales — Percentages

	2001			2002			2003[2]			2004[3]		
	All	Males	Females	All	Males	Females	All	Males	Females	All	Males	Females
Targets for 11-year-olds [Key Stage 2 task/test]												
By 2004												
80-85% of 11-year-olds to achieve **level 4 or above** in												
English	77	72	82	79	75	84	79	74	84	79	74	84
Welsh (first language)	71	65	78	75	68	82	78	72	83	79	72	86
mathematics	74	73	76	73	72	74	75	74	75	78	77	80
science	82	81	83	86	85	87	88	87	88	89	88	91
Targets for 14-year-olds [Key Stage 3 task/test]												
By 2004												
80-85% of 14-year-olds to achieve **level 5 or above** in												
English	62	53	71	61	53	70	63	55	72	65	57	74
Welsh (first language)	71	63	79	71	63	79	74	66	81	73	67	80
mathematics	62	60	63	62	62	62	68	67	69	71	69	72
science	63	63	64	67	67	67	69	70	69	74	74	74
Targets for 15-year-olds [10] **[Key Stage 4]**												
By 2004												
58% of 15-year-olds to achieve at least **5 GCSEs at**												
Grades A*-C or vocational equivalent	50	45	55	50	45	56	51	46	57	51	46	57
95% of 15-year-olds to achieve at least **5 GCSEs at**												
Grades A*-G or vocational equivalent	85	82	87	85	82	88	85	82	88	85	83	88

Numbers

	All	Males	Females	All	Males	Females	All	Males	Females	All	Males	Females
the number of pupils leaving full-time education												
without a recognised qualification to be 25%												
lower than in 1999 [11]	1,122	625	497	1,113	613	500	1,064	643	421	..	..	..

Percentages

	All	Males	Females	All	Males	Females	All	Males	Females	All	Males	Females
Targets for young people [10]												
By 2004												
To reduce the number of 16-18 year-olds without												
qualifications to **1 in 20 (5%)**	12	12	12	11	11	10	..	..	..	..	..	..
To reduce the number of 19-year-olds without **NVQ "level 2"**												
or equivalent qualification [7] to less than **1 in 5 (<20%)**	25	25	25	25	28	22	..	..	..	..	..	..
Targets for Adults [6]												
By 2004												
To reduce the number of adults without												
qualifications to less than **1 in 8 (<13%)**	21	20	23	19	17	20	..	..	..	..	..	..
Over 7 in 10 (>70%) of adults to attain a **NVQ "level 2"**												
or equivalent qualification [7]	60	65	56	63	67	60	..	..	..	..	..	..
Over 5 in 10 (>50%) of adults to attain a **NVQ "level 3"**												
or equivalent qualification [5]	40	44	35	42	46	37	..	..	..	..	..	..

Source: Department for Education and Skills; Labour Force Survey, Spring Quarter of each year (in England); National Assembly for Wales; Welsh Local Labour Force Survey [9]

See previous page for footnotes.

QUALIFICATIONS AND DESTINATIONS
4.8
Students[1] obtaining higher education qualifications[2,3] by level, gender and subject group, 2002/03

United Kingdom

Thousands

	Sub-degree[4]	First Degree	Postgraduate PhD & equivalent	Postgraduate Masters and Others	Postgraduate Total	Total Higher Education
All						
Medicine & Dentistry	0.1	6.1	0.9	1.7	2.7	8.9
Subjects Allied to Medicine	27.8	22.3	0.8	5.8	6.5	56.6
Biological Sciences	1.5	23.2	1.9	3.8	5.7	30.5
Vet. Science, Agriculture & related	1.2	2.7	0.3	0.9	1.1	5.0
Physical Sciences	1.0	12.1	1.8	2.7	4.5	17.6
Mathematical and Computer Sciences	6.2	22.5	0.6	7.8	8.5	37.2
Engineering & Technology	4.0	18.8	1.7	6.7	8.3	31.1
Architecture, Building & Planning	1.8	6.3	0.1	3.2	3.3	11.4
Social Sciences[5]	9.2	35.9	1.2	20.1	21.3	66.5
Business & Administrative Studies	11.0	38.7	0.5	27.1	27.6	77.3
Librarianship & Info Science	0.8	7.2	-	3.0	3.0	11.0
Languages	2.5	19.7	0.7	3.8	4.6	26.8
Humanities	1.0	13.1	0.7	3.4	4.1	18.2
Creative Arts & Design	3.9	26.1	0.3	4.8	5.0	35.0
Education[6]	7.6	9.3	0.5	32.1	32.6	49.6
Combined, general	14.8	9.3	-	4.8	4.8	28.9
All subjects	**94.4**	**273.4**	**11.8**	**131.9**	**143.7**	**511.5**
Males						
Medicine & Dentistry	-	2.8	0.4	0.7	1.2	4.0
Subjects Allied to Medicine	3.3	4.2	0.3	1.4	1.8	9.3
Biological Sciences	0.7	8.0	0.8	1.3	2.1	10.8
Vet. Science, Agriculture & related	0.5	1.0	0.1	0.4	0.6	2.1
Physical Sciences	0.7	6.9	1.2	1.4	2.6	10.2
Mathematical and Computer Sciences	4.6	16.3	0.5	5.4	5.9	26.7
Engineering & Technology	3.6	15.7	1.4	5.4	6.7	26.0
Architecture, Building & Planning	1.3	4.5	0.1	1.9	2.0	7.8
Social Sciences[5]	2.5	14.0	0.7	8.6	9.2	25.7
Business & Administrative Studies	4.5	17.5	0.3	14.3	14.6	36.6
Librarianship & Info Science	0.4	2.6	-	1.0	1.0	4.0
Languages	1.0	5.2	0.3	1.1	1.5	7.6
Humanities	0.4	5.7	0.4	1.5	2.0	8.1
Creative Arts & Design	1.8	10.1	0.2	1.9	2.1	14.0
Education[6]	2.1	1.8	0.2	9.0	9.3	13.2
Combined, general	5.0	3.9	-	2.8	2.8	11.7
All subjects	**32.4**	**120.3**	**6.9**	**58.2**	**65.1**	**217.9**
Females						
Medicine & Dentistry	0.1	3.3	0.5	1.0	1.5	4.9
Subjects Allied to Medicine	24.5	18.1	0.4	4.4	4.8	47.3
Biological Sciences	0.8	15.2	1.1	2.6	3.7	19.7
Vet. Science, Agriculture & related	0.6	1.7	0.1	0.4	0.6	2.9
Physical Sciences	0.3	5.2	0.6	1.3	1.9	7.4
Mathematical and Computer Sciences	1.6	6.3	0.1	2.4	2.6	10.5
Engineering & Technology	0.4	3.1	0.3	1.3	1.6	5.1
Architecture, Building & Planning	0.5	1.8	-	1.3	1.3	3.6
Social Sciences[5]	6.7	21.9	0.5	11.6	12.1	40.7
Business & Administrative Studies	6.4	21.2	0.2	12.9	13.0	40.6
Librarianship & Info Science	0.4	4.6	-	2.0	2.0	7.0
Languages	1.5	14.6	0.4	2.7	3.1	19.2
Humanities	0.6	7.4	0.3	1.9	2.1	10.1
Creative Arts & Design	2.1	16.0	0.1	2.8	2.9	21.0
Education[6]	5.5	7.5	0.3	23.1	23.4	36.4
Combined, general	9.7	5.4	-	2.0	2.0	17.2
All subjects	**61.9**	**153.1**	**4.9**	**73.7**	**78.6**	**293.6**

Sources: Department for Education and Skills; Higher Education Statistics Agency (HESA)

1   Includes students on Open University courses.
2   Excludes qualifications from the private sector.
3   Includes higher education in higher education institutions in the United Kingdom only. Higher education qualifications in further education institutions (approximately 6% of the total number of students) are excluded.
4   Excludes students who successfully completed courses for which formal qualifications are not awarded.
5   Including Law.
6   Including ITT and INSET.

4.9 QUALIFICATIONS AND DESTINATIONS

Highest qualification held by people of working age[1], by gender, age, region and economic activity and, for employees of working age[1], by occupation, 2004

United Kingdom

Thousands and percentages

	All people of working age[1] (000s)	Percentage of people of working age					
		NVQ level 5[2]	NVQ level 4[3]	NVQ level 3[4]	NVQ level 2[5]	Below NVQ level 2[6]	No qualifications
Personal and economic characteristics							
By gender							
Males	18,622	6	21	23	21	16	14
Females	17,657	5	21	15	22	20	16
By age							
16-19	3,045	*	1	21	36	21	21
20-24	3,613	2	18	34	22	16	8
25-29	3,543	6	31	19	19	16	8
30-39	8,786	7	25	16	21	21	10
40-49	8,307	6	23	17	20	19	15
50-64	8,985	5	20	17	19	16	24
By ethnic origin [7]							
White	33,078	5	21	20	22	18	15
Non-white	3,182	6	19	16	21	20	19
of which:							
Mixed	264	6	22	23	22	15	12
Asian or Asian British	1,562	6	18	15	20	19	23
Black or Black British	792	5	20	17	22	22	14
Chinese	154	12	21	15	17	20	15
Other Ethnic Group	410	8	18	11	20	23	20
By Government Office region [8]							
United Kingdom	36,279	5	21	19	22	18	15
North East	1,525	4	18	19	22	21	17
North West	4,091	4	20	20	22	17	17
Yorkshire & the Humber	3,035	5	19	20	22	20	15
East Midlands	2,578	4	20	20	21	19	15
West Midlands	3,195	4	19	19	21	19	18
Eastern	3,305	5	20	18	24	20	13
London	4,767	8	24	16	20	19	14
South East	4,920	6	23	20	21	18	11
South West	2,949	5	21	21	22	20	11
England	30,367	5	21	19	22	19	14
Wales	1,744	5	19	20	24	15	18
Scotland	3,126	5	25	21	19	15	15
Northern Ireland	1,041	5	18	17	24	11	25
By economic activity							
Employees [7,9,10]	23,510	6	25	20	22	18	9
of which:							
Managers and senior officials	3,368	8	36	21	18	13	4
Professional occupations	2,968	28	55	8	6	3	1
Associate professional and technical	3,264	6	46	18	17	10	2
Administrative and secretarial	3,218	2	18	20	30	25	6
Skilled trades	2,029	1	9	38	27	16	10
Personal service occupations	1,875	1	17	22	28	22	10
Sales and customer service occupations	2,095	1	10	22	30	24	14
Process, plant and machine operatives	1,775	*	4	18	26	31	20
Elementary occupations	2,905	-	5	17	24	28	26
Self-employed [8,11]	3,304	5	22	23	22	15	13
ILO unemployed [12]	1,343	3	12	16	24	25	20
Inactive [13]	7,920	2	11	17	20	18	31

Labour Force Survey, Spring 2004 [14,15]

1 Working age is defined as males aged 16-64 and females 16-59. These figures include unpaid family workers, those on government employment and training programmes, or those who did not answer, who are excluded from the economic activity analyses below.
2 Includes Higher degrees and other qualifications at Level 5.
3 Includes First degree, Other degree and sub-degree higher education qualifications such as teaching and nursing certificates, HNC/HNDs, other HE diplomas and other qualifications at Level 4.
4 Vocational qualifications include those with RSA Advanced Diploma, BTEC Nationals, ONC/ONDs, City and Guilds Advanced Craft or trade apprenticeships and other professional or vocational qualifications at Level 3. Academic qualifications include those with more than one GCE A level or SCE Highers/Scottish Certificates of Sixth Year Studies (CSYS) at Level 3.
5 Vocational qualifications include those with RSA Diplomas, City and Guilds Craft, BTEC Firsts or trade apprenticeships and other professional or vocational qualifications at Level 2. Academic qualifications include those with one GCE A level, five or more GCSE grades A*-C or equivalent or AS examinations/SCE Highers/CSYS at Level 2.
6 Vocational qualifications include those with BTEC general certificates, YT certificates, other RSA qualifications, other City and Guilds or other professional or vocational qualifications at Level 1. Academic qualifications include those with one or more GCSE grade G or equivalent (but less than five at grades A*-C) or AS examinations at Level 1.
7 Apart from rounding, figures may not sum to grand totals because of questions in the LFS which were unanswered or did not apply.
8 Usual region of residence - Government Office Regions in England and each UK country.
9 Employees are those in employment excluding the self-employed, unpaid family workers and those on government employment and training programmes.
10 The split into employees and self-employed is based on respondents' own assessment of their employment status.
11 Self-employed are those in employment excluding employees, unpaid family workers and those on government employment and training programmes.
12 Unemployed according to the International Labour Organization (ILO) definition.
13 People who are neither in employment nor ILO unemployed.
14 Users of these data should read the LFS entry Annex A, as it contains important information about the LFS and the concepts and definitions used.
15 More up-to-date information may be available through the DfES Research and Statistics Gateway 'www.dfes.gov.uk/rsgateway/'.

4.10 QUALIFICATIONS AND DESTINATIONS
People[1] currently working towards a qualification[2], 2004

United Kingdom

Thousands and percentages

	Total working towards a qualification		Of which, percentage working towards[3,4]				
	Number (thousands)	Percentage (%)[5]	Degree or equivalent	Higher Education qualification (below degree level)	GCE A level or equivalent	GCSE grades A* to C or equivalent	Other qualification
All people[1]	**6,434**	**17.8**	**26.4**	**11.3**	**21.8**	**13.4**	**26.6**
Economic activity							
Employees [6,7]	3,782	16.1	21.9	13.8	22.3	9.6	31.8
Self-employed [7,8]	192	5.8	14.9	12.7	11.7	8.9	51.8
ILO unemployed [9]	256	19.1	22.5	8.2	19.7	18.4	30.3
Economically inactive [10]	2,105	26.7	36.8	7.1	21.3	19.8	14.3
All aged							
All	6,434	17.8	26.4	11.3	21.8	13.4	26.6
16-19	2,145	70.9	12.1	5.0	46.5	26.5	9.2
20-24	1,274	35.3	57.1	12.1	9.4	4.2	16.8
25-29	628	17.8	32.6	15.9	8.9	6.4	35.4
30-39	1,138	13.0	23.9	16.5	9.6	8.5	40.9
40-49	815	9.8	20.3	15.5	9.7	8.1	46.1
50-64	434	4.8	15.1	11.3	9.7	9.3	54.1
Males aged							
All	2,933	15.8	27.6	9.8	22.8	12.8	26.5
16-19	1,070	69.4	10.9	5.0	47.6	26.2	9.6
20-24	621	34.8	58.1	10.7	10.5	3.4	16.9
25-29	297	17.2	35.8	14.2	8.5	3.8	36.9
30-39	464	10.8	26.3	15.2	6.8	5.7	45.0
40-49	305	7.5	23.0	11.8	8.5	7.2	49.3
50-64	176	3.4	17.6	9.8	6.9	7.9	57.2
Females aged							
All	3,500	19.9	25.3	12.5	21.0	14.0	26.6
16-19	1,075	72.4	13.2	4.9	45.5	26.7	8.9
20-24	653	35.7	56.1	13.3	8.3	5.0	16.7
25-29	331	18.3	29.7	17.4	9.2	8.7	34.0
30-39	674	15.0	22.3	17.5	11.6	10.4	38.0
40-49	510	12.1	18.7	17.8	10.3	8.6	44.2
50-59	258	6.8	13.3	12.4	11.6	10.3	51.9
By highest qualification held [4]							
Degree or equivalent	1,004	16.2	40.7	16.8	3.7	2.8	35.7
Higher Education qualification (below degree level)	546	17.5	36.8	23.8	5.6	3.1	30.5
GCE A level or equivalent	1,975	22.8	45.6	12.1	19.8	3.4	18.9
GCSE grades A* to C, or equivalent	1,565	20.1	4.6	6.6	48.4	13.1	26.8
Other qualification	695	14.4	13.8	9.4	20.3	16.5	38.7
No qualification	621	11.5	1.9	2.5	6.5	69.3	18.8
By ethnic origin							
White	5,552	16.8	25.0	11.2	22.4	13.6	27.3
Non-white	878	27.7	35.1	11.8	17.7	12.2	22.1
Mixed	93	35.7	33.0	*	25.0	17.1	19.6
Asian or Asian British	390	25.1	37.2	11.5	18.6	12.9	18.8
Black or Black British	236	29.9	26.8	13.6	19.6	12.9	26.0
Chinese	63	40.7	61.3	*	*	*	15.9
Other ethnic group	96	23.3	32.3	15.9	*	*	32.3
Employees							
Full-time & part-time							
All	3,782	16.1	21.9	13.8	22.3	9.6	31.8
Males	1,656	13.7	22.2	12.6	23.4	7.9	33.4
Females	2,125	18.7	21.6	14.8	21.6	11.0	30.6
Full-time							
All	2,182	12.4	19.2	16.4	15.3	7.3	41.8
Males	1,144	10.4	18.7	14.5	16.3	6.4	43.6
Females	1,039	15.8	19.5	18.3	14.1	8.1	39.4
Part-time							
All	1,598	27.2	25.9	10.5	32.2	12.8	18.5
Males	512	46.9	30.2	8.4	39.3	11.0	10.6
Females	1,086	22.7	23.7	11.4	28.7	13.7	22.1

Source: Labour Force Survey, Spring 2004 [11]

1 Only those of working age; males aged 16-64 and females aged 16-59. These figures include unpaid family workers, those on government employment and training programmes, or those who did not answer, who are excluded from the Economic activity analyses below.
2 For those who are working towards more than one qualification the highest is recorded.
3 Expressed as a percentage of those in the group working towards a qualification.
4 Apart from rounding, figures may not sum to grand totals because of questions in the LFS which were unanswered or did not apply.
5 Expressed as a percentage of the total number of people in the group.
6 Employees are those in employment excluding the self-employed, unpaid family workers and those on government employment and training programmes.
7 The split into employee and self-employed is based on respondents' own assessment of their employment status.
8 Self-employed are those in employment excluding employees, unpaid family workers and those on government employment and training programmes.
9 Unemployed according to the International Labour Organization (ILO) definition.
10 People who are neither in employment nor ILO unemployed.
11 Users of these data should read the LFS entry in Annex A, as it contains important information about the LFS and the concepts and definitions used.

QUALIFICATIONS AND DESTINATIONS

4.11 Destinations of school leavers by country - time series

United Kingdom   Thousands and percentages[1]

	1991	1996	2001 [2]	2002 [2]	2003
United Kingdom					
Number of school leavers	638.3	683.3	702.9	711.6	730.1
Destination at end of compulsory schooling					
England					
Number of school leavers	522.8	562.1	582.8	592.3	608.8
of which (%):					
Education	61	68	72	72	72
Government supported training [3]	15	10	7	7	7
Employment	10	8	12	11	11
Unemployed or not available for work	9	7	7	8	8
Unknown or left area	6	8	5	5	4
Wales [4]					
Number of school leavers	34.9	36.9	36.9	36.4	37.7
of which (%):					
Education	62	70	74	73	74
Government supported training [3]	16	8	8	9	8
Employment	8	9	7	6	7
Unemployed or not available for work	8	7	6	7	6
Unknown or left area	6	6	6	5	5
Northern Ireland					
Number of school leavers	25.4	26.9	26.1	26.3	26.3
of which (%):					
Education	58	67	67	68	70
Training	27	22	21	19	19
Employment	5	5	6	6	5
Unemployed or not available for work	4	4	3	3	2
Unknown or left area	6	3	3	4	4
Destination of all school leavers					
Scotland [5]					
Number of school leavers	55.2	57.4	57.1	56.5	57.3
of which (%):					
Education	32	45	52	52	52
Training	25	14	6	6	5
Employment	24	23	24	23	23
Unemployed [2,6]	9	..	14	16	16
Miscellaneous/other known destinations [2]	11	14	-	-	-
Destinations not known	..	4	4	3	4

Sources: School Leavers Destinations Surveys; Careers Service Activity Survey (England); Careers Wales Association Ltd; Scottish Executive; Northern Ireland Department of Employment and Learning

1 Figures may not sum to 100% due to rounding.

2 Includes revised data.

3 Including those who have employed status under Work-based training/learning for young people schemes.

4 Figures recorded in the table for Wales, after 1996, are not classified as 'National Statistics'.

5 These figures cannot be directly compared with those for England, Wales and Northern Ireland as they cover the destinations of pupils from classes S4, S5 and S6 who left Education Authority schools during or at the end of the years academic session. England and Wales figures relate to destinations of year 11 pupils leaving secondary school, while figures for Northern Ireland relate to year 12 pupils.

6 In recent years this category includes those school leavers who are not actively seeking employment or training (for example those who are caring for others or who are working on a part-time basis).

QUALIFICATIONS AND DESTINATIONS
Destinations of full-time first degree home and EU graduates [1] by gender and subject group [2], 2002/03 [3]

United Kingdom   Numbers of first degree graduates - by destination   Thousands

	UK Employment only	Overseas Employment only	Combination of Employment and Study	Further Study only	Not available for Employment	Believed to be unemployed	Other known destinations [4]	Total of known destinations	Unknown destinations [5]	Total First Degree Graduates [6]
All										
Medicine & Dentistry	4.0	-	0.2	0.4	-	-	-	4.6	0.7	5.3
Subjects Allied to Medicine	9.5	0.1	1.4	1.1	0.3	0.4	0.1	12.9	2.7	15.5
Biological Sciences	9.9	0.4	1.4	3.7	1.1	1.2	0.2	17.8	3.9	21.7
Vet. Science, Agriculture & related	1.3	0.1	0.1	0.3	0.1	0.1	-	2.1	0.4	2.4
Physical Sciences	4.8	0.2	0.6	2.5	0.6	0.8	0.1	9.6	1.9	11.5
Mathematical and Computing Sciences	9.1	0.3	1.2	2.2	0.7	1.7	0.1	15.4	3.8	19.1
Engineering & Technology	6.3	0.4	0.7	1.7	0.5	1.1	0.1	10.9	3.3	14.3
Architecture, Building & Planning	2.2	0.1	0.4	0.4	0.1	0.2	-	3.5	0.9	4.4
Social Sciences (inc Law)	12.6	0.6	2.2	6.2	1.5	1.4	0.3	24.8	6.4	31.3
Business & Administrative Studies	15.6	0.8	2.4	2.0	1.6	1.7	0.2	24.3	7.2	31.5
Mass Communications & Documentation	3.5	0.1	0.3	0.4	0.3	0.5	0.1	5.1	1.6	6.7
Languages	7.9	0.9	1.2	3.0	0.9	0.9	0.1	14.9	3.5	18.4
Historical and Philosophical Studies	5.0	0.3	0.8	2.4	0.6	0.7	0.1	9.9	2.3	12.2
Creative Arts & Design	11.9	0.4	1.2	2.1	0.9	2.0	0.3	18.7	5.6	24.3
Education	5.3	0.1	0.3	0.6	0.2	0.2	-	6.6	1.2	7.8
Combined	0.7	-	0.1	0.2	0.1	0.1	-	1.1	0.3	1.5
All subjects	**109.6**	**4.8**	**14.5**	**29.1**	**9.6**	**12.9**	**1.8**	**182.3**	**45.6**	**227.9**
Males										
Medicine & Dentistry	1.8	-	0.1	0.1	-	-	-	2.1	0.3	2.4
Subjects Allied to Medicine	1.6	-	0.3	0.4	0.1	0.1	-	2.5	0.6	3.1
Biological Sciences	3.3	0.1	0.4	1.2	0.4	0.5	0.1	6.0	1.5	7.5
Vet. Science, Agriculture & related	0.5	-	-	0.1	0.1	-	-	0.7	0.1	0.9
Physical Sciences	2.6	0.1	0.3	1.4	0.4	0.5	0.1	5.5	1.1	6.6
Mathematical and Computing Sciences	6.7	0.2	0.7	1.5	0.5	1.4	0.1	11.1	2.8	14.0
Engineering & Technology	5.2	0.4	0.6	1.4	0.4	1.0	0.1	9.1	2.8	11.9
Architecture, Building & Planning	1.6	0.1	0.3	0.3	0.1	0.1	-	2.5	0.6	3.1
Social Sciences (inc Law)	4.5	0.3	0.8	2.4	0.7	0.7	0.1	9.4	2.8	12.2
Business & Administrative Studies	6.8	0.4	1.1	0.9	0.7	0.9	0.1	10.9	3.6	14.4
Mass Communications & Documentation	1.2	-	0.1	0.1	0.1	0.2	-	1.8	0.6	2.4
Languages	1.9	0.2	0.2	0.8	0.2	0.3	0.1	3.8	1.0	4.8
Historical and Philosophical Studies	2.1	0.1	0.3	1.0	0.3	0.4	0.1	4.2	1.1	5.3
Creative Arts & Design	4.6	0.2	0.4	0.7	0.3	1.0	0.1	7.2	2.4	9.6
Education	0.9	-	-	0.1	-	-	-	1.1	0.3	1.4
Combined	0.2	-	-	0.1	-	-	-	0.4	0.1	0.5
All subjects	**45.5**	**2.2**	**5.7**	**12.4**	**4.3**	**7.2**	**0.9**	**78.3**	**21.7**	**100.1**
Females										
Medicine & Dentistry	2.2	-	0.1	0.2	-	-	-	2.6	0.3	2.9
Subjects Allied to Medicine	7.9	0.1	1.0	0.8	0.3	0.3	0.1	10.3	2.1	12.4
Biological Sciences	6.5	0.2	1.0	2.5	0.7	0.7	0.1	11.8	2.4	14.2
Vet. Science, Agriculture & related	0.8	-	0.1	0.2	0.1	-	-	1.3	0.2	1.6
Physical Sciences	2.1	0.1	0.3	1.1	0.2	0.2	-	4.1	0.8	4.9
Mathematical and Computing Sciences	2.4	-	0.4	0.7	0.2	0.4	-	4.3	0.9	5.1
Engineering & Technology	1.1	0.1	0.1	0.3	0.1	0.1	-	1.9	0.5	2.4
Architecture, Building & Planning	0.6	-	0.1	0.2	-	0.1	-	1.0	0.3	1.3
Social Sciences (inc Law)	8.0	0.4	1.5	3.8	0.9	0.8	0.1	15.4	3.7	19.1
Business & Administrative Studies	8.9	0.4	1.4	1.1	0.8	0.8	0.1	13.4	3.6	17.1
Mass Communications & Documentation	2.3	0.1	0.2	0.2	0.2	0.2	-	3.3	1.0	4.3
Languages	6.0	0.7	0.9	2.3	0.6	0.6	0.1	11.1	2.5	13.6
Historical and Philosophical Studies	2.9	0.2	0.5	1.4	0.3	0.3	0.1	5.6	1.2	6.8
Creative Arts & Design	7.3	0.3	0.8	1.5	0.6	1.0	0.2	11.5	3.3	14.8
Education	4.4	0.1	0.2	0.5	0.1	0.2	-	5.5	0.9	6.4
Combined	0.4	-	0.1	0.1	-	0.1	-	0.8	0.2	0.9
All subjects	**64.1**	**2.6**	**8.8**	**16.7**	**5.3**	**5.6**	**0.9**	**104.0**	**23.9**	**127.8**

Source: Department for Education and Skills; Higher Education Statistics Agency (HESA)

1 Home and EU students graduating from higher education institutions in 2003. As from 1999/00 the target population excludes non-EU overseas domiciled students, consequently direct comparisons with earlier years cannot be made.
2 In 2002/03, the Joint Academic Coding System (JACS) was used, which is not identical to the previous subject classification used.
3 Destinations from the academic year 2002/03, collected from the Destinations of Leavers from Higher Education (DLHE) record, which replaced the First Destination Supplement (FDS) used in previous years.
4 Including students not in study who were not looking for employment, further study or training.
5 Includes non-respondents and explicit refusals.
6 Includes known and unknown destinations.

Chapter 5
Population

CHAPTER 5: POPULATION

Key Facts

- UK population aged 2 and over at January 2004 was 58.1 million (28.4 million males and 29.8 million females). **(Table 5.1)**

- UK working age population at Spring 2004 was 36.3 million, of which 23.5 million were Employees, 3.3 million were Self employed, 1.3 million were ILO unemployed and 7.9 million were Economically inactive. **(Table 5.1)**

- UK population aged 2 and over increased by 4.3 per cent between 1991 (55.7 million) and 2004 (58.1 million). Over the same period the working age population increased by 4.2 per cent, from 34.8 million (regrossed) to 36.3 million. **(Table 5.2)**

- Of people of working age, between 1991 (regrossed figures) and 2004, Employees increased by 8.3 per cent (21.7 million to 23.5 million), Self employed increased by 3.0 per cent (3.2 million to 3.3 million), Economically inactive increased by 11.5 per cent (7.1 million to 7.9 million), and ILO unemployed decreased by 42.9 per cent from 2.4 million to 1.3 million. **(Table 5.2)**

CHAPTER 5: POPULATION - LIST OF TABLES

POPULATION

5.1

Population[1] at 1 January by age[2] and gender at the beginning of the academic year[2], 2004

United Kingdom

Thousands

| | 2004 [2] | | | | | | | | | | | | | | |
| | All[3] | | | | | Males | | | | | Females | | | | |
	United Kingdom	England	Wales	Scotland	Northern Ireland	United Kingdom	England	Wales	Scotland	Northern Ireland	United Kingdom	England	Wales	Scotland	Northern Ireland
Ages															
Under 5	2,030	1,704	98	160	67	1,039	872	50	82	35	991	832	48	78	33
5-10	4,377	3,659	219	355	146	2,240	1,872	112	181	75	2,138	1,787	107	173	71
11-15	3,911	3,260	198	322	131	2,006	1,672	102	165	67	1,905	1,588	96	157	64
16-19	3,063	2,540	156	261	106	1,572	1,305	79	133	55	1,491	1,236	76	128	52
20-24	3,726	3,108	179	323	115	1,863	1,553	89	163	58	1,863	1,555	91	160	57
25-29	3,664	3,116	153	287	108	1,823	1,555	74	141	53	1,841	1,561	79	146	55
30-39	9,081	7,675	400	751	255	4,503	3,825	192	361	125	4,577	3,851	208	389	130
40-49	8,275	6,905	394	745	232	4,100	3,431	193	363	114	4,175	3,474	201	382	117
50-59	7,548	6,308	394	653	192	3,732	3,121	195	322	95	3,816	3,187	200	331	97
60-64	2,960	2,455	162	265	79	1,448	1,204	79	126	38	1,513	1,251	82	139	41
65+	9,513	7,952	512	819	230	4,042	3,393	218	336	96	5,471	4,559	294	483	135
Total aged 2 +	**58,149**	**48,683**	**2,865**	**4,941**	**1,660**	**28,368**	**23,802**	**1,383**	**2,374**	**810**	**29,781**	**24,882**	**1,482**	**2,567**	**850**
of which working age[4]	36,279	30,367	1,744	3,126	1,041	18,622	15,599	895	1,594	534	17,657	14,768	849	1,532	507
of which															
Employees[5,6]	23,510	19,734	1,113	2,085	577	12,144	10,219	579	1,057	289	11,365	9,514	535	1,028	288
Self employed[6,7]	3,304	2,836	141	223	104	2,450	2,095	105	165	85	854	741	35	58	19
ILO unemployed[8]	1,343	1,096	63	149	35	778	629	31	92	25	565	467	31	57	10
Economically inactive[9]	7,920	6,532	419	657	312	3,145	2,571	173	274	127	4,776	3,961	245	384	186

Sources: Department for Education and Skills; Labour Force Survey [10]; Office for National Statistics; Government Actuary's Department

1 Estimated and projected numbers based on demographic data provided by the Office for National Statistics (ONS) and the Government Actuary's Department (GAD). Population estimates incorporate post-2001 Census revisions.
2 Age at 31 August 2003. For the Labour Force Survey economic data only, age is based on the age of respondents at the time of the survey.
3 Males and Females may not sum to All totals due to rounding.
4 Working age is defined as males aged 16-64 and females aged 16-59. These figures include unpaid family workers, those on government employment and training programmes, or those who did not answer, who are excluded from the separate analyses below.
5 Employees are those in employment excluding the self-employed, unpaid family workers and those on government employment and training programmes.
6 The split into employees and self-employed is based on respondents' own assessment of their employment status.
7 Self-employed are those in employment excluding employees, unpaid family workers and those on government employment and training programmes.
8 Unemployed according to the International Labour Organization (ILO) definition.
9 Economically inactive are those who are neither in employment nor ILO unemployed.
10 Users of these data should read the LFS entry in Annex A, as it contains important information about the LFS and the concepts and definitions used.

POPULATION

5.2

Population[1] at 1 January by age[2] at the beginning of the academic year - time series

United Kingdom

Thousands

Ages	1991[3]	1996[3]	2001[3]	2002[3]	2003[3]	2004
Under 5	2,289	2,319	2,161	2,131	2,078	2,030
5-10	4,379	4,598	4,569	4,509	4,447	4,377
11-15	3,391	3,614	3,835	3,861	3,900	3,911
16-19	3,180	2,686	2,881	2,937	3,006	3,063
20-24	4,502	3,872	3,507	3,584	3,651	3,726
25-29	4,668	4,486	4,023	3,905	3,753	3,664
30-39	7,870	8,722	9,158	9,218	9,184	9,081
40-49	7,522	7,835	7,816	7,959	8,113	8,275
50-59	6,027	6,364	7,289	7,420	7,508	7,548
60-64	2,904	2,790	2,895	2,882	2,898	2,960
65+	9,013	9,193	9,306	9,373	9,442	9,513
Total aged 2 +	**55,744**	**56,478**	**57,439**	**57,779**	**57,979**	**58,149**
of which working age [4]	34,823	35,053	35,774	35,974	36,127	36,279
of which						
Employees[5,6]	21,714	21,486	23,322	23,414	23,497	23,510
Self employed[6,7]	3,209	3,250	3,038	3,075	3,237	3,304
ILO unemployed[8]	2,350	2,262	1,351	1,451	1,396	1,343
Economically inactive[9]	7,100	7,711	7,833	7,851	7,840	7,920

Sources: Department for Education and Skills; Labour Force Survey [10]; Office for National Statistics; Government Actuary's Department

1   Estimated and projected numbers based on demographic data provided by the Office for National Statistics (ONS) and the Government Actuary's Department (GAD). Population estimates incorporate post-2001 Census revisions.

2   Age at 31 August of the previous year. For the Labour Force Survey economic data only, age is based on the age of respondents at the time of the survey.

3   Includes revised data.

4   Working age is defined as males aged 16-64 and females aged 16-59. These figures include unpaid family workers, those on government employment and training programmes, or those who did not answer, who are excluded from the separate analyses below.

5   Employees are those in employment excluding the self-employed, unpaid family workers and those on government employment and training programmes.

6   The split into employees and self-employed is based on respondents' own assessment of their employment status.

7   Self-employed are those in employment excluding employees, unpaid family workers and those on government employment and training programmes.

8   Unemployed according to the International Labour Organization (ILO) definition.

9   Economically inactive are those who are neither in employment nor ILO unemployed.

10   Users of these data should read the LFS entry in Annex A, as it contains important information about the LFS and the concepts and definitions used.

Chapter 6
International Comparisons

CHAPTER 6: INTERNATIONAL COMPARISONS

Introduction

International comparisons of the functioning of education and training systems can help countries to identify their strengths and weaknesses and evaluate their performance against their main competitors. Governments are increasingly looking towards these comparisons as they develop and monitor education and training policies.

The United Kingdom participates in the continuing development of international comparisons of education and training. With help from the National Assembly for Wales, Scottish Executive, the Northern Ireland Department of Education and the Northern Ireland Department for Employment and Learning, DfES supply detailed statistics on education and training in the UK, drawn from this volume and other sources, to the Organisation for Economic Co-operation and Development (OECD), the Statistical Office of the European Union (EUROSTAT) and the United Nations Educational, Scientific and Cultural Organisation (UNESCO).

Based on information supplied by various countries to the international bodies, and the results of international studies, a range of 'indicators' is now available, seeking to compare different aspects of countries' education and training systems and their respective performance.

The comparative tables shown here draw from OECD's "Education at a Glance" (2004 Edition), which includes *trends* in international comparisons.

It is important to note, however, that international comparisons of education and training are very difficult and should therefore be treated with caution. In addition, some knowledge of the underlying systems in different countries is extremely useful in interpreting the data.

To ensure comparability, most educational activity in different countries has been assigned to 6 internationally-agreed "ISCED" (International Standard Classification of Education) levels of education. The best comparisons are based on such internationally agreed definitions and procedures, backed up by controls to ensure that each country meets these. Despite these efforts, there may still be comparability problems that persist - some of the more important ones are noted below:

Notes:

Classifying education
- Coverage of what is considered to be "education" may vary, especially at the pre-compulsory and post-compulsory level e.g. early childhood provision, apprenticeships, adult learning etc.

Expenditure on education
- Where institutions cover more than one of the education levels (e.g. "lower" (age 11-13) and "upper" (age 14+) secondary school education in the UK), estimates are often required to assign expenditure figures between levels.

- The range of public and private provision varies considerably between countries. As a proportion of total spending on education, that coming from private sources varies from less than 5% in Denmark, Finland, Norway, Portugal, the Slovak Republic, Sweden and Turkey to around 30% in the United States and over 40% in Korea. The equivalent figure for the UK was about 15%.

- Public expenditure on education, as a percentage of GDP, is influenced by a number of factors. An obvious one is the proportion of the population of school age, which can vary widely between different countries.

- Expenditure coverage, especially at the HE level, differs according to the extent to which countries include elements such as student support and research and development.

Participation in education
- Many of the measures shown are on the basis of headcounts, no distinction being possible between full-time and part-time study. Some countries do not even recognise the concept of part-time study, although many of their students would be classified as "part-time" in the UK.

- When comparing expected years of schooling in different countries, the length of the school year and the quality of education offered is not necessarily the same.

- The reasons why adults in some countries are so much less likely than others to participate in university-level education are varied. One important factor may be the extensive provision of vocational education and apprenticeships in continental Europe, likely to have reduced the perceived need to enrol in formal university-level studies as preparation for work.

Teachers
- A clear definition of a "teacher", especially in higher education, has not been well established in international data collections. Some countries include professional staff such as guidance counsellors and school psychologists in their "teacher" counts.

CHAPTER 6: INTERNATIONAL COMPARISONS

Explanatory Note

In the following 'Key Facts' section the UK position is sometimes compared to the 'OECD average'. This 'average' is calculated as the ***unweighted*** mean of the data values of all countries for which data are available or can be estimated.

Key Facts

- Public expenditure on all levels of education in the UK represented 4.7% of Gross Domestic Product in 2001, below the OECD average of 5.3%. This was higher than Japan (3.6%) and Germany (4.6%), but lower than New Zealand (6.7%), France (5.7%), the US (5.6%), Australia (5.0%), Italy (5.0%) and all of the Scandinavian countries. **(Table 6.1)**

- In 2001, average expenditure per student per year at the pre-primary level in the UK (US$7,595) was significantly above the OECD average (US$4,187). The average UK expenditure per secondary level student (US$5,933) was 9% less than the OECD average (US$6,510). Spending per student at primary level in the UK (US$4,415) was also 9% less than the OECD average (US$4,850). **(Table 6.2)**

- Average expenditure per higher education student in the UK in 2001 (US$10,753) was 7% above the OECD average (US$10,052). However, the US spent over twice the amount per higher education student as the UK. **(Table 6.2)**

- In 2002, given current conditions, a UK 5 year old could expect to enrol in 20.4 years of full-time and part-time education during their lifetime, compared with the OECD average of 17.2 years. Expected years in education in the UK increased by 19% between 1995 and 2002. They are currently second only to those in Australia, where a 5 year old can expect to enrol in 21.1 years of full-time and part-time education. **(Table 6.3)**

- The ratio of students to teaching staff in the UK was above the OECD average at all levels of education in 2002. In primary education, the UK rate was 19.9 students per teacher, compared to the OECD average of 16.6. In secondary education, the UK rate was 14.8 students per teacher, compared to the OECD average of 13.6. **(Table 6.4)**

- In the Progress in International Reading Literacy Study (PIRLS2001) of "4th grade" students (10-year-olds), for reading literacy England came third of the 35 countries taking part and third of the 16 OECD countries in the study. Only Sweden and the Netherlands gained higher scores. The mean scores in reading literacy for 10 year old boys and girls in England (boys 541; girls 564) and in Scotland (boys 519; girls 537) were above the PIRLS averages (boys 490; girls 510). **(Table 6.5)**

- In 2002, the UK graduation rate for all first degrees (35.9%) was above the OECD average (31.8%). The UK had the 6th highest rate out of 17 countries for first degree programmes and the 6th highest out of 26 countries for advanced research programmes. **(Table 6.6)**

- In 2002, the proportion of primary education teachers in the UK aged less than 30 was relatively high at 22.0%. Only Korea (27.0%), Luxembourg (27.0%) and the Slovak Republic (22.1%) had a higher proportion in this age group. At the other end of the age range, the UK had relatively few primary education teachers aged 60 or more (0.8%). The figure for this age group exceeded 5.0% in Denmark, Germany, Iceland, New Zealand, the Slovak Republic and Sweden. **(Table 6.7)**

- In 2002, of the 20 countries providing data, the UK had the 8th highest proportion of secondary education teachers aged less than 30. As with teachers in primary education, the UK had relatively few secondary teachers aged 60 or more, at 1.3% - the 4th lowest figure. **(Table 6.7)**

CHAPTER 6: INTERNATIONAL COMPARISONS – LIST OF TABLES

6.1 INTERNATIONAL COMPARISONS
Public expenditure on education as a percentage of GDP, 1995 and 2001

	Public expenditure on education[1] as a percentage of GDP			
	2001			1995
	Primary, Secondary and Post-Secondary Non-Tertiary Education	Tertiary Education	All levels[2]	All levels[2]
Australia	3.8	1.2	5.0	5.2
Austria	3.8	1.4	5.8	6.2
Belgium	4.0	1.4	6.1	..
Canada[3]	3.1	1.9	5.2	6.5
Czech Republic	3.0	0.9	4.4	4.9
Denmark[4]	4.8	2.7	8.5	7.7
Finland	3.9	2.1	6.2	6.8
France	4.0	1.0	5.7	6.0
Germany	3.0	1.1	4.6	4.6
Greece	2.4	1.2	3.9	3.1
Hungary	3.2	1.1	5.1	5.4
Iceland	5.1	1.1	6.5	..
Ireland	3.0	1.2	4.3	5.1
Italy	3.7	0.8	5.0	4.9
Japan[4]	2.7	0.5	3.6	3.5
Korea	3.5	0.5	4.9	..
Luxembourg	3.3	..	3.8	..
Mexico	3.8	0.7	5.1	4.6
Netherlands	3.3	1.3	5.0	5.1
New Zealand	4.7	1.8	6.7	5.7
Norway	4.8	1.8	7.0	7.4
Poland	4.1	1.1	5.6	5.7
Portugal	4.3	1.1	5.9	5.4
Slovak Republic	2.7	0.8	4.0	5.0
Spain	3.0	1.0	4.4	4.7
Sweden	4.8	2.0	7.3	7.2
Switzerland	3.9	1.3	5.5	5.5
Turkey	2.5	1.2	3.7	2.4
United Kingdom	**3.4**	**0.8**	**4.7**	**5.2**
United States[3]	3.8	1.5	5.6	..
Country mean	**3.6**	**1.3**	**5.3**	**5.3**

Source: OECD, Education at a Glance, 2004

1 Direct expenditure for institutions and public subsidies to households e.g. for tuition fees and living costs. The definition of "education expenditure" used by OECD is different from the definition used in Chapter 1 of this Volume.
2 Includes expenditure for early childhood education and other miscellaneous expenditure.
3 Post-secondary non-tertiary is included in 'tertiary education' and is excluded from 'primary, secondary and post-secondary non-tertiary education'.
4 Post-secondary non-tertiary is included in both 'primary, secondary and post-secondary non-tertiary education' and in 'tertiary education'.

| | Expenditure per full-time equivalent student per year[1] | | | | |
| | (US$ converted using purchasing power parities) | | | | |
	Early childhood education[2]	Primary education	Secondary education	Tertiary education	Cumulative expenditure per student over the average duration of tertiary education studies[3]
Australia	..	5,052	7,239	12,688	32,101
Austria	5,713	6,571	8,562	11,274	62,459
Belgium[4]	4,062	5,321	7,912	11,589	..
Canada	..	..	..	..	..
Czech Republic	2,449	1,871	3,448	5,555	..
Denmark[5]	4,542	7,572	8,113	14,280	59,834
Finland[4]	3,640	4,708	6,537	10,981	49,972
France	4,323	4,777	8,107	8,837	41,372
Germany	4,956	4,237	6,620	10,504	55,426
Greece[6]	..	3,299	3,768	4,280	24,255
Hungary[7]	2,882	2,592	2,633	7,122	28,844
Iceland[7]	..	6,373	7,265	7,674	20,566
Ireland	4,026	3,743	5,245	10,003	32,411
Italy[7]	5,972	6,783	8,258	8,347	45,824
Japan[5]	3,478	5,771	6,534	11,164	42,970
Korea	1,913	3,714	5,159	6,618	22,701
Luxembourg[5,6]	..	7,873	11,091	..	..
Mexico	1,410	1,357	1,915	4,341	14,858
Netherlands	4,228	4,862	6,403	12,974	63,186
New Zealand	..	..	..	..	..
Norway[4]	8,246	7,404	9,040	13,189	..
Poland[8]	2,220	2,322	..	3,579	..
Portugal	..	4,181	5,976	5,199	..
Slovak Republic[4]	1,740	1,252	1,874	5,285	..
Spain[4]	3,608	4,168	5,442	7,455	33,920
Sweden	3,504	6,295	6,482	15,188	69,981
Switzerland[7]	3,080	6,889	10,916	20,230	73,320
Turkey	..	..	..	..	..
United Kingdom[4]	**7,595**	**4,415**	**5,933**	**10,753**	**41,209**
United States[9]	8,522	7,560	8,779	22,234	..
Country mean	**4,187**	**4,850**	**6,510**	**10,052**	**42,906**

Source: OECD, Education at a Glance, 2004

1 Calendar year 2001. Where the financial year and/or school year do not match the calendar year, corresponding weightings are made.

2 For children aged 3 years and older.

3 Calculated by multiplying the expenditure per full-time equivalent student per year by the average number of years of duration of tertiary education studies. Includes students who do not complete their course.

4 Includes post-secondary non-tertiary expenditure in the secondary figure.

5 Includes some post-secondary non-tertiary expenditure in both the secondary and tertiary figures.

6 Includes pre-primary expenditure in the primary figure.

7 Public institutions only in the final column.

8 Includes lower secondary expenditure in the primary figure. Secondary expenditure thus refers only to upper secondary expenditure.

9 Includes post-secondary non-tertiary expenditure in the tertiary figure.

INTERNATIONAL COMPARISONS
Participation in education, 2002

	Context			Expected years of education[1]	
	Compulsory school starting age[2]	Ending age of compulsory schooling[3]	Age range at which over 90% of the population are enrolled	Expected years of full-time and part time education from age 5	Index of change between 1995 and 2002 (1995 = 100)
Australia	6	15	5 - 16	21.1	110
Austria	6	15	5 - 16	16.0	103
Belgium	6	18	3 - 17	19.4	108
Canada	6	16	..	..	..
Czech Republic	6	15	5 - 17	16.2	114
Denmark	7	16	4 - 16	18.0	107
Finland	7	16	6 - 17	19.4	113
France	6	16	3 - 17	16.6	100
Germany	6	18	6 - 17	17.1	104
Greece	6	14.5	6 - 16	16.3	117
Hungary	6	16	4 - 16	16.8	117
Iceland	6	16	3 - 16	18.5	111
Ireland	6	15	5 - 16	16.5	107
Italy	6	15	3 - 15	16.7	..
Japan	6	15	4 - 17	..	..
Korea	6	14	6 - 17	16.2	113
Luxembourg	6	15	4 - 15	14.4	..
Mexico	6	15	6 - 12	12.9	107
Netherlands	5	18	4 - 16	17.2	..
New Zealand	6	16	4 - 15	18.3	..
Norway	7	16	6 - 17	17.9	102
Poland	7	15	6 - 17	17.0	118
Portugal	6	14	5 - 15	17.0	103
Slovak Republic	6	16	6 - 16	15.1	..
Spain	6	16	3 - 16	17.3	102
Sweden	7	16	6 - 18	20.1	146
Switzerland	6	15	6 - 16	16.5	..
Turkey	6	14	..	..	..
United Kingdom	**5**	**16**	**4 - 15**	**20.4**	**119**
United States	6	17	6 - 15	16.8	..
Country mean	**6**	**16**	**.**	**17.2**	**111**

Sources: OECD, Education at a Glance, 2004

1 Calculated as the sum of the net enrolment rates in education for each single year of age from age 5 onwards, divided by 100.
2 Age at start of academic year.
3 Age at end of academic year.

6.4

INTERNATIONAL COMPARISONS
Ratio of students to teaching staff[1] by level of education (based on full-time equivalents), 2002

	Level of education (full-time equivalents)			
	Pre-primary education	Primary education	Secondary education	Tertiary education
Australia	..	16.9	12.5	..
Austria	18.2	14.4	10.0	13.0
Belgium[2]	16.3	13.1	9.3	18.7
Canada	..	..	..	..
Czech Republic[2]	12.9	18.9	13.6	16.1
Denmark	6.6	10.9	..	..
Finland[2]	12.7	15.8	13.4	12.6
France	19.0	19.4	12.2	17.9
Germany	24.2	18.9	15.1	12.6
Greece	13.9	12.5	9.3	32.2
Hungary	10.9	10.8	11.7	13.8
Iceland	5.2	11.4	..	8.7
Ireland	13.5	19.5	..	16.3
Italy	12.8	10.6	10.2	23.1
Japan	18.1	20.3	14.8	11.2
Korea	21.7	31.4	18.4	..
Luxembourg	14.5	11.6	9.0	..
Mexico	21.6	26.9	28.8	15.3
Netherlands[2,3]	..	17.0	15.9	13.0
New Zealand	5.6	19.6	16.6	15.0
Norway[2]	..	11.5	10.4	13.2
Poland	13.5	12.8	13.9	18.0
Portugal	..	11.0	8.3	..
Slovak Republic	9.8	20.1	13.7	10.5
Spain[2]	15.8	14.6	11.2	13.0
Sweden	10.7	12.5	13.2	9.1
Switzerland	..	..	..	..
Turkey	14.9	27.5	17.7	16.2
United Kingdom	**26.6**	**19.9**	**14.8**	**18.3**
United States	15.5	15.5	15.5	17.1
Country mean	**14.8**	**16.6**	**13.6**	**15.4**

Source: OECD, Education at a Glance, 2004

1   Includes head teachers and administrative personnel involved in teaching, pro-rata.
2   Secondary figure includes post-secondary non-tertiary education programmes.
3   Primary figure includes pre-primary education programmes.

6.5

	Reading literacy		
	Females	**Males**	**Difference[2]**
	Mean score	Mean score	Mean Score difference
Czech Republic	543	531	12
England[3,4]	**564**	**541**	**22**
France	531	520	11
Germany	545	533	13
Greece[4]	535	514	21
Hungary	550	536	14
Iceland	522	503	19
Italy	545	537	8
Netherlands[3]	562	547	15
New Zealand	542	516	27
Norway	510	489	21
Scotland[3]	**537**	**519**	**17**
Slovak Republic	526	510	16
Sweden	572	550	22
Turkey	459	440	19
United States[3]	551	533	18
OECD country mean	**538**	**521**	**17**
PIRLS country mean[5]	**510**	**490**	**20**

Source: OECD, Education at a Glance, 2004; IEA Progress in Reading Literacy Study (PIRLS) 2001

1 Year 5 in England, P5 in Scotland.
2 Positive differences indicate that females perform better than males while negative differences indicate that males perform better than females.
3 Met guidelines for sample participation rates only after replacement schools were included.
4 National Defined Population covers less than 95% of National Desired Population.
5 Over 140,000 pupils in 35 countries participated in PIRLS 2001.

	Participation		Graduation rates[1]			
			University level[2]			Postgraduate[3]
				First Degree		
	Expected years of Tertiary education	Non-university level[2]	All First Degrees	Medium[4]	Long[5]	Doctorate
Australia	3.6	..	45.4	35.9	9.5	1.3
Austria	2.1	..	18.0	2.7	15.3	1.7
Belgium	2.8	..	..	..	..	1.1
Canada	..	..	..	..	..	..
Czech Republic	1.8	4.5	14.9	2.1	12.9	0.8
Denmark[6]	2.7	9.5	..	..	..	0.9
Finland[6]	4.3	3.7	45.4	27.3	18.1	1.9
France[6]	2.6	18.5	24.8	8.6	16.2	1.4
Germany	2.1	9.8	19.2	6.5	12.7	2.0
Greece	3.3	..	..	..	..	0.7
Hungary	2.4	1.3	37.2	..	..	0.7
Iceland	2.7	6.4	41.2	33.3	7.6	0.1
Ireland	2.7	12.7	31.1	23.8	7.3	0.8
Italy[6]	2.5	0.9	22.7	2.5	20.2	0.5
Japan	..	26.7	33.8	29.3	4.5	0.7
Korea	4.0	..	..	..	..	0.9
Luxembourg	..	..	..	..	..	..
Mexico	1.1	..	..	..	..	0.1
Netherlands	2.6	..	..	..	..	1.3
New Zealand	3.3	..	..	..	..	0.9
Norway	3.3	4.8	..	..	..	1.1
Poland	3.1	..	41.5	..	..	0.8
Portugal	2.6	..	..	..	..	..
Slovak Republic	1.7	2.7	23.0	5.0	17.9	0.8
Spain	3.0	13.8	33.5	..	..	1.0
Sweden	3.4	3.8	32.7	31.5	1.2	2.8
Switzerland	1.8	18.9	17.9	..	..	2.6
Turkey	..	..	..	..	..	..
United Kingdom	**2.8**	**11.5**	**35.9**	**33.3**	**2.6**	**1.6**
United States	4.1	8.8	..	..	..	1.3
Country mean	**2.7**	**9.8**	**31.8**	**21.2**	**13.3**	**1.2**

Source: OECD, Education at a Glance, 2004

1 Calculated as the ratio of graduates to the population at the typical age of graduation, multiplied by 100, except for Postgraduate.

2 "University-level" tertiary education refers to "largely theoretically based" courses with a minimum of 3 years full-time-equivalent duration. In the UK, this comprises first and higher degrees. "Non university-level tertiary education" courses are "more practically-oriented and occupationally specific". In the UK, this level comprises "sub-degree" tertiary education courses, such as HNCs, HNDs, Dip HEs.

3 Calculated by summing the graduation rates by single year of age, except for France, Italy, Japan, Korea, Mexico, the Netherlands and the United States.

4 Three to less than 5 years duration.

5 Five or more years duration.

6 Year of reference for graduation rates is 2001.

INTERNATIONAL COMPARISONS

6.7 Age distribution of teachers in primary and secondary education, 2002

Percentages

	Primary education					Secondary education				
	Age range					Age range				
	< 30	30 - 39	40 - 49	50 - 59	>= 60	< 30	30 - 39	40 - 49	50 - 59	>= 60
Australia	..	..	..	..	..	..	..	..	..	..
Austria	14.2	27.7	37.7	19.2	1.2	9.8	29.1	42.6	17.7	0.9
Belgium[1]	21.9	28.9	28.6	19.6	1.0	13.2	21.9	34.6	27.7	2.5
Canada	..	..	..	..	..	..	..	..	..	..
Czech Republic	..	..	..	..	..	..	..	..	..	..
Denmark	7.9	21.0	25.8	36.9	8.3	..	..	..	..	..
Finland	13.5	32.9	29.6	23.0	1.0	7.8	25.7	30.3	32.5	3.8
France	14.3	28.0	33.6	23.8	0.2	13.0	27.1	25.1	33.8	1.0
Germany	6.8	16.2	30.0	40.4	6.6	4.2	14.6	32.5	41.6	7.1
Greece	..	..	..	..	..	..	..	..	..	..
Hungary	16.4	33.0	35.6	13.2	1.8	15.3	25.9	33.1	22.3	3.4
Iceland[2]	15.3	29.2	29.8	19.8	5.9	6.9	21.4	32.3	27.9	11.6
Ireland	20.8	23.7	32.7	18.2	4.7	11.4	26.1	29.8	27.0	5.8
Italy	3.0	25.6	36.7	30.4	4.2	0.6	11.1	40.3	43.8	4.2
Japan	8.8	30.1	43.9	17.0	0.2	10.9	32.2	36.4	18.8	1.7
Korea	27.0	30.2	25.4	16.5	0.7	17.5	37.3	34.6	9.9	0.7
Luxembourg[3]	27.0	23.1	25.2	24.1	0.6	13.8	26.7	28.8	29.0	1.7
Mexico	..	..	..	..	..	..	..	..	..	..
Netherlands	18.4	20.5	36.2	23.2	1.7	9.1	16.8	35.9	35.0	3.2
New Zealand	16.6	20.7	32.1	25.0	5.8	13.7	19.5	32.3	27.9	6.6
Norway[4]	..	..	..	..	..	12.0	23.2	27.2	30.4	7.2
Poland	..	..	..	..	..	..	..	..	..	..
Portugal	14.6	24.8	39.2	18.6	2.7	22.5	37.0	26.8	11.5	2.3
Slovak Republic	22.1	24.9	24.8	22.6	5.7	18.8	24.2	28.8	22.5	5.7
Spain	..	..	..	..	..	..	..	..	..	..
Sweden	12.3	18.4	26.2	35.9	7.1	11.4	20.2	24.3	35.0	9.1
Switzerland[3]	..	..	..	..	..	..	..	..	..	..
Turkey	..	..	..	..	..	..	..	..	..	..
United Kingdom	**22.0**	**22.2**	**28.1**	**27.0**	**0.8**	**13.5**	**22.1**	**33.4**	**29.7**	**1.3**
United States	18.3	22.2	30.3	25.7	3.5	16.9	21.9	31.6	26.5	3.1
Country mean	**16.4**	**25.3**	**31.5**	**23.7**	**3.1**	**12.3**	**24.2**	**32.2**	**27.4**	**4.0**

Source: OECD website, Education at a Glance Indicator Tables D7.1 and D7.3

1   Secondary figures include staff employed in post-secondary non-tertiary programmes.
2   Secondary figures exclude staff employed in lower secondary programmes.
3   Public institutions only.
4   Secondary figures include staff employed in primary programmes.

Annex A

SOURCES OF EDUCATION AND TRAINING STATISTICS

This Annex gives details of the current major sources of education and training statistics used in this publication.

List of Sources

1   Education Expenditure

2   Further Education Statistics

3   Government Supported Work-Based Learning for Young People (WBLYP)

4   Higher Education Statistics Agency (HESA)

5   International Comparisons

6   Labour Force Survey (LFS)

7   Population

8   Public Examinations: GCSE/GNVQ, GCE, SCE Standard Grade and National Qualifications (NQ)

9   School Leaver Destinations

10 Schools Statistics

11 Vocational Qualifications

1   EDUCATION EXPENDITURE

HM Treasury provided education expenditure figures in Tables 1.1 and 1.2 from their Public Expenditure Statistical Analysis (PESA). Total Expenditure on Services (TES) is a definition of aggregate public spending and covers most expenditure by the public sector that is included in Total Managed Expenditure (TME), where TME is a measure of public sector expenditure drawn from components in national accounts produced by the Office for National Statistics (ONS). TES broadly represents the sum of current and capital expenditure of central and local government, and public corporations, but excludes general government capital consumption and other accounting adjustments. Gross Domestic Product (GDP) figures and deflators are based on the March 2004 National Accounts release. Table 1.3 reports UK identifiable expenditure on education services by country, and is also derived from PESA.

2   FURTHER EDUCATION STATISTICS

In April 2001 the publication of data on further education in England became the responsibility of the Learning and Skills Council (LSC), which took over responsibility for funding the further education sector in England from the Further Education Funding Council (FEFC). The source used for the FE data for England is the Individualised Student Record (ISR). At the same time the National Council for Education and Training for Wales (ELWa) became responsible for collection of information in Wales - statistics are provided by the National Assembly for Wales (NAfW). Statistical information on further education students in Scotland are provided by the Scottish Executive, from the Scottish Further Education Funding Council (SFEFC), and institutes of further education provide data for Northern Ireland to the Department for Employment and Learning (DELNI). The Higher Education Statistics Agency (HESA) provides data on FE students in higher education institutions in the UK.

3   GOVERNMENT SUPPORTED WORK-BASED LEARNING FOR YOUNG PEOPLE (WBLYP)

The main Government supported work-based learning programmes for young people (aged 15-24) in England are Advanced Modern Apprenticeships (AMA) (formerly Modern Apprenticeships), Foundation Modern Apprenticeships (FMA) (formerly National Traineeships), and, since September 2002, 'Entry to Employment', which replaced Other Training for Young People. The Department for Education and Skills funds these programmes in England.

Modern apprenticeships (MAs) prepare young people for an economy based on high level skills. MAs aim to radically increase the supply of skills at craft, supervisory and technician (intermediate) level within industry. They provide quality work-based learning for young people to achieve qualifications at FMA (national vocational qualification level 2) and AMA (national vocational qualification level 3) levels.

'Entry to Employment' is a high quality programme for young people who are not ready for apprenticeship, which aims to give them the help they need to enter modern apprenticeships or other employment.

Until 25 March 2001, WBLYP was delivered through the network of Training and Enterprise Councils (TECs), however, since 26 March 2001, work-based learning for young people has been delivered through the Learning and Skills Council (LSC) in England.

Until 25 March 2001, the statistics came from three sources: aggregate management information returns provided by TECs, certificates that training providers completed for each individual joining a programme (starts certificates) and a postal questionnaire sent to each trainee[1] six months[2] after leaving the programme, asking for information on whether they completed their training, usefulness of the training, their current activity and what qualifications they gained. While the questionnaires have changed several times since their introduction, the core questions have remained consistent. From 26 March 2001, the statistics for England come from the LSC-maintained Individualised Learner Record.

Since 1 April 2001, work-based learning for adults in England has been delivered through the Employment Service (ES) as an integral part of provision for long term unemployed adults. ES is now part of the Department for Work and Pensions (DWP) and data for work-based learning for Adults are no longer shown in this Volume.

Further details of WBLYP can be obtained from the Statistical First Releases (SFRs) at the websites shown in section 1.2 of Annex B.

4   HIGHER EDUCATION STATISTICS AGENCY (HESA)

From the academic year 1994/95 onwards, the Higher Education Statistics Agency (HESA) has collected information for HE students within UK HE institutions. The data collected include enrolment numbers, qualifiers and first destinations (home and EU students only from 1999/00) of qualifiers. The HESA student figures in this volume from 2001/02 are taken from the July 'standard registration' count and are not directly

---

1 Apart from those known to have ceased training as a result of serious injury, serious illness or death.

2   In the past, follow-up surveys have been carried out 3 months after leaving up to December 1990 leavers for Employment Training and up to September 1990 leavers for Youth Training.

comparable with those previously recorded from the December 'snapshot' count.

5 INTERNATIONAL COMPARISONS

The tables in Chapter 6, International Comparisons, are taken from the Organisation for Economic Co-operation and Development (OECD) 2004 edition of the publication *Education at a Glance (EAG)*, the OECD website EAG Indicators, and the IEA (International Association for the Evaluation of Educational Achievement) PIRLS (Progress in Reading Literacy Study) 2001. It is important to note, however, that international comparisons of education and training are very difficult and should therefore be treated with caution. In addition, some knowledge of the underlying systems in different countries is extremely useful in interpreting the data.

6 LABOUR FORCE SURVEY (LFS)

Please note that in the LFS tables some separate analyses will not sum to base figures shown because of unpaid family workers, those on government-supported training and employment programmes, or those who did not answer, who are excluded from the separate analyses (see below for details).

The Labour Force Survey (LFS) was first carried out in the United Kingdom in 1973, as part of the UK's obligations as members of the European Economic Community, and was repeated every two years until 1983. Between 1984 and 1991, the survey was carried out annually, with results published relating to the March to May quarter.

From spring (March to May) 1992 the survey was carried out in Great Britain on a quarterly basis. In Northern Ireland the LFS was conducted in spring 1992 and spring 1993, and was then carried out quarterly from winter (December to February) 1994-95. For about the last ten years, there has been a quarterly survey covering the whole of the UK. The International Labour Organization (ILO) - an agency of the United Nations - agrees the concepts and definitions used in the LFS.

The survey is a continuous sample carried out throughout the whole of the United Kingdom by interviewing people about personal circumstances and work. The LFS sample is selected on a systematic, unclustered basis and includes some 56,000 private addresses throughout the UK every quarter. As well as these private households, the survey covers two groups of people living in a type of accommodation called *communal establishments*. These two groups are students in halls of residence (whose parents usually answer the survey questions on the students' behalf) and people living in NHS accommodation (which used to be called nurses' homes). The survey does not sample people living in other forms of accommodation - for example, army camps, local authority homes, or hospitals.

Details of the labour force and other characteristics of around 105,000 people aged 16 and over are collected every quarter; basic personal details are also collected for around 28,000 children aged under 16. The results of each survey are processed and 'grossed', to provide estimates that cover the whole population. This allows us to say that there are about 27 million people in employment, even though the sample itself has only identified about 60,000 employed people.

In 2004, ONS issued re-grossed figures revising LFS estimates which are reflected in time series LFS data used in *Education and Training Statistics for the United Kingdom*.

CONCEPTS AND DEFINITIONS

All People
This group includes everyone of working age (Males aged 16-64 and Females aged 16-59) and comprises; employees, the self-employed, those on government supported programmes, unpaid family workers, the ILO unemployed and the economically inactive.

Economically active – people aged 16 and over who are either in employment (did some paid work in the reference week) or ILO unemployed.

Employees / Self-employed – the division between employees and self-employed is based on survey respondents' own assessment of their employment status.

Full-time / part-time – the classification of full-time and part-time is on the basis of self-assessment. People on Government-supported training and employment programmes who are at college in the survey reference week are classified, by convention, as part-time.

Temporary employees – in the LFS these are defined as those employees who say that their main job is non-permanent in one of the following ways: fixed period contract; agency temping; casual work; seasonal work; other temporary work.

Government-supported training and employment programmes – This group comprises all people aged 16 and over participating in one of the Government's employment and training programmes administered by the Learning and Skills Councils in England, the National Council for Education and Training (ELWa) in Wales, local enterprise companies in Scotland, or the Training and Employment Agency in Northern Ireland. This group of people has been excluded from the separate economic analyses in the tables as the LFS generally undercounts the numbers involved. Administrative sources provide much more reliable information about this group (see separate source number 3).

Unpaid Family Workers – This group comprises persons doing unpaid work for a business they own or for a business that a relative owns. This group of people has been excluded from the separate economic analyses as it is relatively small (around 100,000) and when disaggregated many of the estimates fall below the publication threshold of 10,000.

ILO unemployment – the International Labour Organization (ILO) measure of unemployment refers to people without a job who were available to start work in the two weeks following their LFS interview and who had either looked for work in the four weeks prior to interview or were waiting to start a job they had already obtained.

Economically inactive – people who are neither in employment nor unemployed on the ILO measure. This group includes, for example, all those who were looking after a home or retired (as well as those aged under 16).

Industry – the classification of respondents' industry of employment is based on the Standard Industrial Classification 1992, SIC (92).

Occupation – the classification of respondents' occupations are based on the Standard Occupational Classification (SOC2000), introduced in spring 2001.

7 POPULATION

The population figures in Chapter 5 are estimated and projected numbers based on demographic data provided by the Office for National Statistics and the Government Actuary's Department, which incorporate post-2001 Census revisions. Data for the 'working age' category and sub-analyses, however, are taken from the Labour Force Survey (see source No 6 for further information) and contain reweighted data.

8 PUBLIC EXAMINATIONS: GCSE/GNVQ, GCE, SCE STANDARD GRADE AND NATIONAL QUALIFICATIONS (NQ)

Data for England and Wales are produced from data provided by the GCSE and GCE examining boards and groups. GCSE and GCE data for Northern Ireland are derived from the Summary of Annual Examination Results and Further Education examination results. In Scotland pupils study for the SCE Standard grade (a two-year course leading to examinations at the end of the fourth year of secondary schooling) and Higher grade, which requires at least a further year of secondary schooling. The data source is the Scottish Qualifications Authority (formerly Scottish Examination Board). From 1999/00 additional new National Qualifications (NQ) were introduced in Scotland to allow greater flexibility and choice in the Scottish examination system. NQ include Intermediate 1 & 2 designed primarily for candidates in the fifth and sixth year of secondary schooling.

9 SCHOOL LEAVER DESTINATIONS

From 1996, information on the early destinations of year 11 pupils in England has been collected via the Careers Service Activity Survey. This replaced the former School Leavers Destination Survey, which collected information on the destinations of year 11 pupils in England and Wales. It provides data about the choices of around half a million young people finishing compulsory education each year. In Scotland, data on destinations of leavers of all ages are collated by Careers Scotland. School leaver information is provided by the Department for Employment and Learning in Northern Ireland. Data for school leavers in Wales are now provided by Careers Wales Association Ltd, and although included in Table 4.11, are not classified as 'National Statistics'.

10 SCHOOLS STATISTICS

The Department for Education and Skills carries out an annual Census of schools in England on the third Thursday in January. Data are collected on the number of schools by type; number of pupils by age and sex; number of admissions; pupils' school meal arrangements; number of teaching and non-teaching staff; course of study followed by pupils aged 16 and over; number of classes as taught and number of pupils with statements of special educational needs. Data collected in January 2004 were published the following September in the publication *Statistics of Education: Schools in England*. From January 2002 onwards, maintained primary, secondary and special schools, as well as CTC's, have reported data at an individual pupil level. In January 2003, the pupil level coverage expanded to include non-maintained special schools and academies.

Corresponding annual schools census counts are also carried out in January for pupils in Wales (at individual pupil level from 2003) and October for pupils in Northern Ireland. The annual schools census count for pupils in Scotland is carried out in September (excluding information on school meals, which is collected in a separate survey in January) - although the course of study followed by pupils aged 16 and over is not collected, but examination results for each subject are received in August.

11 VOCATIONAL QUALIFICATIONS

Information on awards of National Vocational Qualifications (NVQs)/Scottish Vocational Qualifications (SVQs), General National Vocational Qualifications (GNVQs) (up to 1999/00)/Advanced Vocational Certificates of Education (VCEs)/General

Scottish Vocational Qualifications (GSVQs) and Vocationally Related Qualifications (VRQs) made by UK awarding bodies has been taken from the National Information System for Vocational Qualifications (NISVQ) held by DfES. GNVQ figures from 2000/01, based on the Secondary School and College Performance Tables, are not included in Table 4.5. As part of the NISVQ project, the Qualifications and Curriculum Authority (QCA) provides annual totals (October-September) of NVQ awards by framework area and level. This is used for grossing up the more detailed NVQ award information, collected from the awarding bodies who participate in NISVQ, in order to produce UK NVQ estimates. QCA's totals are based on quarterly returns sent by all NVQ awarding bodies. UK NVQ/SVQ estimates are based on grossed-up numbers of NVQs plus all SVQs.

NISVQ receives detailed information on awards made by four of the largest awarding bodies: City and Guilds, Edexcel, OCR and SQA. However, in 2000/01 the SQA were only able to supply a small amount of information on their qualifications, which meant that it was excluded from any analysis by level.

More detailed statistical information on the awards of Vocational Qualifications is presented in the DfES Statistical Bulletin: Vocational Qualifications in the UK: 2002/03, which can be found on the DfES Research and Statistics Gateway (www.dfes.gov.uk/rsgateway).

Annex B

UNITED KINGDOM EDUCATION AND TRAINING STATISTICS: OTHER REFERENCE MATERIAL

1 GENERAL

1.1 Various summaries of education and training statistics for all four parts of the United Kingdom are contained in the *Annual Abstract of Statistics*, *Regional Trends* and *Social Trends* publications prepared by the Office for National Statistics. Some education statistics also appear in the *Digest of Welsh Statistics*, *Scottish Social Statistics* and the *Annual Abstract of Statistics, Northern Ireland*.

1.2 Each of the home education departments also publishes statistics in a variety of press notices, bulletins and statistical volumes. The relevant websites are as follows:

England: http://www.dfes.gov.uk/rsgateway
Wales: http://www.wales.gov.uk/
Scotland: http://www.scotland.gov.uk
N. Ireland: http://www.deni.gov.uk
http://www.delni.gov.uk

2 OFFICE FOR NATIONAL STATISTICS (ONS) PUBLICATIONS

Social Trends is produced annually, No 34 2004 (£41.00. ISBN 0 11 621732 4) being the current edition. This publication brings together some of the more significant statistical series relating to social polices and conditions and presents a series of articles, followed by tables and charts. One chapter concentrates on education and training.

Regional Trends is also published annually, No 38 2004 (£41.00. ISBN 0 11 621650 6) being the current edition. The publication brings together detailed information highlighting regional variations in the United Kingdom and covers a wide range of social, demographic and economic topics. One chapter concentrates on education and training.

UK 2004 (£37.50. ISBN 0 11 621661 1), formerly known as The Britain Yearbook, is one of the best known and most respected reference works available on the UK. This 55th Edition provides a mix of statistics, maps, photographs, tables and text covering all aspects of life in the UK. One chapter concentrates on education and training. 'UK 2005' is due to be published on 31st January 2005.

Guide to Official Statistics 2000 Edition (£32.00. ISBN 0 11 621 161 X) is a comprehensive guide to UK statistics, listing all the statistical censuses, surveys, administrative systems, press releases, publications, databases, CD-ROMs, and other services, by industry sector. The information is also available on StatBase at: http://www.statistics.gov.uk.

Labour Market Trends (incorporating the *Employment Gazette*) is a monthly publication with over 70 pages of labour market statistical tables. It also contains regular analytical articles using Labour Force Survey data and every month includes an LFS Help Line feature, which presents information frequently requested by users of the LFS. The price per issue is £10.00 and it is available from The Stationery Office Bookshops.

The Office for National Statistics on behalf of The Government Statistical Service (GSS) has created StatBase ® as an on-line access system for deposited official data. The data comes from a variety of individual sources throughout GSS. This can be accessed via the ONS website - the home page can be found at: http://www.statistics.gov.uk.

3. INTERNATIONAL STATISTICS

A number of publications providing comparative statistics and indicators on education and training in different countries are now available - some of the most important are listed below.

Education at a Glance: OECD Indicators 2004. Organisation for Economic Co-operation and Development. Stationery Office, 2004. £34.00. ISBN 92 640 1567 1.

Key Data on Education in Europe 2002. Eurydice, Eurostat. Stationery Office, 2003. £12.00. ISBN 92 844635 8.

Education across Europe 2003. Eurostat, European Commission. Stationery Office, 2004. £26.00. ISBN 92 8945783 X.

W

Y